AF674541

The Business of Business Is (Not) Just Business

The Business of Business Is (Not) Just Business

How Behavioural Tools Can Drive Real Change

EDITED BY

Sutapa Banerjee

HarperCollins *Publishers* India

First published in India by HarperCollins *Publishers* 2026
HarperCollins *Publishers* India, Cyber City,
Building 10-A, Gurugram, Haryana – 122002, India
www.harpercollins.co.in

2 4 6 8 10 9 7 5 3 1

Anthology copyright © Samruddha Bharat Foundation 2026
Copyright for the individual pieces vests with their respective authors

P-ISBN: 978-93-7307-469-6
E-ISBN: 978-93-7307-365-1

The views and opinions expressed in this book are the authors' own and the facts are as reported by them, and the publishers are not in any way liable for the same.

Sutapa Banerjee asserts the moral right to be identified as the editor of this work.

All rights reserved. No part of this publication may be reproduced, stored in a retrieval system, or transmitted, in any form or by any means, electronic, mechanical, photocopying, recording or otherwise, without the prior permission of the publishers.

Without limiting the exclusive rights of any author, contributor or the publisher of this publication, any unauthorized use of this publication to train generative artificial intelligence (AI) technologies is expressly prohibited. HarperCollins also exercise their rights under Article 4(3) of the Digital Single Market Directive 2019/790 and expressly reserve this publication from the text and data-mining exception.

Typeset in 11.5/15.2 Minion Pro
by HarperCollins *Publishers* India Pvt. Ltd

Printed and bound at
Manipal Technologies Limited, Manipal

MIX
Paper | Supporting responsible forestry
FSC™ C043100

This book is produced from independently certified FSC* paper to ensure responsible forest management.

HarperCollins *Publishers*, Macken House, 39/40 Mayor Street Upper,
Dublin 1, D01 C9W8, Ireland

For the two people who, in many ways, helped me become the person I am today—
my mother, Nibedita,
and my daughter, Diya.

Contents

Foreword

NADIR GODREJ

There's a capitalistic strain
that enthrones shareholder gain.
And Milton Friedman could see
that this simplistic philosophy
could lead to great efficiency.
But wherever there's externality,
this capitalism, red in tooth and claw,
can prove to be a dismal flaw.

Correction can come from regulation
or even from self-remediation.
And Adam Smith himself foresaw
that business could address this flaw.

It should be clearly understood:
One can do well by doing good.
Doing it smartly we do better—
so why not be the trendsetter!

And here I think that we all ought to
pay careful heed to Michael Porter.
With shared value, there's no cost
for doing good, as nothing's lost.

All it takes is a thinking brain
to remove a societal pain
and combine it with a business gain
to create a sustainable chain
of endless mutual benefit.
This concept is a tremendous hit!

This proposition is easy to state
But yet we find that we wait and wait!
Sutapa Banerjee took a fresh look
and came up with this interesting book.
All of us, I'm sure, will learn
a socially responsible way to earn.

Behavioural science is the key.
It's a refreshing way to see.
For those who choose not to budge,
can we provide them with a 'nudge'?

The book is filled with ideas galore!
Two important themes are at the core:
Women's economic participation
and incentives and legislation
to make business socially constructive.
It turns out the interactions are instructive.

Academic experts point the way.
Business practitioners have their say.
In each part insights arise;
Sutapa then does synthesize
The learnings across diverse fields.
Practical solutions are what this yields.

There is no excuse to shirk,
as we find solutions that can work!
The final chapter links it all—
all of us should take the call!

Always keep these facts in sight;
Don't hesitate to do what's right.
This strategy is tried and tested;
in the long haul it can't be bested.

Now ESG will take you far.
Don't just be a shooting star,
rising high before you fall—
instead take the enduring call.

All of us can forge ahead
if we only learn to shed
the barriers that can divide.
And if cooperation's tried,
with the help of business, I foresee
a helpful, thriving society.

This book can show us all the way
To reach that glorious, bright new day!

The Experiment

SUTAPA BANERJEE

WHEN I FIRST CONCEPTUALIZED THIS book, I was clear what it is *not* meant to be, what it *is* intended to be and what it *could* potentially evolve into.

At its core, this book is best viewed as a structured thought experiment, similar in nature to the experiments at the heart of behavioural economics and psychology. These disciplines, particularly behavioural science (which intersects economics and psychology and draws insights from neuroscience, sociology and evolutionary biology), are central to the book's narrative. My own chapter, 'Men and Money', as well as the concluding chapters of each section and the final chapter of the book, draw extensively from these fields.

Behavioural science, despite its empirical strength and decades of research, remains underutilized in India. The opening chapter, authored by a renowned behavioural economist, introduces the fundamentals of this field, which is woven into the thematic fabric of the book.

Structuring the book as a thought experiment allowed me to test two hypotheses:

Can bringing together diverse perspectives from key stakeholders on a specific problem not only enhance our understanding but also reveal approaches, frameworks, and practices that can be scaled across sectors?

Does examining three distinct yet interrelated challenges within a single volume help uncover common approaches and practices that cut across different domains and their respective ecosystems?

The insights addressing the first hypothesis are reflected in the final chapters of each of the three sections. The more ambitious second hypothesis is explored in the concluding chapter of the book.

What this book is

At a glance, this book is a curated collection of essays written by a diverse group of contributors—economists, domain experts, business leaders from both traditional and digital enterprises, investors and catalytic agents. Each contributor offers a perspective on one of three urgent challenges currently confronting India: the environmental sustainability of economic growth; unemployment, with a particular focus on the low economic participation of women; and deeply entrenched societal norms and stereotypes that hinder progress.

These issues were selected because they are domains where businesses and their supply chains have an outsized impact. This book seeks to explore how that impact can be harnessed positively or how its adverse effects can be mitigated.

It comprises separate sections, each dedicated to one of these challenges. Within each section, the perspectives of a wide array of stakeholders from the relevant ecosystem are presented. These diverse viewpoints help both in gaining a deeper, more nuanced understanding of a complex problem and in identifying the different approaches, practices and measures that have proved effective in countering and improving the situation. Notably, they highlight the key factors the contributors believe made these approaches successful.

But do these diverse perspectives of key stakeholders reveal approaches, frameworks and practices that may work across sectors? I test this hypothesis and share *the outcome* along with my own perspective on the use of evidence-based research and behavioural tools in the concluding chapter of each section. In the process, I explore the interplay of pulls, pressures and measures that may have created a compelling motive for businesses to adopt the strategies they did. I also identify the common threads, if any, that run across different businesses, and the key drivers in the ecosystem that could help scale impact by encouraging broader adoption.

The attempt is to shift the discourse from what businesses *should do* to *what* may actually *propel* more of them to take meaningful action. Drawing on the insights and experiences of domain experts, business leaders, and my own analysis, the book evaluates a combination of tools—legislation, incentives, 'behavioural nudges'[1] and others—that may hold a greater promise of success.

While most chapters focus on the Indian context, several include examples of practices that succeeded in other countries and may offer valuable lessons for India.

What this book could be

Are there frameworks, practices and approaches that, though developed in one context, may be applicable to others?

This question forms the basis for structuring the book into three sections, each focused on a distinct challenge. By bringing these diverse issues together, the aim is to evaluate whether common frameworks and practices exist that have been *successfully used in two, or even all three, problem areas.*

In the concluding chapter, 'Towards a New Playbook', I explore the shared practices and approaches that emerge and consider how they may be applied across domains, possibly with appropriate contextual adaptations.

Cross-cutting themes

Two themes run prominently through the book and are explored in depth:

1. **Low economic participation of women:** This issue is examined from multiple angles to uncover approaches and tools that might address the persistent underrepresentation of women in the economy. Most of the corrective interventions and tools suggested here have not seen concerted, widespread use in India. I examine these in detail in 'Men and Money', as well as in the concluding chapters of each section.
2. **Role of behavioural insights in policy design:** What remains insufficiently understood, and therefore rarely applied, is the role of behavioural insights in shaping policies and incentives. For instance, a well-designed behavioural nudge, tailored to a specific context, may significantly increase the likelihood of successfully influencing business behaviour.

In short, at the very least, this book is a collection of perspectives on issues that affect us all—individually to varying degrees, and collectively in significant ways. These perspectives come from individuals who are either leading businesses in specific areas or are domain experts, offering a deeper, more nuanced understanding of the challenges and complexities involved. The breadth of sectors and domains represented ensures, hopefully, that every reader will find something of relevance and interest.

The book could go a step further by helping to identify measures that might encourage more businesses to move in a direction that benefits society, within the context of each specific problem. This is the hypothesis I test and reflect on in the concluding chapter of each section.

It could go even further by uncovering and highlighting frameworks, practices, approaches and insights that may have cross-domain applicability. This broader synthesis is presented in the final section, 'The Outcome'.

What this book is not

It is equally important to state clearly what this book does not set out to do.

It does not attempt to highlight every area where businesses impact society. Nor does it seek to examine threadbare any single issue. It does not cover the full range of sectors in which businesses operate, nor does it include the views of every significant voice and business leader who could meaningfully contribute to these discussions.

The book focuses specifically on the private sector, even though the public sector plays a vital role in the Indian economy.

Most importantly, this book is not intended to be prescriptive. Rather than offering definitive answers or directives, it aims to shift the discourse towards identifying approaches, tools and enablers that stakeholders—government, regulators and businesses—might consider adopting in their pursuit of systemic change.

PART I

The Context

1

The Business of Behaviour

A Behavioural Economist's Perspective

DILIP SOMAN

As a researcher and university professor, I have had the honour and privilege of working with several organizations over the course of my career. These engagements have taken the form of joint research projects, co-creational projects, consulting and advising, executive training, conducting workshops and coaching. Over the years, I have worked with governments, ministries and bureaus, for-profit enterprises, advised startups and served in an advisory capacity to many large global organizations.

A few years ago, I was asked about the diverse types of organizations I had worked with, and whether it was a challenge to extend my work across such a wide range. The question was appropriate—I had indeed worked with organizations that were large and small, hierarchical and flat, that varied across multiple dimensions of culture and geography.

So, was there anything common at all?

The basic goal of organizations

On reflection, it struck me that there was one fundamental commonality across all of these, and indeed, across all organizations—they are all in the business of changing somebody's behaviour. For example, governments are interested in ensuring that businesses comply with regulations; for-profit corporations are obviously interested in getting their customers to purchase products and make better choices; human resource departments want employees to avail of the many benefits offered to them; dietitians seek to encourage people to eat a more balanced diet rather than loading up on unhealthy foods; and as an educator, I am always trying to get my students to behave differently as a function of the education I impart.

It is therefore no exaggeration to claim that we are all in the business of changing somebody's behaviour.

The behavioural change challenges faced by organizations can take many forms. **Compliance** involves getting individuals or other organizations to accomplish tasks in a prescribed format and within a prescribed timeline. **Switching** refers to influencing people who are currently making a particular choice (say, a competitor's product, a sub-optimal mobile phone plan or an unhealthy lifestyle) to opt for a better alternative (say, your product, the better mobile plan, a healthy lifestyle). **Consumption** focuses on changing behaviours to encourage the use of beneficial items (such as medication, leisure activities or information). **Acceleration** involves prompting people to engage in certain behaviours sooner, before it is too late (for example, beginning to exercise or saving for retirement).

Note that across these four categories of behavioural change challenges, the entity whose behaviour needs to be changed could be an individual, a group or an organization. Moreover, this entity could be external (e.g., customer, vendor, citizen, client) or internal (e.g., employee, affiliates, departments) to a firm.

Behavioural science

Over the last several decades, a burgeoning field in the areas of psychology, behavioural economics and judgment and decision-making has comprehensively studied the choices people make and how those choices can be influenced.

In 2008, University of Chicago professor Richard Thaler and current Harvard professor Cass Sunstein authored an influential book titled *Nudge*. The book reviews the copious research in the behavioural sciences and makes the simple but important observation that human behaviour is shaped not only by one's likes and dislikes, but more importantly, by the situation and context in which an individual finds themselves. For example, the same person might make a different decision when asked a question in person versus online, when alone versus with family, when stressed versus relaxed or in the summer versus the winter. Indeed, behaviour can vary across an exceptionally large number of contextual variables.

Nudge poses an important question: If we know that human behaviour is a function of context, can we not create context to steer people towards the behaviour that they, or we, would like them to display?

The process by which this is accomplished is called **choice architecture**—an approach that involves altering the context in which a choice is made, either by either presenting the information differently or by changing the surrounding situation, with the goal of steering people towards a desired choice. It is a form of behavioural change that does not involve persuasion, relies on minimal additional information, and requires no regulations, mandates or changes in monetary incentives.

The publication of the book also transformed behavioural science into an applied discipline. Since 2008, more than six hundred teams in organizations across the world have been applying behavioural science principles to practical organizational problems. Indeed, at the very extreme, one could claim that any business problem, in any part of an organization, is a behavioural change problem. **Compliance** requires a set of actors to do things differently and at different points in time. **Marketing** seeks to shift customer preferences and influence choices. **Product design and innovation** rely extensively on user insights. **Human resources** involves the management of, well, humans. In fact, even **corporate culture** can be broken down into a series of behaviours that must be changed for that culture to thrive.

Other parts of the organization, including operations, strategy, finance and accounting, consumer protection and client success, also hinge on some agent changing behaviour. While many of these disciplines have flourished through an understanding of behaviour, it is less clear whether they have actually adopted the scientific method in their processes. Behavioural science, in particular, offers more than a set of well-demonstrated empirical principles for understanding human behaviour and diagnosing behavioural change challenges. It provides both research methods for evaluating ideas and generating evidence, as well as a lens through which to view the world differently. For instance, rather than regarding a process as a series of activities, an alternative approach is to see it as a pipeline of customer interactions or decisions, each of which may generate a different cognitive, emotional or motivational response. More generally, it allows us to shift our understanding of human behaviour from an art—

where some individuals are gifted with the ability to understand humans and gain insights—to a science.

While we can celebrate the fact that there are six hundred teams applying behavioural science, we must also keep in mind that there are an estimated three hundred million organizations across the world. If human behaviour is so central to organizations, and if we have a robust science that understands human behaviour, then why are organizations not adopting it as widely as we might expect? One simple answer is the relative newness of the science. Another is the lack of exposure to compelling use cases and success stories.

The applications of the science

There are two central ideas in the behavioural sciences that have significant implications for how organizations operate. The first is the gap between intentions and actions. Many of us set goals to become better versions of ourselves. We want to exercise more, spend more time with family, adopt healthier diets or save more for retirement and for the care of our loved ones. Yet when it comes time follow through, everyday life often gets in the way.

American author Augusten Burroughs wrote one of my favourite books, *Magical Thinking*. One particular quote from the book has stuck with me: 'I myself am made entirely of flaws stitched together with good intentions.' In my view, this describes human behaviour perfectly. Everybody intends to be good—we intend to eat healthy food, exercise regularly and save money for the future. But as mentioned, there is usually a gap between our intentions and our actions. As a result, the solution to last-mile problems is not so much about creating awareness or persuading people, as it is about facilitating action.

Indeed, many people who do not save enough for retirement or fail to lead healthy lifestyles do not need to be persuaded to do these things—they are fully on board with the idea. The problem is that the stresses, strains and constraints of short-term goals keep getting in the way. At other times, the barrier is psychological. For instance, in many Western countries that rely on defined contribution retirement plans, employees can be overwhelmed by the volume of information on numerous fund options and might therefore choose not to participate. The problem is not a lack of conviction about the need to save, but rather the challenge of overcoming the cognitive difficulties involved in making suitable choices.

A second concept from the behavioural sciences is that sometimes, small things in the environment can have significant effects on behaviour. For example, several years ago, I was interested in studying why members of an insurance plan—who had prepaid for an annual check-up—often failed to see their doctor for that check-up. When asked, these individuals would simply say they were too busy. However, an investigation into the process revealed that the individual had to telephone the doctor's office to make an appointment. While this seems like a trivial task, it was a source of annoyance and procrastination. By simply changing the default and automatically giving people an appointment, which they were free to reschedule, we were able to significantly increase the number of people who got their annual check-up.

There are several other examples where relatively minor changes at the last mile (the touchpoints that end users face) have had a significant impact on both user and organizational outcomes. In the United Kingdom, reformatting a letter sent to small and medium enterprises informing them that 90 per cent of other enterprises paid their taxes on time reduced delays in tax filing and the associated costs. In Canada, simplifying an organ donation form and adding messaging that encouraged potential donors to empathize with potential recipients significantly increased donation rates. In Australia, a bank increased transparency in credit card advertising by highlighting both the positives and the negatives of their card. This resulted in greater customer satisfaction, better choices, more cross-purchasing of other products from the bank and a higher lifetime value. In Mexico, redesigning quarterly pension statements to minimize behavioural frictions coupled with a series of SMS reminders boosted voluntary pension contributions. Across South Asia and Africa, pairing financial literacy initiatives with simple behavioural interventions such as planning prompts or budgeting worksheets allowed users to convert their newly gained financial knowledge into concrete behaviours.

These are all examples of the successful deployment of behavioural science at the last mile—at the point where stakeholders come into contact with an organization's products, policies or programmes. Organizations typically outsource last-mile activities: sales is often handled by contractors; webpages and communications are designed by agencies; and even merchandising and displays are managed by retailers. This can be a mistake, because there is considerable power in the touchpoints at the last mile. Simple changes in forms, webpages, communications and field staff scripts have had significant effects on the uptake of products, processes and programmes. It is often the little things that matter most.

From the last mile to the first

The applications of behavioural science are not restricted to the last mile; the science can contribute to several first-mile areas as well. I have already written about its applications to corporate culture. The science has been successfully used by organizations in product and process design, human resources, rethinking fundamental concepts like segmentation, and indeed, as a strategic way of looking at the organization. More generally, rather than thinking of behavioural science as merely a tool—something specific to be used to address a concrete problem—there is a lot of value in thinking of it as a lens, a different way of looking at existing problems.

One example of a first-mile behavioural solution is in the area of diversity and inclusion. Many corporations use quotas and other interventions to hire women and minorities. However, not much attention is paid to the career trajectories of these underrepresented groups. In many organizations, employees—in some way or the other—must actively ask for promotion. My colleagues Joyce He, Sonia Kang and Nico Lacetera point out that women and minorities tend to be less overconfident and are less likely to self-promote. As a result, many remain in the lower ranks of the organization. The behavioural solution is to change the process. If organizations were to automatically consider all employees for promotion, say, every three years (or at another appropriate interval) while allowing individuals to opt out, a greater number of women and minorities would likely progress through the ranks.

There are other examples of behavioural science being used to tackle thorny social problems using a mix of first-mile and last-mile solutions. In the area of human resources—especially hiring and staffing—gender and other stereotypes (for example, ethnic) on the part of management have often prevented minority employees from securing impactful roles. Stereotypes create a halo effect—the presence of a stereotype tends to change how individuals interpret information. For example, knowing that an applicant for a sales or technical job is female might cause the hiring manager to attribute her past experience or academic performance to factors other than competence.

One popular intervention to counter this problem is the use of recruitment platforms that hide performance-irrelevant factors that can cast a halo, thereby helping recruiters focus solely on performance-relevant attributes. A successful, behaviourally-informed platform that improves the quality of recruits, reduces stereotype bias and increases diversity is Applied (beapplied.com).

In the domain of environment and climate change, behavioural interventions—such as visualization (showing pictures of sea life trapped in plastic), process improvements (moving recycling receptacles closer to homes), social influences and tangible demonstrations of the consequences of climate change—have been shown to encourage a range of sustainable behaviours, including a reduction in plastic usage, increased purchase of sustainable products, greater reuse and recycling and lower energy consumption. The hallmark of these solutions is their cost-effectiveness and relative ease of implementation over traditional tools such as regulation, financial incentives, advertising campaigns or penalties.

Conclusion

Over a dozen years since the publication of Thaler and Sunstein's highly influential book *Nudge*, people still do not exercise as much as they should; they still do not take public transit often enough; and they still work too hard and spend too little time with their families. As indicated herein, it is not that people do not want to do these things—but given human nature, organizations must take proactive steps to help facilitate these and other desirable behaviours.

Recent global developments have only served to underscore the importance of behavioural science. The COVID-19 pandemic showed us that while humankind succeeded in creating, testing and approving a new vaccine in record time, psychology created a barrier at the last mile—getting the vaccine into people's arms. Climate change has taught us that while many are aware of its perils, psychology often hinders us from doing something about it. Poverty alleviation programmes around the world have shown that, despite innovative and potentially impactful cash transfer schemes devised by governments and non-profits, psychology has limited their uptake. And many of us can relate to the human behaviour of sharing information online without verifying its authenticity, which has contributed to the misinformation pandemic.

Looking ahead, much work remains to be done to successfully embed the science of behavioural insights into the DNA of both governments and for-profit organizations. Hopefully, we will all embrace the challenge and apply behavioural insights to create value—for individuals as customers and citizens, for organizations of all shapes and sizes, for nations, and more broadly, for society and humankind.

2

Sustainability and Inclusion

An Economist's View

ABHEEK BARUA

FIRST THINGS FIRST. WHAT IS sustainability from an economist's perspective? The chatter around sustainability has focused disproportionately on climate change and decarbonization. However, for a lower-middle-income emerging economy (EE) like India, 'sustainable' growth is about much more than caps on greenhouse gases. Water pollution through industrial effluents, and indeed water availability itself, is a major challenge. According to the government's own think tank, NITI Aayog, 600 million Indians suffered from 'acute water shortages in 2018, when the last nation-wide comprehensive water survey was done'.[1] Particulate matter (especially PM 10 and PM 2.5) pollution in urban areas threatens the health of India's workforce. The leaching of soil nutrients through excessive inorganic fertilizer use also needs to be addressed.

There is another dimension to sustainability that economists emphasize: inclusive growth. For growth to be sustained in the long term, an increasing proportion of the income pyramid must benefit.

Rising inequality ultimately shrinks markets and impedes economic momentum. Studies have shown a significant increase in India's inequality in the post-liberalization period. In 2022–23, the top 1 per cent wealth share was 39.5 per cent, 29 percentage points went just to the top 0.1 per cent, 22 percentage points to just the top 0.01 per cent and 16 percentage points to just the top 0.001 per cent. (source: 'Income and Wealth Inequality in India, 1922–2023: The Rise of the Billionaire Raj' Working Paper, 2024/09 World Inequality Lab)

For labour-surplus economies like India, the mantra for inclusivity perhaps lies in making growth more labour-intensive and in creating better-quality (and hence more remunerative) jobs. Much has been written on why Indian industry has chosen capital over labour in its growth strategy. The absence of skills and labour market flexibility invariably tops this list.

A related issue is the low participation of women in India's workforce. While there is some disagreement on the reliability of available data, it is broadly accepted that India has one of the lowest rates of women working outside the home. The World Economic Forum's *Gender Gap Report 2025* ranked India 131 out of 148 countries.[2] Economists point out that reversing this gender bias could itself act as a force multiplier, putting the economy on a more sustainable, high-growth track. India's neighbour Bangladesh—ranked 24 in the same report—has shown how greater female participation can drive growth. Its ready-made garments industry, the second-largest exporter in the world, contributes roughly a tenth of its annual GDP, with the majority of its workers being women.[3]

The quest for sustainable growth thus presents a broad spectrum of challenges. It would take much more than a single essay to explore these problems. This essay focuses on environmental sustainability.

Pushback from emerging economies

Policymakers and CEOs in the emerging world have their own misgivings about 'sustainability'. Shorn of all the frills and furbelows of policy statements, the principal focus of EE governments is to boost per capita income growth as much and as quickly as possible. While there is some debate about whether per capita income is the right metric to target, it has historically correlated well with poverty reduction and welfare parameters such as access to healthcare, sanitation and education.

How does this 'growth chase' clash with environmental sustainability? For one thing, there is a strong belief in a significant trade-off between the two. Excessive emphasis on sustainability could hamper growth—or so policymakers believe. At the micro level, this is reflected in a widely held perception among companies that making production processes sustainable imposes financial costs, reduces profitability and ultimately constrains growth.

Thus, when India continues to invest in coal-fired power plants despite its commitment to net-zero carbon emissions by 2070 (it plans to add up to 56 gigawatts of coal-based capacity over the next decade), it does so because it sees it as a cost-effective, reliable way to achieve economic growth and its associated benefits.

A related belief is that sustainability is a luxury only more affluent countries can afford. A common extension of this argument is that the cart must come before the horse—as average incomes rise through growth, sustainability standards will improve automatically. History appears to support this view. Take the US as an example. Its Environmental Protection Agency (EPA)—the country's 'sustainability watchdog'—was set up as late as 1970, when per capita income was a hefty $5,234 (about $41,000 in today's terms). India's current per capita income is about $2,400.

China is another case in point. Its manufacturing success and sustained, double-digit economic growth over decades is often attributed to the twin engines of cheap labour and lax environmental norms. It wasn't until 2013 that Chinese authorities really started paying attention to environmental issues. By then, China's per capita income was over $7,000, about five times that of India's.

Can trade help? The compensation question

Economists recognize that environmental sustainability is a uniquely global problem. The environment cannot be segmented along national boundaries. Thus, the solutions—be it limiting greenhouse gases or reversing deforestation to preserve carbon sinks—must be globally coordinated. Prima facie, international trade, which provides the principal economic link between economies, promises a solution.

However, efforts to leverage trade to achieve sustainability have pitted developed economies (DEs) against EEs. For the latter, lax environmental norms have historically been the very source of their competitive advantage. The aggressive offshoring of 'dirty' manufacturing from DEs to EEs has driven growth and livelihoods. Emerging economies argue that raising sustainability standards in line with DE demands will erode this advantage, putting them in direct competition with DE producers. They are therefore unwilling to sacrifice their edge in the market without adequate compensation.

Some of the demands from DEs have indeed been stringent. The European Union, for instance, has introduced the Carbon Border Adjustment Mechanism (CBAM)—effectively a carbon tax on suppliers—which came into effect in October 2023. This significantly affects exports of iron and steel, cement and clinker, aluminium, steel and fertilizers.

There is another grouse against the trade arrangements that is likely to emerge from the template specified by DCs. The more sophisticated emission control technologies have, somewhat predictably, been created in the developed world. DCs have been reluctant to either transfer this technology or invest significantly in producing emission control equipment in the emerging economies. EEs could face a proverbial 'double whammy'—trade barriers like CBAM will reduce exports, and the forced purchase of expensive equipment will skew the trade balance further.

International trade can be a useful ally in global environmental sustainability only if there is a sense of fairness, of give and take between regions. For this, the DEs must be willing to share technology and make significant investments in the EEs for the latter to see it as a fair, level playing field.

On the question of fairness, it would be remiss not to mention the sense of historical injustice that underpins the sustainability dialogue. Estimates show that since 1850, humans have emitted around 2,500 billion tonnes of carbon dioxide into the atmosphere.[4] This build-up has largely been driven by the DEs. The US is responsible for 20 per cent of this, Germany for 4 per cent and the UK for 3 per cent.[5] This accounts only for direct emissions. Indonesia and Brazil also place high on the emission league tables because of aggressive deforestation, much of it carried out by their colonizers in the late nineteenth and early twentieth centuries. Thus, the question of who is responsible for the present state of the world invariably arises in climate talks, as does the related question of fair compensation for the DE's legacy of environmental damage.

Global versus local—enlightened self-interest

Whatever the misgivings and reservations about the developed world, sheer self-interest should drive EEs like ours to address sustainability issues with an increased sense of urgency. The United Nations report on climate change found that most of the global hotspots of human vulnerability due to climate change are in the developing nations of Asia, Africa, and South and Central America.[6] The damage to the holy grail of growth from environmental degradation is enormous. We need to wake up to the fact that crumbling hillsides, choking cities and the growing intensity of adverse climate do not portend well for future growth. In short, the hard-wired notion of a trade-off between growth and sustainability is spurious. Growth needs sustainable production practices.

Legislations on sustainability and environment

a) The Environment Protection Act, 1986
b) Forest Conservation Act, 1980
c) Energy Conservation Act, 2001
d) Renewable Purchase Obligations (under Electricity Act), 2003

The battle for sustainable growth must be fought on two fronts. The first is to create and enforce standards. The second is to raise funds for technologies that enable sustainable production. As with all 'externalities', such as environmental damage, the government perhaps has the biggest role to play. For one thing, it is critical to paint the big picture in formulating a national sustainability strategy that aligns and encompasses various policies across sectors. The identification and articulation of aggregate targets, such as those on carbon emissions or safe drinking water, is the government's job. The government is also, through its budget allocation, the biggest financier of projects that can drive sustainability.

Then there is the business of 'nudges'—both away from unsustainable practices through rules and penalties, and towards positive behaviour through subsidies and incentives to conserve the environment. Economists often tend to be sceptical about the effective implementation of rules and typically prefer market forces to do the job. The government can play a key role in creating these market platforms.

Positive 'nudges' to promote sustainability and conservation

1. *Carbon trading market*: Trading of energy savings and carbon credit certificates
2. *Solar-powered agricultural pumps*: To reduce dependence on fossil fuels for irrigation
3. *Green building ratings and efficient streetlights*: Concessional financing and government support
4. *Solid waste management*: Partial funding for setting up waste-to-energy plants
5. *Support for water conservation and efficiency*: Through the National Water Mission
6. *Exemptions and waivers*: On duties and levies for renewable energy projects
7. *Clean energy finance support*: Through production-linked incentives for battery manufacturing, credit guarantees for energy-efficient projects, sovereign green bond issuance, priority lending for small renewable projects and more

The cap-and-trade model for carbon emissions is an example of how markets can help create both incentives and costs. Under this model, if companies reduce emissions beyond what is mandated by the so-called 'credit', they can sell the unused credit to those who fall short. Indian companies have been net exporters in the international carbon credit market for a while now. In October 2022, the government took the first steps towards creating a national carbon market through the Energy Conservation (Amendment) Bill. This will not only help in meeting India's long-term goals, but attractive margins on carbon offsets (Indian carbon credit exporters have long complained about being short-changed on international carbon exchanges) could also drive the evolution of cheaper, indigenous, energy-efficient technologies.

Rules and practices for discouraging climate negative practices

1. Environmental standards and impact assessment—industry-specific mandatory norms and assessment of pollutants and environmental impact
2. Prohibition of manufacture and import of inefficient machinery not conforming to norms
3. Penal provision for breaching environmental norms
4. Conservation and pollution norms for buildings and vehicles—energy conservation codes for buildings using more than 100 kW of power and BS VI pollution norms for vehicles

Home-grown technologies have fared well in some countries, not just in carbon conservation but also in other areas of environmental protection. Egypt's organic farming company Sekem is a widely cited example of meeting multiple sustainability goals. Their innovations in organic cotton farming, starting in the early 1990s, helped reclaim arable land from the Sahara, which then absorbed carbon dioxide from the atmosphere and reduced water needs by 20 to 40 per cent.

Interestingly, the cap-and-trade model for particulate matter, the first of its kind in the world, was introduced in Surat, Gujarat, to address city air pollution. Preliminary findings suggest that industries participating in the pilot scheme reduced their particulate matter emissions by 24 per cent from 2019 to 2021, compared to those that remained under the business-as-usual regulation of complying with ambient air quality standards. Given that particulate pollution is highly heterogeneous in both composition and sources, the success of the Surat model offers hope that similar mechanisms could be applied to other pollutants, such as industrial water effluents.

Punitive congestion charges on vehicles, another form of market-based intervention, have helped many Western cities address the twin problems of traffic and related pollution. Once called the 'Great Smoke' for its overwhelming air pollution, London today has an average AQI of 25 compared to Delhi's 215.

Mass transport facilities such as metros have improved significantly in Indian cities. Shared transport aggregators like Uber have reached a critical size in some cities and should be encouraged to adopt electric vehicles and address problems like passenger safety. As alternative transport options grow, commuters must be nudged to make better use of them through the clear choice of either paying through their nose for private transport or switching to cleaner alternatives.

Economists are often criticized for providing neat solutions that pay little heed to political imperatives or budget constraints. That is certainly true in India. A major contributor to groundwater depletion is agriculture, which guzzles 80 per cent of the country's water. Free power for farmers encourages overuse of electric pumps to extract as much groundwater as possible. The obvious solution seems to be the phasing out of power subsidies. However, as every Indian politician knows, this is easier said than done. That said, the political narrative is changing.

The government cannot do this alone. Indian industry must play a bigger role in the sustainability effort. It is reasonable to expect bigger firms to take the lead, instead of treating sustainability as another box to tick on their corporate social responsibility (CSR) checklist. After all, they are better informed about the issues and the options available than a small and medium enterprise (SME) vendor.

One could visualize a large company as a mini economy, with vendors and distributors trading with it. The key advantage that bigger corporations have is that they exercise significant control over the supply and distribution chain. They can use this power to ensure that sustainability practices are followed throughout the chain. This might lead to some cost escalation as suppliers adopt new practices, with inevitable repercussions for near-term profits. However, firms must recognize that prioritizing long-term competitiveness, and indeed survival in the face of an environmental apocalypse, trumps short-sighted demands of near-term profitability.

Sustainable finance

The effort to finance sustainability has gained considerable traction over the past decade and a half. The European Investment Bank issued the world's first green bond, focused exclusively on climate change, in 2007. These bonds are issued solely to finance sustainable projects and can be issued by financial institutions such as the European Investment Bank, central banks and private companies.

By 2021, the global green bond market had reached $2.1 trillion, with issuers from eighty countries. A parallel market for non-climate sustainable projects has also emerged, with a size of around $200 billion. While the bulk of issuance has come from the private sector, sovereign issuers, often with much larger average issuances, have added significant heft. Europe has led the way, but the sovereign response is now truly global.

Emerging economies, particularly through their development banks, have rapidly increased their participation. In 2021, 21 per cent of green bond issuance came from these economies, with the Asia–Pacific region leading the growth. Indian companies have contributed about $8 billion in issuance, although this still represents only 1 per cent of total bond issuance. The Indian government made its debut in 2022–23 with around $3 billion in local-currency green bonds.

The success of green finance ultimately depends on the availability of liquidity for lending. While banks and bond investors provide this, there is a growing discourse around how central banks, such as the Reserve Bank of India, can nudge them towards financing green projects. Environmental damage can affect economic and financial stability: adverse climate events can trigger spikes in the prices of critical items, leading to inflationary spillovers across prices. Central banks have started to take note of this, which is encouraging.

A raft of tools is available to central banks to direct credit towards sustainable sectors and away from environmentally harmful ones. China has introduced restrictions on bank lending to sectors based on their carbon compliance. Brazil has incorporated green considerations into their capital adequacy norms, that is, the amount of capital (which comes at a cost) to be held against a loan. The RBI has included lending to small sustainable projects in its mandated priority sector lending. The European Central Bank has purchased green bonds as part of its monetary operations. This is just the beginning. If central banks can get past the debates over mandates and legal frameworks and recognize the enormity of the environmental challenge, they can make a critical difference to the flow of funds to the sustainability cause.

Perhaps the most encouraging news comes from the world of equity finance. A meta-study by New York University's Stern School and Rockefeller Asset Management, covering more than 1,000 research papers that examined the link between financial performance and environmental, social and governance (ESG) factors, reported the following finding:

> [A] positive relationship between ESG and financial performance for 58 per cent of the 'corporate' studies focused on operational metrics such as ROE, ROA, or stock price with 13 per cent showing neutral impact, 21 per cent mixed results (the same study finding a positive, neutral or negative results) and only 8 per cent showing a negative relationship. For investment studies typically focused on risk-adjusted attributes such as alpha or the Sharpe ratio on a portfolio of stocks, 59 per cent (*of portfolios that invested in ESG compliant firms*) showed similar or better performance relative to conventional investment approaches while only 14 per cent found negative results.[7]

The results suggest that the often-assumed inverse relationship between corporate performance and sustainability is greatly exaggerated. Sustainable firms can, in fact, deliver superior results in both financial and equity performance.

Why this counterintuitive result? More granular, company-level studies show that a focus on sustainability ultimately leads to better resource utilization. Firms that prioritize ESG tend to achieve gains in overall resource efficiency (productivity of factors), which in turn boosts corporate performance.[8]

Nudges, restrictions, caps and barriers work to a degree. Companies want to 'see the money' before committing to large-scale innovation, and so do investors. These analyses underscore the fact that the financial opportunity may lie in chasing sustainability rather than resisting it.

Examples of sustainability initiatives by leading corporates in india

1. *Godrej Consumer Products:* 100 per cent Extended Producer Responsibility compliant, ensuring that producers are responsible for product disposal at the end of their life cycles.
2. *ITC Limited:* Waste-to-energy for over 79,000 tonnes of waste and greening of over 39,000 hectares of land.
3. *Ambuja Cement*: Promotes sprinkler and micro-irrigation systems, supports tech-enabled scientific farming to improve agricultural efficiency, facilitates access to safe drinking water, among other initiatives.
4. *Reliance Industries, Tata Power and the Adani Group*: Have announced major investment pipelines over the next decade and beyond for renewable energy projects.
5. *ReNew Power and Suzlon Energy*: Globally recognized for their leadership in solar and wind energy.

PART II

Environment and Sustainability

3

From Compliance to Leadership

A Climate Educator's View

KARTIKEYA SARABHAI

CLIMATE CHANGE IS BY FAR the greatest threat to the survival of life as we know it on this planet. Not just human life, but all animals and plants are under threat. It is a creeping calamity that began when we learned the secrets of using fossil fuels 275 years ago. While our actions till the middle of the 20th century could be put down to ignorance, that excuse no longer holds. Increasingly, we have been warned about the consequences of neglecting the environmental impact of fossil fuel use on the climate.

As I write this, I am sitting on my veranda in Ahmedabad, looking out at a thunderstorm and heavy rain, and it is only 28 May, the day of the IPL finals between Gujarat and Chennai. However, the cancelled match is the least of our problems. India is a country where the monsoon rains govern the water cycle. The onset of the southwest and northeast monsoons used to be predictably timed: 1 June in Kerala, 10 June in Mumbai, and 15 June in Ahmedabad. But unseasonal rains throw things out of gear, causing a tremendous impact on the rural economy. Farmers have far less resilience than IPL cricketers.

India is a large country on the way to becoming the most populous country in the world. In the seventy-five years since independence, it has made remarkable progress on several fronts. From a life expectancy of just thirty-two years[1] at the time of independence in 1947, the figure has risen to nearly seventy years[2] today. India also has the largest youth population, accounting for nearly 20 per cent[3] of global youth. Its economy is one of the fastest-growing among large countries. Starting from a very low per-capita carbon and environmental footprint, India needs more equitable carbon space as it develops. It cannot follow the classical development model, which is fossil fuel intensive.

India remains a developing country and still has a long way to go before catching up with first-world standards. Almost 10 per cent[4] of the population still lives below the poverty line. On several other indicators, there is work to be done. The prime minister has set a target for 2047, when India completes 100 years of independence, for the country to be considered 'developed'.[5] But the challenge remains: to maintain rapid growth while also being climate and environmentally responsible.

Background

Over the past decades, the Indian government has undergone a sea change in the way it views business and private enterprise. In the early years after independence, the state and public sector enterprises were expected to lead India's growth. Under the 'License Raj' regime, businesses were not seen as partners in development. The belief was that, without strict regulation, businesses would not align their interests with those of nation-building. When environmental awareness grew, and the first environmental legislations were enacted, this attitude persisted. The government focused on control, while industry primarily lobbied to stop or dilute regulations.[6] The majority of businesses saw their role as essentially meeting compliance requirements.

It was only in the early 1990s, when the first steps were taken to liberalize the economy, that one saw a perceptible change in the way businesses were perceived. The policy shift saw the unlocking of entrepreneurship. The growth of the private sector was now seen as a part of India's development strategy. The period was marked by a gradual shift from regulations to incentives. At the same time, internationally, the role of business in environmental conservation was evolving. This international discourse, especially within the United Nations system, in which India actively participates, had a significant impact on domestic thinking as well.

Some of the measures and policies that India initiated regarding the role of businesses in development and sustainability went beyond prevailing international thinking. A significant milestone was the enactment of corporate social responsibility (CSR) regulations through the Companies Act, 2013. Until then, industry saw its role as limited to cleaning up its own production. CSR regulations required large businesses to directly engage in development work. Promoting environmental sustainability was one of the areas identified for CSR spending. This led to businesses working with non-governmental organizations (NGOs) and getting directly involved in looking at developmental issues. However, this legislation was confined to large enterprises.

Since the publication of books such as *Cradle to Cradle*,[7] the earlier concept of 'cradle to grave' responsibility began to be replaced. While this model focused on responsibility for a product's entire life cycle, the newer concept introduced the idea of circularity[8]—one of nature's most powerful concepts—which is now influencing global economic thinking. Businesses have started looking not only at the entire value chain but beyond it as well. The effort has been to build processes to achieve circularity. Small and medium enterprises (SMEs) and the informal sector are increasingly becoming a part of the 'circle'.

The concept of net zero emerged from the global dialogue on achieving climate neutrality. At the opening of COP26 in Glasgow, Prime Minister Narendra Modi announced that India would cut its emissions to reach net zero by 2070.[9] This is an ambitious target and requires a multi-sectoral strategy. Commenting on the role of business, the Observer Research Foundation noted:

> Businesses have a pivotal role to play in this. Their actions, resources, capacity to innovate and greater reach are vital to swiftly decarbonise sectors, infrastructure, value chains, and the products and services they provide. Businesses are already playing a key role in the climate fight, helped by the growing customer and investor focus on sustainability, as well as increasing regulatory and disclosure requirements. Solving a problem at the national or international level is also becoming a key driver with this collaboration.[10]

Several business houses have since announced their own net-zero targets and developed action plans to achieve them.

Businesses are now not just looking at their own impact but also at their extended producer responsibilities, the sustainability of their supply chains and, ultimately, the circularity of their business models. CSR has prompted large businesses to examine development issues in the community as well as environmental concerns. In so doing, these businesses must work closely with micro, small and medium enterprises (MSMEs), local and national governments and NGOs on sustainability initiatives.

Businesses are now taking on the challenge of climate change at the national and international levels. To address this, business groups are collaborating with one another and with the United Nations and national bodies to act at a scale that will make a real impact on the climate crisis.

The United Nations has provided a forum for countries to evolve policies that delineate the increasing responsibilities of businesses towards sustainability. It is important to understand the various concepts that have evolved at the international level and how they have impacted India's thinking on climate change.

The international context

A little over fifty years ago, the United Nations Conference on the Human Environment, held in Stockholm, Sweden, in 1972, marked the first global recognition of the environmental crisis humanity was bringing upon itself. India recognized the gravity of the situation, and the then prime minister, Indira Gandhi, was the only head of government other than the host country to attend. In her speech, she emphasized the intimate link between environmental and poverty-related issues.[11]

Twenty years later, in 1992, the United Nations Conference on Environment and Development (UNCED) was held in Rio de Janeiro, Brazil. By then, it had been firmly established that human development and the environment are intricately linked. The conference led to several actions, including the adoption of the Rio Principles, such as 'polluter pays'[12] and 'common but differentiated responsibilities' (CBDR)[13]. It also led to the conventions on climate change, biodiversity and desertification. The conference was the first to acknowledge and establish the concept of 'major groups'.[14] Business and industry were among these, and their participation was recognized as necessary to achieve sustainable development.

Reporting and dialogue

The United Nations Framework Convention on Climate Change (UNFCCC), created to address global climate change concerns, emerged as an important outcome of the Rio Conference. It was one of the three important conventions established there. The UNFCCC convenes annually as the Conference of the Parties (COP) to discuss and negotiate climate policies.

Globally, as businesses became more actively involved in sustainability dialogues, concepts such as cleaner production began gaining ground. Cleaner production meant adopting preventive environmental strategies to stop pollution at the source, managing the environmental impact of the production process, not just impacts on its output. It addresses the root causes of environmental problems rather than their effects. Several multilateral environmental agreements (MEA) were signed in the period post-1992.

The cleaner production initiative was gradually extended to include product design, life-cycle thinking and consumption. These developments were reflected in the growth of regional round tables on cleaner production and a growth in the number of United Nations Industrial Development Organization (UNIDO)/ United Nations Environment Programme (UNEP) National Cleaner Production Centres globally.

In 1997, the Global Reporting Initiative (GRI), an independent international standards organization, was launched to help businesses, governments and organizations understand and communicate their impacts on issues such as climate change.

While the COP process addresses several issues directly relevant to businesses, it does not include them as partners. There was a need, therefore, for an apex United Nations body in which corporates could participate. In 2000, then United Nations Secretary-General Kofi Annan launched an initiative to include companies and organizations in improving sustainable development practices. This led to the creation of the United Nations Global Compact (UNGC), a non-binding United Nations pact. Its mandate is to encourage businesses to adopt ethical, moral, socially responsible and sustainable business practices, and to report on their implementation. It asks CEOs and top executives to commit to particular sustainability and social responsibility targets in exchange for access to training, peer networks and a practical framework for accountability.

While many commitments were made at UNCED in 1992 and a vision for the future was set, there was a need for a review. This led to the Rio+20 process, which culminated in the 2012 United Nations Conference on Sustainable Development, also held in Rio de Janeiro, Brazil. The conference led to the adoption of a political outcome document titled 'The Future We Want',[15] which expanded on the concept of responsible entrepreneurship. Some companies took on the responsibility of improving conditions in all parts of the world where they operate. Many governments introduced initiatives to support start-ups and foster entrepreneurship with a sustainability profile. Support included training on transforming ideas into profitable businesses, including administrative assistance and facilitation of investment decisions.[16]

Global actions

Even as increasing evidence of anthropocentric climate change emerged, and various modelling exercises showed the devastating consequences of mean global temperatures rising by more than 1.5°C, a global international agreement continued to elude successive COPs. At Copenhagen, 2009, an agreement was nearly reached but ultimately did not materialize. Finally, in 2015, at COP21 in Paris, a breakthrough was achieved. The Paris Agreement introduced a new approach to climate action through nationally determined contributions (NDCs). It established mechanisms for regular review and enhancement of countries' NDCs and set international standards for business action, especially in emissions reduction. Parties were encouraged to communicate or update their NDCs every five years to increase their ambitions over time.

Over the years, the UNFCCC has fostered several international collaborations and partnerships involving industries and businesses. These efforts aim to support and promote sustainable practices, technology transfer and financing for climate change mitigation and adaptation. One such initiative is the Climate Technology Centre and Network (CTCN), hosted by UNEP. It serves as the operational arm of the UNFCCC's Technology Mechanism.

Several contemporary instruments and initiatives have since emerged to support and promote green businesses. Incentives for green enterprises were put in place to address environmental issues, advance the shift to a low-carbon economy, meet consumer expectations, generate economic possibilities, improve resilience, and encourage stakeholder engagement. These tools aided in building an ecosystem that supports the adoption of sustainable business practices, which benefit the environment, society and the economy.

An initiative like the Carbon Disclosure Project (CDP) was set up as a global non-profit organization to encourage companies and cities to disclose their environmental impacts, including carbon emissions, water usage and deforestation risks. Carbon trading, which began after the Kyoto Protocol in 2005, continues as a voluntary mechanism and is fuelled by net-zero commitments of countries and industries.

Extended Producer Responsibility (EPR), another important regulation, was conceptualized globally and adopted in India in 2016. EPR regulations hold manufacturers accountable for managing the impacts of their products at the end of their useful life. This motivates businesses to design products that can be recycled and to take responsibility for waste management.

Environmental, social and governance (ESG) is another widely adopted concept. It serves as a business framework for integrating social and environmental issues into corporate governance. Several businesses are incorporating ESG principles into their organizational strategies. The framework considers the requirements and opportunities for generating value for all parties involved in the organization, including employees, clients, suppliers and financiers.

The Indian view

As international thinking on the role of business evolved, Indian business and industry were also changing their outlook towards environmental sustainability and climate change. Initially, this began with the development of compliance mechanisms for the various new laws enacted in India after the 1972 United Nations Conference. Several new pieces of legislation were passed, beginning with the Water (Prevention and Control of Pollution) Act of 1974. In general, the perception was one of industry versus the environment. This perception was seen as a new reality that had to become part of the cost of doing business. There was little conviction, and environmentalists were, in general, seen as anti-development activists.

The Ministry of Environment and Forests was formed in 1985. Recognizing that the transformation to a more sustainable society needed strong education, public awareness and capacity-building, the Centre for Environment Education (CEE) was set up simultaneously as a Centre of Excellence under the ministry. In 1993, CEE, the organization we established, launched its industries initiative. The programme aimed to create broader awareness among businesses and industry about environmental issues and legislation, and to demonstrate new ideas through pilot projects. Our work focused mostly on SMEs located in industrial estates around Ahmedabad.

Initially, success was moderate at best. At the time, Gujarat was witnessing a significant increase in the export of dyes and dye intermediates. Europe had banned the production of several of these chemicals due to environmental concerns, and industries here saw this as an opportunity. Some of these chemicals—such as K acid and H acid—were toxic and harmful to the environment. As pollution intensified, the Gujarat High Court, in 1995, ordered the shutdown of over 600 SMEs for violating pollution control laws.[17]

Suddenly, there was a surge of interest in environmental management and the search for solutions. These included better manufacturing practices, effluent treatment and the setting up of common effluent treatment plants at industrial estates. At the time, the interest largely revolved around understanding the laws and new standards and how to comply with them to avoid fines and closures.

For several years, environmental issues were still largely seen as related to pollution, protecting wildlife and preventing the cutting down of trees. I was once on a government committee to approve a new textile plant. The applicant, Arvind Mills, had represented that the proposed plant was non-polluting and involved no disturbance to wildlife. At the time, groundwater was not seen as an environmental issue. When the committee pointed out that depletion and lowering of groundwater levels could dry up nearly eighty village wells, the company said they would redesign the plan.

Within a few months, a new proposal was submitted that involved recycling over 90 per cent of the water.[18] Furthermore, the company took responsibility for ensuring that wells in the nearby villages would not dry up. Not only did they succeed in recycling the water, but having developed expertise in better water management, they started a company to consult with others on how this could be done.[19] Environmental issues were no longer seen as a hindrance but rather as a challenge and an opportunity—what we today refer to as the green economy—with new enterprises and jobs.

Increasing consumer consciousness and certification is another driver for companies moving towards responsible environmental behaviour. For example, CII has promoted its GreenCo certification programme, under which industries are evaluated on parameters such as greenhouse gas (GHG) reduction and renewable energy use.

One of the earlier initiatives, the Ecomark, an environmental certification mark for products was launched by the Ministry of Environment and Forests. We at CEE were asked to design the label and selected the Indian *matka* as a symbol of perfect design steeped in Indian tradition. Today, there are a number of labels that drive both industry and consumers. The star rating by the Bureau of Energy Efficiency (BEE) is widely accepted for white goods, and energy saving has become a significant consideration, for instance, when buying a refrigerator. Several green ratings for buildings have also emerged, including LEED and GRIHA certifications.

Market-based mechanisms have also been tried and have shown a lot of potential. In Surat, a government-anchored programme to tackle air pollution from industrial point sources was introduced in 2019. It was the world's first pilot programme for particulate matter emissions trading, known as the Emission Trading Scheme for Particulate Matter (ETS-PM). It was a collaboration between the Ministry of Environment, Forest and Climate Change (MoEFCC), the Central Pollution Control Board (CPCB) and the Gujarat Pollution Control Board (GPCB) on the government side, and J-PAL South Asia, the University of Chicago and Yale University on the research side. The programme uses CPCB-mandated continuous emission monitoring systems (CEMS). The Surat ETS-PM pilot has demonstrated the feasibility of using market-based mechanisms as a powerful tool to mitigate the impacts of air pollution.

Industry initiatives

Increasingly, industries have been moving towards cleaner production and taking responsibility for their environmental impact. From a climate change perspective, industries are now undertaking various measures to make processes more efficient, save electricity and other resources, and adopt responsible practices. To encourage and recognize this leadership by industry, JSW and the *Times of India*, as part of the Earth Care Awards, dedicated a special category for industry. Some examples of corporate initiatives include:

- Geocycle India, the in-house waste management arm of Ambuja Cements and ACC, has co-processed about 2 million tons of waste. It operates six pre-processing and fourteen co-processing facilities, handling close to 1 million tons of waste annually and diverting it from landfills.[20]

- Mahindra & Mahindra's Susten comprises the group's renewable engineering, procurement and construction unit (with more than 4 GW of capacity constructed) as well as an independent power production unit with around 1.54 GW of operational solar plants.[21]
- Godrej Industries installed a unique heat recovery system at one of their units. The system helps reduce carbon emissions by decarbonizing the heating and cooling system and is scalable wherever substantial heat recovery is possible. Godrej has also made environmental sustainability an integral part of its manufacturing and supply chain processes.[22]
- The Oil and Natural Gas Corporation (ONGC) introduced a waste heat recovery project to recover flare gases, along with a gas flaring reduction project. These and several other initiatives have helped reduce CO2 emissions by approximately 1 million tons per annum.[23]
- TATA Sponge Iron Ltd uses kiln gas to generate power in its waste heat recovery power plants. The project has generated 26 MW of electricity from waste gases for in-house consumption.[24]
- ITC's Sustainability 2.0 vision is anchored in the inclusive and innovative business models the company has implemented on a large scale over many years. Its vision and goals are to ensure water security for all, restore biodiversity by adopting nature-based solutions, create an effective circular economy for post-consumer packaging waste and scale up programmes that support sustainable livelihoods.[25]

- Mother Dairy, a wholly owned subsidiary of the National Dairy Development Board, is the first Indian dairy cooperative to acquire CPCB registration and implement EPR. Their efforts follow a holistic approach and include the collection and recycling/co-processing of post-consumer single-layered plastic (SLP) and multi-layered plastic (MLP) waste.[26]
- Hindustan Unilever is redesigning its products and business models based on 'reduce, reuse and recycle'. The plastic they use is kept within the system and out of the environment by purchasing post-consumer recycled plastic and adopting waste-free manufacturing methods.[27]
- Procter & Gamble has reduced absolute emissions across global operations by 57 per cent through energy efficiency measures and renewable energy sourcing.[28]

Most of these examples are from larger industries. Today, many of them are not only implementing cleaner production practices within their own industries but also innovating and impacting the industry sector as a whole. However, much more effort is still required to create the same level of awareness and responsibility among small and medium enterprises.

Most industry associations have also taken important steps in this direction. The Confederation of Indian Industry (CII) has a Climate Change Council, while the Federation of Indian Chambers of Commerce and Industry (FICCI) has set up an Environment and Climate Change Division that focuses on climate and policy issues. Currently, FICCI is promoting clean developmental mechanisms (CDM) and carbon credits among industries.

Afforestation and greening

While the primary responsibility for greening lies with the Forest Department and other government agencies, businesses have also started taking major initiatives towards afforestation. For instance, Reliance Industries undertook an extensive mangrove plantation initiative, successfully planting mangroves across 875 acres of land. This effort contributes not only to climate change mitigation but also to the conservation and restoration of these vital coastal ecosystems[29] by providing valuable habitats for a wide range of species. This proactive approach sets an example for corporate responsibility in preserving natural ecosystems. Governments are also collaborating with corporate efforts. Reliance Industries and the government of Gujarat have entered into a memorandum of understanding (MoU) to establish a mangrove forest across approximately 3500 acres in the Marine National Park.[30]

Another example is Godrej & Boyce, who, in collaboration with CII and the World Wide Fund for Nature (WWF), India, launched the India Mangroves Coalition to protect and sustainably manage mangrove ecosystems in India.[31] The initiative focuses on raising awareness, conducting research, advocating policy interventions and fostering collaborations among various stakeholders. It signifies a commitment to mangrove conservation and highlights the importance of cooperation between industry, environmental organizations and the business community.[32]

HCL Harit, the flagship programme for environmental action by HCL, focuses on increasing green cover, conserving and rejuvenating water bodies, improving coastal and marine habitats and promoting environmental education with the help of innovative tools and techniques.[33]

Net zero and India

Top Indian corporations are increasing their sustainability quotient through investments in improving operational sustainability by enhancing efficiency, responsibly procuring materials and upgrading disclosures. However, much work remains to be done to fulfil the net-zero targets set for the country. Several major Indian companies are already working towards achieving net-zero emissions on or before 2050. These commitments align with global efforts to combat climate change and reduce greenhouse gas emissions.

Companies are exploring strategies and initiatives to transition towards cleaner and more sustainable practices. This includes investing in renewable energy, implementing energy-efficient technologies, and adopting sustainable business models. To lessen their carbon footprint, Indian businesses have boosted their investments in renewable energy, waste heat recovery systems, more efficient equipment and renewable fuels.

Some examples include Wipro,[34] Aditya Birla Group,[35] JSW Steel,[36] UltraTech[37] and Adani,[38] which has set a target of 2050 for achieving net-zero emissions. Others have set more aggressive targets, such as Reliance (2035);[39] Dalmia Cement,[40] Proctor and Gamble[41] and Mahindra & Mahindra Group (2040);[42] Dabur (2040);[43] Tata Steel (2045);[44] and Indian Oil (2046).[45] Certain companies, like Infosys,[46] have already achieved their net-zero targets.

As per the Business Responsibility and Sustainability Reporting (BRSR) criteria introduced by India's market regulator, the Securities and Exchange Board of India (SEBI), around 100 companies voluntarily disclosed information for the fiscal year 2021-2022. From the fiscal year 2022-2023 onwards,

BRSR reporting will be mandatory for the top 1000 listed companies in India.

The Carbon Disclosure Project (CDP) reported a significant 40 per cent rise in environmental disclosures across its three focus areas—climate change, water security and forests—by Indian corporates in 2022. This increase is in response to requests from investors for greater transparency on environmental issues. The proactive efforts of some companies reflect a growing awareness of climate-related risks and a commitment to environmental sustainability within India's corporate sector.[47]

GRI South Asia and the Bombay Stock Exchange (BSE) have signed an MoU to work together to promote sustainability reporting practices among listed companies. This includes conducting workshops and trainings with local companies to build their capacity. The GRI Universal Standards 2021 update includes revised reporting principles, requirements and structure, to fully reflect the environmental and human rights due diligence expectations set in intergovernmental instruments. The linkage document also takes into account the new GRI Sector Standards.[48]

Over thirty Indian companies have also committed to the Science-Based Targets initiative (SBTi), pledging to achieve net-zero emissions by 2050 or earlier.[49] SBTi—a collaboration between the CDP, the UN Global Compact, the World Resources Institute and WWF—provides businesses with guidance and techniques to set environmental sustainability targets.

To finance their expansion plans, companies are increasingly turning to sustainability-linked loans (SLL), which offer lower interest rates. Some Indian companies that have recently raised SLLs include JSW Cement, Birla Carbon and Glenmark Pharmaceuticals.[50]

However, considering the substantial capital required to achieve net-zero ambitions, there is a need for accelerated fundraising in this sector. According to a report by the Council on Energy, Environment and Water (CEEW), India will require an investment of $10.1 trillion (over Rs 830 lakh crore) by 2070 to achieve net-zero emissions.[51] This translates to an annual investment of over $200 billion.

Modelling and research commissioned by the High-level Policy Commission on Getting Asia to Net Zero suggest that achieving net-zero emissions by 2070 in India could have significant positive impacts on the economy. It is estimated that the transition to net zero could boost India's GDP by as much as 4.7 per cent above the projected baseline growth by 2036, amounting to a total of $371 billion.[52] Furthermore, the shift to a net-zero economy would create additional employment opportunities, creating 15 million jobs by 2047 compared to a baseline scenario. Additionally, households could save approximately $9.7 billion in energy costs by 2060.[53]

To support India's transition to net zero, the report suggests leveraging carbon revenues or other domestic tax-raising mechanisms to fund green investments. It also emphasizes the importance of international support, as this would free up domestic finance for development, poverty reduction and managing social impacts. Such an approach would help mitigate the potential negative impacts on households from higher prices and taxes.

Overall, the findings highlight the potential economic and societal benefits of pursuing a net-zero emissions target in India. The transition would not only contribute to climate change mitigation but also unlock opportunities for economic growth, job creation and cost savings for households.[54]

The push towards net-zero emissions reflects the growing recognition among Indian companies of the need to address climate change and contribute to global sustainability goals. Achieving net-zero emissions by 2050 is a significant commitment that requires substantial effort and collaboration across sectors.[55]

Towards a circular economy

There is no concept of waste in nature. What we consider the end of one system or cycle marks the start of another one. The output of one process is the input for another—this is the essence of a circular model.

Human development, especially after the Industrial Revolution, changed this. With the discovery of coal, natural gas and petroleum—the fossilized remains of ancient forests and biomass—vast energy reserves became available for the taking. The invention of machines of all types increased our capabilities far beyond what even kings could have imagined a few centuries earlier. Modernization, development and growth were all linear concepts. It was assumed that the waste generated would be taken care of by nature and the environment. After all, how much damage could human activity do? Until then, human existence had largely involved biodegradable materials, and with relatively low population levels, natural systems could manage the resulting waste. However, this was no longer true with the rise of fossil fuels and the discovery of new, non-biodegradable substances.

Our organization has been working on three areas of the circular economy: plastics, textiles and used oils. The circular economy concept requires industries at various stages of the value chain to work together. In India, part of this value chain inevitably involves the informal sector, which plays an important role in waste recycling. It also involves many small and medium enterprises.

A recent conference on used oils, organized by Rosefield Energy Tech along with CEE in June 2023, provided a good example of how insights from one part of the value chain can benefit others. It is estimated that out of the nearly 2.8 million tons of virgin oil consumed, only 15 per cent of used oil is collected and reprocessed, despite India having a re-refining capacity of nearly 1.18 million tons. The conference brought together various stakeholders, including producers, importers, brand owners and small aggregators of used oils. In particular, they deliberated on a recent notification by the Ministry of Environment, Forest and Climate Change on Extended Producer Responsibility (EPR) and explored ways to develop a circularity model for used oils.

To strengthen circularity practices in the textile sector, GIZ and Aditya Birla Fashion and Retail Limited are collaborating on a project titled 'Approaches for Circular Textiles and Apparel Industry in India'. The project, being implemented by our organization, aims to help India's textile and apparel industry embrace circular economy principles by developing guidelines and training modules, as well as collaborating with start-ups through an innovation challenge. Eventually, the project is expected to result in a policy paper for the Ministry of Textiles.

We are also working with HDFC to help set up a circular economy model for the plastics industry.

MSMEs must play a major part in the transition to a circular economy. According to the Ministry of Micro, Small and Medium Enterprises, MSMEs accounted for 30.27 per cent of India's GDP in 2018-19.[56] However, a part of this sector is unorganized and utilizes crude technologies to increase production. Due to capital constraints and the informal nature of some enterprises, many rely on limited end-of-pipe solutions. As a result, the MSME sector is projected to continue contributing significantly to industrial pollution in India.[57]

Circular economy opportunities for MSMEs exist across all stages of the value chain, not just in the more common downstream activities (recycling, reuse), but also in the upstream stage through pollution avoidance, design changes, resource-efficient production, and substituting secondary materials for primary resources.[58]

Some challenges in implementing circular economy practices for SMEs are the lack of technically skilled human resources with the know-how to transform industrial processes and inadequate training for the teams involved. Top management is often reluctant to move from a linear economy to a circular one due to the transition costs. SMEs also expect financial benefits and subsidies for making such a change, which entails investments.

Government policy support

The Government of India brought out a National Action Plan on Climate Change (NAPCC), which has eight missions, in response to India's global commitments to address climate change. A Perform, Achieve and Trade (PAT) scheme under the National Mission on Enhanced Energy Efficiency (NMEEE), implemented by the Bureau of Energy Efficiency, Ministry of Power, aims at reducing specific energy consumption—i.e., energy use per unit of production—for designated consumers in energy-intensive sectors. This is done with an associated market mechanism to enhance cost-effectiveness through the certification of excess energy savings, which can be traded. The savings are converted into tradable instruments called Energy Saving Certificates (ESCerts), which are traded on power exchanges.

Governments at all levels and industries need to work together closely to evolve policies that support net zero and circularity. Some immediate steps that can be taken are:

- Get industry sectors to work together to develop circular economy models. This will help identify gaps in technology, policy, skilling and capacity building. Industry-wise action plans can be drawn up with clear goals and milestones.
- Connect with the vast informal recycling sector and bring them into the emerging circular economy with better skills, tools and dignity.
- Work closely with local industry associations to create awareness. When local bodies and their members take the lead, the shift to a cleaner production process is far more impactful, and experience sharing is more focused and actionable.
- Ensure ministries, local government and pollution control boards are continuously engaged in the process, working as partners while being strict with violators and those deliberately breaking the environmental regulations and laws.
- Develop financial instruments that can better assist the required transformation.
- Encourage innovation. Promote in-company research and development, research institutions and start-ups; encourage companies to share innovations, which could be via consulting or turnkey assignments; and adapt global best practices to Indian conditions.
- Make annual sustainability reporting mandatory for all companies. This will at least make units conscious of the issues pertinent to their industry.

- Use recognition and awards to encourage companies to move towards more responsible production and distribution. Look into certification as a means of prompting consumers to make better choices.
- Support efforts to increase public awareness, technical training, green skilling and the greening of curricula so that entrants to the workforce already have a fairly good understanding of the climate change crisis and the actions required.
- Continue to involve businesses in afforestation and greening efforts in areas they control or can influence.

Conclusion

As I conclude this chapter, news reports are declaring that July 2023 has been the hottest month in recorded history. United Nations Secretary-General Antonio Guterres has stated that the planet is entering an 'era of global boiling'. Scientists widely agree that this extreme heat is primarily linked to fossil fuel use.[59] Fuel consumption is tied to nearly every business process, from electricity generation to waste management. Business is now very much at the core of the sustainability and climate change efforts needed to achieve both national and global targets. Larger corporations are already gearing up for this challenge. Smaller businesses, too, must be equally involved. The circular economy model offers both the inspiration and the opportunity for achieving sustainable development. Solving the climate crisis demands that businesses work together and feel a sense of shared ownership and responsibility.

4

The Chemicals Industry

A Business View

R. MUKUNDAN

'In a free enterprise, community is not just another stakeholder but is the very purpose of its existence.'

—JAMSETJI NUSSERWANJI TATA

BUSINESS IS A FORCE FOR good, but headline-making news reports indicate the reverse—ranging from the Bhopal gas tragedy to stories of runaway tycoons and financial frauds. They fuel the impression that businesses can't be trusted to act in the public interest. However, the speed and scale of the COVID-19 vaccination effort demonstrated the potential of businesses rising to the challenge to serve the greater good. So, what can businesses do to earn the trust of all stakeholders? What steps can business leaders take to drive positive change, both within their companies and in their broader impact on the environment and society? It boils down to being responsible, building coalitions, maintaining transparency and taking action to deliver on promises.

This essay is divided into four sections, each highlighting specific examples of voluntary corporate action and how they can lead to meaningful change.

Be responsible

> *'No success or achievement in material terms is worthwhile unless it serves the needs or interests of the country and its people and is achieved by fair and honest means.'*
>
> —J.R.D. TATA

Responsible Care—started in Canada in 1985—is a global, voluntary initiative developed by the chemical industry for the chemical industry. It operates in sixty-seven countries, whose combined chemical sectors account for nearly 90 per cent of global chemical production. Ninety-six of the world's 100 largest chemical producers have adopted Responsible Care. It reflects the industry's commitment to improving health, safety and environmental performance.

Signatory companies pledge to enhance performance in environmental protection, occupational safety and health, plant safety, product stewardship and logistics. They also commit to continuously enhancing dialogue with local communities and the public, independent of legal requirements. In essence, Responsible Care is about ethical leadership that benefits society, the economy and the environment. This creates the necessary conditions for change through peer pressure and mutual assistance. The outcomes are dramatic, with improvements in a wide range of areas.

According to the American Chemistry Council, an industry trade association for American chemical companies, Responsible

Care companies have achieved a 26 per cent reduction in recordable injuries, five times better safety management than other US manufacturing sectors and three times better worker safety compared to the broader chemical industry. These companies have also recorded a 39 per cent reduction in Nox emissions, an 18 per cent reduction in SOx and a 12 per cent reduction in greenhouse gas intensity. Collectively, they have invested over $27 billion in enhancing facility security.

In India, implementation amongst major chemical companies has been equally impressive, increasing trust with policymakers and regulators, and yielding tangible benefits for the companies involved. As of April 2022, 160 companies were Responsible Care signatories, working to implement the Responsible Care Codes Management System, and seventy-nine of these were Responsible Care logo holders. The chemical industry is heavily concentrated in Gujarat and Tamil Nadu, where state regulators are giving increased importance to the adoption of Responsible Care. In Gujarat, Responsible Care-registered companies are given an additional two-year environmental consent validity and fast-track clearance for projects.

Additionally, the Government of India is a signatory to SAICM (Strategic Approach to International Chemicals Management)[1] among other international conventions, making Responsible Care not merely a choice but an imperative for sustained business growth.

This recognition—that being responsible is good for business—is backed by several research studies, especially those involving early adopters who distinguished themselves through improved environmental performance.

The Responsible Care approach began by building the case for change. Although it was initially shaped by the 1984 Bhopal gas tragedy, over the years, the programme has evolved to include independent performance reviews, the adoption of specific measures to evaluate industry performance, greater public transparency and more value to business operations. It transformed from a company- or site-specific tool into a value chain and supply chain initiative, including a network of suppliers, distributors and customers.

The success of the Responsible Care programme can be attributed to the following measures:

1. Adopting a progressive Responsible Care Management System (RCMS) that incorporates appropriate business elements and yields operational reliability and performance improvement.
2. Instituting independent third-party certification for all member companies.
3. Integrating several quality certifications, including ISO 14001.
4. Expanding performance metrics to measure individual company and industry performance.
5. Enhancing both physical and cyber security.

The outcomes, while visible now, were not easy to measure in the initial years, as implementing Responsible Care requires a long-term perspective. It involves considerable investment in measures can that impact short-term profitability, but in the long run, reduce the risk faced by organizations. These investments should be viewed as an ongoing commitment to environmental improvement, required for competitiveness and reducing risks. Increasingly, they are also leading to faster approvals and longer durations for permits and operating consents.

There is also an inevitable impact on corporate culture. Such investments enhance employee pride and satisfaction, creating a cadre of ambassadors in the community. This, in turn, contributes positively to government policy and the industry's public image.

Build a coalition of stakeholders

> '*I suggest that the most significant contribution organised industry can make is by identifying itself with the life and the problems of the people of the community to which it belongs, and by applying its resources, skills and talents to the extent that they can reasonably spare them, to serve and help them.*'
>
> —J.R.D. TATA

While the chemical industry often evokes images of disasters that have impacted communities, there is growing recognition of the agri-value chain's significant impact on sustainability, particularly in relation to deforestation, biodiversity and water resources. Hence, sustainability has rapidly become a key challenge for agribusiness companies, regardless of their position along the supply chain or geographic focus.

In response, agribusiness firms are interacting with a much broader set of stakeholders, including not only supply chain actors and investors, but also governments, knowledge institutions, non-governmental organizations (NGOs) and other civil society groups. This has led to a proliferation of initiatives and multi-stakeholder movements such as the Sustainable Agriculture Initiative Platform, GAIN Business Alliance, Rainforest Alliance and the Water Footprint Network.

In this context, it is worth highlighting the efforts of coffee and tea plantations in India to work towards a sustainable future.

Coffee is grown extensively in the Western Ghats, a region recognized as a global biodiversity hotspot that holds about 30 per cent of India's plant and vertebrate species diversity in less than 6 per cent of the country's land area. Much of the large-scale conversion of forests and grasslands into plantations for crops like tea, coffee and timber had already occurred in many areas prior to 1920.

Among the various plantations in the Western Ghats, crops such as coffee and cardamom, traditionally grown under the shade of trees, occupy a special place. In areas such as the Annamalai hills, where hunting is prohibited, one can walk through coffee plantations and see even endangered or endemic species such as great hornbills, lion-tailed macaques and Nilgiri langurs. A large body of research from around the world has established that shade-grown coffee plantations can support many forest species, including birds, arboreal mammals, invertebrates such as ants and bees, as well as native trees and epiphytic plants.

Two aspects must be remembered when considering the value of shade-grown coffee for biodiversity. First, although coffee plantations can support significant biodiversity, many species are restricted to forests and will only survive if remnant forests in the landscape—such as reserved forests, rainforest fragments and sacred groves—are also protected. Second, just as there are many brews of coffee, there are many 'brews' of coffee estates. Farms that rely on a limited or even just a single shade tree species, particularly alien (exotic) species like silver oak, provide poorer habitats than farms that maintain a diversity of native shade tree species.

Here, Indian coffee plantations had a window of opportunity. Unlike newer coffee-growing regions such as Vietnam and Sumatra, where plantations are often established through deforestation, many of India's coffee estates are decades-old, well-established plantations with a variety of native shade tree species, with reserved forests and sacred groves integrated into the landscape. The revival of traditional practices—using native shade trees, protecting sacred groves and forests and adopting a no-hunting policy—has highlighted how conservation can benefit coffee.

Globally, there is increasing recognition of the economic value of biodiversity and forests to plantations. These benefits include ecosystem services such as pollination, carbon sequestration and watershed benefits for farms. Besides these direct advantages, many schemes are being implemented as incentives for conservation in production landscapes. These include conservation easements, direct payments or credits for biodiversity and ecosystem services, carbon sequestration and trading, land purchases, conservation certification of produce, corporate social responsibility initiatives and voluntary efforts. The Rainforest Alliance certification for sustainable agriculture in coffee plantations is one such example.

While large plantations do benefit significantly from these efforts, small plantations, while gaining from better technical expertise and farm practices, often do not seem to receive the same financial benefits from these certifications. It is in this context that the efforts of Trustea deserve appreciation. Trustea is an Indian initiative to deliver all the elements of sustainable agriculture in plantations while simultaneously providing value for small growers.

The initial funders included Tata Consumer, Unilever and IDH (Initiatief Duurzame Handel). The programme committee comprised the Tea Board of India (Chair), IDH (Vice-Chair), Unilever, Tata Consumer, Solidaridad, Rainforest Alliance and the Ethical Tea partnership. This inclusive approach of bringing together a quasi-government industry body like the Tea Board with multiple stakeholders, including the plantation workforce, has led to widespread adoption of the Trustea programme and high-impact results.

By 2019, 663 million kilograms of tea were Trustea-verified, constituting about 48 per cent of total production. Traceability was as high as 89 per cent in the northeast, while south India (63 per cent) and West Bengal (56 per cent) were improving on this score. The project achieved 100 per cent soil testing in the northeast and south India, and implemented about 60 per cent of the best water management practices. The impact on the workforce, through better work practices, was 100 per cent.

This overarching approach of linking the environment with safety (both food and workforce) and livelihoods has delivered a highly impactful outcome.

Be transparent

> '*Business, as I have seen it, places one great demand on you: it needs you to self-impose a framework of ethics, values, fairness, and objectivity on yourself at all times*'
>
> —Ratan Tata

The key aspects of business integrity are fairness, honesty and transparency. Transparency and disclosure (T&D) are critical components of corporate governance and essential for resolving information gaps. Corporate disclosures help bridge the divide between external and internal stakeholders, playing an essential role in the functioning of stock markets.

It is empirically proven that when companies provide accurate and timely reports on their performance, they build trust with shareholders. T&D also protects investors' rights by reducing risks associated with share prices. Corporate governance relies heavily on T&D policies, which help reduce information asymmetry and agency bottlenecks. T&D improves corporate governance procedures and helps increase operational efficiency.

The number of Indian companies now reporting ESG in their disclosures is increasing partly due to encouragement and push by the Securities and Exchange Board of India (SEBI), the government regulator for listed firms. We need to continue this effort to enforce and encourage such disclosures through legislated requirements, standards and recommendations. These ESG disclosures will improve Indian firms' corporate image, provide a better understanding of their products and services, and, most importantly, improve their relationships with various stakeholders.

Act: Deliver on the promise

> '*There are solutions for most problems. The barriers and roadblocks that we face are usually of our own making, and these can only be demolished by having determination to find a solution—even if contrary to conventional wisdom that prevails around us—by breaking tradition.*'
>
> —Ratan Tata

Annual climate summits are usually marked by a flurry of new corporate commitments. But what set the year 2023 apart was the heightened scepticism among participants, activists and even companies about whether these pledges would result in sufficient and measurable action. This uncertainty comes in the context of a looming global recession, continued conflict in Europe and a slowdown in China. According to the 2023 report from the Intergovernmental Panel on Climate Change, the world is expected to reach a 1.5°C rise in temperatures by the early 2030s. Whether we can limit warming to this threshold—and prevent the most severe climate impacts—will depend on the actions taken in this decade.

Businesses can help innovate and scale solutions to climate change. Or it can perpetuate outdated systems profiting from practices threatening our collective future.

a. Net-zero transition

In recent years, the concept of net-zero has become a popular way for businesses to demonstrate their commitment to climate action. Over 30 per cent of the world's 2000 largest publicly traded companies (by revenue) have promised to achieve net-zero by mid-century. However, not all net-zero pledges are equal. Lack of standardization has led to widely varying interpretations of 'net-zero', including differences in the sources of emissions included in the target boundary, the level and pace of emissions reductions and the strategies used to meet these targets.

The Science-Based Targets initiative (SBTi), co-founded by the World Resources Institute, has introduced a new standard to tackle this issue by providing a science-based definition of net-zero.

What is India doing?

India unveiled its Long-Term Low Emission Development Strategy (LT LEDS) in October 2022. This document not only outlined the pathway to achieving net zero by 2070 but, more importantly, committed to several intermediate targets, some of which are set for as early as 2030. The salient amongst them include:

1. Meeting 50 per cent of India's cumulative electric power installed capacity from non-fossil fuel sources by 2030.
2. Reducing the emission intensity of GDP by 45 per cent below 2005 levels by 2030.
3. Achieving a three-fold increase in nuclear installed capacity by 2032.
4. Proactively shutting down inefficient thermal power units—a total 241 units, with a combined capacity of 17,281 MW, have been retired from the 10th Plan period up to September 2021.
5. Targeting 20 per cent ethanol blending in petrol by 2025, with a savings potential of approximately Rs 30,000 crore per year.
6. Making Indian Railways net-zero by 2030, leading to an annual mitigation of 60 million tonnes of CO2.

b. Commodity-driven deforestation

Despite global lockdowns in 2020, forest loss in the tropics rose by 12 per cent compared to 2019 and continues on an upward trend. Of the 12.2 million hectares lost in 2020, 4.2 million hectares—an area the size of the Netherlands—were cleared from primary tropical rainforests, which are known for their immense biodiversity and role as crucial global carbon sinks. Such clearing often violates the rights of indigenous and local communities who have stewarded these forests over countless generations. Those living in voluntary isolation are some of the most vulnerable, as deforestation can cause displacement, forced contact with outsiders and exposure to illnesses for which they have little or no immunity, among other risks.

What is India doing?

In India, 24.6 per cent of the total geographical area is under forest and tree cover. India has among the lowest rates of gross deforestation in the world, whether measured in absolute terms, per capita terms, or annual rates. The carbon stock in forests is estimated at 7,204 million tonnes.

India's Nationally Determined Contributions (NDCs) include a target to create an additional carbon sink of 2.5 to 3 billion tonnes of CO2 equivalent by 2030.

Major policies and institutions include:

- National Mission for a Green India
- National Afforestation Programme
- Compensatory Afforestation Fund Management and Planning Authority
- Nagar Van Yojana
- National REDD+ (Reducing Emissions from Deforestation and Forest Degradation) Strategy (2018)
- National Rural Livelihoods Mission
- Forest Fire Prevention and Management Scheme
- AMRUT (Atal Mission for Rejuvenation and Urban Transformation)

Other voluntary contributions include:

1. Restoration of 26 million hectares of degraded land by 2030.
2. Adoption of twelve national biodiversity targets, aligned with the twenty global Aichi biodiversity goals.

3. Large-scale greening efforts by the National Highways Authority of India (NHAI) and Indian Railways.

The forest sector employs approximately 6.23 million people and is a source of livelihood for several communities, especially tribal communities.

Just transition to net zero

While the above highlights India's commitments, their delivery depends on joint action by all stakeholders—the government as an enabler, and enterprises in both public and private sectors as drivers of outcomes.

India also needs to rethink its governance systems. For example, there is no unified Ministry of Energy. Instead, the sector is supported by multiple bodies, including the Ministry of Power, Ministry of Coal, Ministry of Petroleum and Natural Gas, Ministry of Renewable Energy, and the Department of Atomic Energy. We need to create a platform for unified action by all these ministries to support India's transition to net zero.

The traditional focus of emissions reduction strategies has been energy. The scale-up of clean energy remains central to decarbonization. Encouragingly, some important tipping points have been reached. The fall in renewable energy costs has been so steep that the transition to zero-carbon electricity now seems inevitable. The automotive industry appears to be at a similar tipping point, although the uptake of zero-emissions vehicles remains low.

In most other sectors, however, the transition to zero carbon remains uncertain. Without diverting attention from finishing the job in the most advanced sectors, net zero is about addressing issues of hard to abate sectors, such as heavy industries, buildings, food and agriculture, aviation and mining. In most of these sectors, while zero-carbon solutions do exist, they are often expensive and not yet as well-established as incumbent technologies and infrastructure.

This transition requires a comprehensive approach, involving multiple stakeholders. Climate change is increasingly being addressed by communities, administrations, boardrooms, regulatory agencies, central banks, financial institutions and even the courts. This broad-based societal support will be essential for a successful net-zero transition.

Much of the work will be sector-specific. For example, in sectors that are less locked into high-carbon practices, there is a need to proactively train a young workforce in twenty-first-century skills and make long-term investment decisions with net zero in mind. In hard-to-abate sectors, the shift will create short-term pressure on some workers, who may have to be reskilled and redeployed, and the risk of stranded assets in high-carbon industries. Addressing these transition challenges is an integral part of delivery, and requires close collaboration between government, industry, labour unions and local communities, along with substantial investment in education, skills and social protection.

Some thoughts for accelerating change

Overall, India and Indian firms have a great opportunity to position themselves at the forefront of green and resilient supply chains. Many positive actions are already underway, and the current pace bodes well for further accelerating change. India Inc. has begun to act responsibly by building coalitions of stakeholders, with transparency at the core, to deliver on commitments. However, the pace of change has been slow when one looks at the task at hand. This can be accelerated by focusing on three key elements:

1. **Deliver on efficiency and near-term targets**: The targets set for 2030 are the catalysts for change, and they drive action. We must accelerate and ensure delivery of the same. These include the already initiated closure of old and inefficient power plants, vehicles and buildings; and improving the efficiency of logistics through improved infrastructure to ensure the smooth flow of materials and people. Rapid digitization, improved digital connectivity and a strong digital infrastructure are equally crucial.
2. **Greater focus on transition fuels and energy systems.** Can we increase support for bioethanol and biodiesel? Can we mandate a 30 per cent blend of biomass in coal boilers by 2030? Can we bring fiscal support to bio-resources? Can we pivot production-linked incentive schemes to procurement incentive schemes to generate demand for early-stage products and solutions? Can we expand land availability and reduce acquisition barriers for renewable deployment?
3. **Foster collaborative innovation at scale**: India can identify a few grand challenges and bring together research and development, the Council of Scientific and Industrial Research (CSIR) and universities on large-scale platforms to drive innovation. Focus areas could include providing green hydrogen at $1 per kg, developing smart and micro grids, designing climate-smart urban spaces and building climate-resilient rural economies.

We began this chapter by asserting that business can be a force for good. To realize this, businesses must move from the sidelines and take a leadership role in this transition, transforming themselves and, in the process, accelerating change and delivering well before the commitments we have all made.

5

Building Sustainably

A Cement Industry Perspective

PARTH JINDAL

Indian cement industry: Driving India's growth story

THE CEMENT SECTOR IS AMONG the fastest-growing core industries in India and is crucial to the country's economic growth and development. India is the second-largest cement producer in the world, with an installed capacity of over 540 million tonnes per annum. In financial year (FY) 21–22, cement production stood at approximately 360 million tonnes, the majority of which was consumed domestically. As India aspires to grow from a $3 trillion economy to a $10 trillion economy over the next decade, cement consumption is expected to show commensurate growth.

The Indian cement industry is relatively consolidated, with the top twenty companies accounting for around 70 per cent of total production. With abundant, geographically dispersed reserves of high-quality limestone and low per capita cement consumption, there is huge potential for growth. Cement demand is expected to reach around 450 million tonnes per annum by FY 24–25.

This demand growth will be driven by sustained investments in housing under the Pradhan Mantri (PM) Awas Yojana, and several other central government initiatives such as the Mahatma Gandhi National Rural Employment Guarantee (MGNREGA), PM Garib Kalyan Rozgar Abhiyan and PM Gati Shakti—the National Master Plan (NMP) for Multimodal Connectivity. State-level schemes, including Matir Srishti (West Bengal) and public works programmes in Jharkhand will also contribute to growth.

To meet the increasing demand, CRISIL Ratings estimates that the cement industry will add approximately 80 million to 100 million tonnes of capacity by FY 24–25, marking the highest capacity expansion in the past decade.

Cement: A hard-to-abate sector in terms of decarbonization

The cement sector contributes around 7 per cent of global anthropogenic CO2 emissions. On average, the production of one tonne of cement releases approximately 600 kg of CO2 emissions. Most of these emissions are generated during the cement manufacturing process (see Figure 1 below), particularly during the production of clinker, an intermediate product. As it is difficult to mitigate these process emissions, the cement sector is considered a 'hard-to-abate' sector with respect to CO2 emissions.

The Indian government recently updated its Nationally Determined Contribution (NDC) target, committing to reduce the emissions intensity of its GDP by 45 per cent by 2030 compared to 2005 levels. This represents a significant step towards achieving India's long-term goal of reaching net zero by 2070, as announced by the prime minister at the 26th Conference of the Parties (COP26) in Glasgow, UK.

Fig: Co2 emissions in the cement value chain

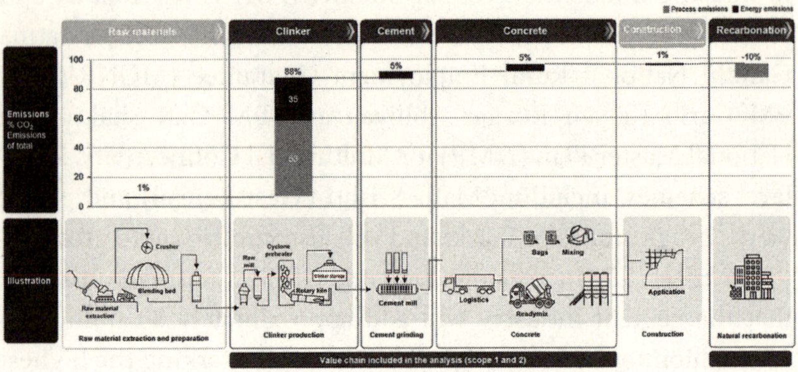

Considering the multifold growth expected in the cement sector over the next decade, India will face a challenge in managing its overall greenhouse gas (GHG) footprint and meeting its medium-term and long-term emission targets. This, in turn, has led to a focus on decarbonizing hard-to-abate sectors such as cement; indeed, the industry has already begun exploring innovative approaches to reduce process emissions.

One of the most common levers to lower process emissions is to reduce the production of ordinary Portland cement (OPC), which has the highest carbon footprint in the sector, and instead increase the manufacture of blended cements. In blended cement production, part of the clinker is substituted with supplementary cementitious materials (SCMs) such as slag and fly ash, which are by-products from steel production and coal-fired power generation, respectively.

In India, the share of blended cement has increased over the past twenty-five years, from around 30 per cent in 1995 to approximately 73 per cent in 2017. The majority of this is Portland pozzolana cement (PPC), which has a carbon footprint about 70 per cent lower than that of OPC. The balance is comprised of Portland slag cement (PSC), which has an even lower carbon footprint—approximately 40 per cent that of OPC. Recently, the industry has seen the introduction of another blended cement variant, Portland composite cement (PCC).

The Indian cement industry's decarbonization journey

The Indian cement industry is a global leader in energy- and resource-efficient cement production. The majority of companies in the sector today have adopted the following decarbonization levers across the manufacturing value chain:

1. Product portfolio management via clinker substitution

As mentioned previously, the Indian cement industry has successfully transitioned towards an increased share of blended cement production. This has been possible due to sustained efforts by industry participants as well as appropriate policy support from the government. Blended cements are environmentally friendly, as they contain a lower proportion of the intermediate product, clinker, which is primarily made of natural limestone. This results in lower CO_2 emissions during the manufacturing process and helps conserve the country's mineral resources. Among blended cements, PSC has the highest potential for clinker substitution (up to 70 per cent); thus, the carbon reduction potential is also quite significant. Simultaneously, the consumption of alternative raw materials such as fly ash and slag avoids the dumping of these in landfills and, consequently, environmental hazards.

Many companies in the industry continue to make headway in this area. Our company, for example, has pioneered the use of ground granulated blast furnace slag (GGBFS) as a replacement for OPC in concrete production. GGBFS is made by grinding slag to a fine powder; it has zero clinker content and, therefore, a minimal carbon footprint. As awareness and acceptance of blended cements and GGBFS increase, this will further reduce the carbon footprint of the cement sector.

2. Use of alternative fuels

Cement manufacturing is an energy-intensive process that has historically relied on traditional fuels such as coal and pet-coke. For several years now, the industry has been using various alternative fuels as partial replacements for traditional fuels to help reduce overall CO2 emissions. Examples include agricultural waste and biomass, municipal solid waste and refuse-derived fuel (RFD), waste tyres and several types of industrial waste, ranging from pharmaceutical waste, spent carbon, spent pot liners (SPL), ETP sludge and oil-soaked cotton rags to waste oil.

The Cement Manufacturers' Association of India estimated that the share of alternative fuel usage in the Indian cement industry was around 4 per cent in 2017; this has undoubtedly increased in recent years. Given that alternative fuel usage in cement kilns can be as high as 90 per cent in certain western European countries, there remains significant potential to further increase its use in India as well. From a technological standpoint, production systems can be modified to accommodate waste co-processing systems. The challenge lies in collecting, segregating, ensuring consistency in pre-processing and transporting alternative fuels. Here, the industry would benefit from collaborations with municipal bodies, tie-ups with agro-waste processors and active promotion of circular economy systems.

Many companies, including ours, have started using other industrial wastes as alternative raw materials, such as steel slag, waste from steel plants and red mud (a by-product of the aluminium production process) in the cement manufacturing process. This not only helps conserve natural resources but also reduces process-related CO_2 emissions.

3. Increasing clean energy consumption

Cement plants consume significant amounts of power in the production process, which has typically been sourced from either captive power plants or the electrical grid. As these legacy power plants have largely used traditional fuel sources, they have contributed to indirect CO_2 emissions (Scope 2 emissions) associated with cement production.

In recent years, several companies have made significant investments in renewable power generation, both wind and solar, as a way to reduce their carbon footprint. We, too, have installed solar systems at two of our plants and have ambitious plans to expand the share of renewable energy in our energy mix. This will be achieved both by building additional solar and wind capacity and through power purchase agreements (PPAs) with other renewable energy producers.

In addition to these measures, there is a potential to generate electricity from waste process gases released during cement manufacturing through waste heat recovery (WHR) power plants. These plants provide clean electricity and are an important lever for decarbonization. The Indian cement industry has been a global leader in installing WHR systems, with the potential to meet up to 70 per cent of the electricity requirement for clinker manufacturing using this clean energy source.

4. Increasing energy efficiency

Unlike in many Western economies, a large part of India's cement production base is relatively new and, therefore, has been set up using modern technology—such as dry horizontal kilns, pre-heaters, etc. This has made the Indian cement industry more efficient than its global counterparts in terms of both thermal and electrical specific energy consumption.

Investing for a sustainable future

Despite the cement industry's best efforts towards decarbonization, we must recognize that achieving net-zero targets will require overcoming several challenges, both short-term and long-term, that the cement industry currently faces or will encounter in the future.

Challenges in decarbonization in the cement sector

Short-term challenges	Long-term challenges
Lack of demand for low-carbon cement/concrete: In the built environment, awareness of green building materials remains low. Additionally, current green building ratings place limited emphasis on the use of such materials. There is a need for increased focus on embodied carbon in the built environment, which will increase the demand for low-carbon cement and concrete.	**Availability of SCMs:** Currently, the industry relies on blast furnace slag and fly ash as supplementary cementitious materials (SCMs) to reduce clinker content in blended cements. However, their availability is expected to decline due to decarbonization efforts in the energy and steel sectors. Basic research is needed to develop new SCMs and alternative materials, such as calcined clay, which our company is also working on.

Short-term challenges	Long-term challenges
Carbon labelling and green procurement: Though Environmental Product Declarations (EPDs) exist, they are not mandated for public procurement. A policy framework is needed to encourage the sourcing of low-carbon materials for public infrastructure projects.	**High cost of future decarbonization technologies:** Technical solutions like carbon capture, utilization and storage (CCUS) are essential for achieving net-zero cement, but their high costs must be passed on to the consumer. While scale and innovation may reduce these costs, we still need a policy framework to incentivize the transition to a net-zero environment.

Addressing these challenges will require collaboration among stakeholders in the cement industry, including manufacturers, policymakers, investors, architects, builders and consumers. While short-term constraints are easier to tackle, aggressive efforts are needed to address long-term challenges. There is a need for significant investments in new products, new production technologies and green energy systems beyond what is technically and commercially feasible today. To succeed, the Indian cement industry must pool its resources through industry associations and academic institutions, collaborate with international companies and associations, and work proactively with the government on the policy front.

Some ways to address the above-mentioned challenges are:

1. Increasing awareness of sustainable construction practices

Government support is essential to promote and popularize green building rating systems such as LEED,[1] GRIHA[2] and IGBC[3] across the country. This would significantly boost the use of eco-friendly building materials. Further, architects and designers must play a proactive role in specifying low-carbon construction materials and emphasizing the importance of embodied carbon reductions. Rating agencies should also increase the weightage given to embodied carbon in line with life cycle analysis of the built environment.

Another way to reduce the industry's carbon footprint is by promoting the reuse of construction and demolition waste in new buildings, which requires supportive policies. The cement industry too has a part to play in educating large cement buyers, both in the public and private sectors, about its innovative and green product offerings.

2. Increasing procurement of green products for public projects

Various government bodies and public sector units in India are, directly or indirectly, large purchasers of cement products. We believe they should take the lead in advancing the procurement of green cement products. There is sufficient precedent for such industry-wide programmes, for example, the mandated use of ethanol-blended petrol across India, which has led to significant foreign exchange savings. In the cement industry, this could take the form of mandating the use of blended cement in public projects to substantially reduce their carbon footprint. Countries such as Canada and France have already taken steps in this direction.

3. Investment in new and emerging 'futuristic' technologies

Several global research projects are analysing ways to reduce the carbon intensity of the cement production chain. At the manufacturing stage, innovations include kiln electrification, use of concentrated solar thermal (CST) energy, reduction in clinker content through the development of new cement variants and standards such as LC3 and geopolymer cement, and identification of alternative waste materials that can be used in clinker production, cement grinding or concrete batching. Financial support will be needed to support basic research and the commercialization of such climate technologies.

Apart from decarbonization in the manufacturing process, carbon capture, utilization and storage (CCUS) is the most important lever for achieving net-zero emissions. However, considerable work needs to be done to make CCUS technically feasible and commercially viable. As other heavy industries like oil and gas and steel also depend on CCUS, a holistic effort is needed to develop a shared infrastructure for transporting captured carbon and developing carbon sinks for its geological sequestration. The government has a major role to play in bringing all industry sectors together, developing enabling policy frameworks, and facilitating financing to make this a reality. Concepts like BECCS (Bioenergy + CCS) could even render cement production carbon-negative, though they entail high capital costs and multiple stakeholders.

4. Introduction of regulations supporting sustainable practices

There are several areas where new regulations would go a long way in enhancing sustainable practices. For example, developing codes and standards to define what constitutes a 'green' product is crucial. Additionally, building a block-chain or digital traceability tool would enable buyers to identify and purchase responsibly produced construction materials.

Finally, the roll-out of a nationwide carbon credit and trading scheme, which is currently under development, would provide a further impetus to the sustainability of the cement sector.

5. Coordinated industry action in technology development

Most Indian cement companies are currently working on research projects to reduce their carbon footprint and increase efficiencies. Given the industry's supply overhang and average capacity utilization of around 70 per cent, companies need to be competitive and make every effort to reduce costs in order to survive. There is a need for greater collaboration in technology development and research work, which could help accelerate the transition to a low-carbon economy.

The way forward

Over the next decade, demand for cement in India will continue to grow in line with the expansion of the Indian economy—consequently, the cement industry will need to further reduce its energy use and carbon intensity.

While cement manufacturers have increased their sustainability through investment and innovation, these changes have largely been incremental. Going forward, the industry must adopt transformational technologies and processes to achieve its net zero targets, and these efforts will be capital-intensive. This will require collaboration across a wide range of stakeholders, including technology suppliers, academia, associations, start-ups, architects and designers, government agencies, green building rating bodies, transporters, builders and end-users. Support from the government on policy, and from banks and financial institutions in the form of new instruments to support capital inflows for sustainability-related projects with much longer tenures will also be essential.

It is imperative that the cement industry maintains a strong commitment to a sustainable future by strengthening its efforts in all three key elements of ESG and sustainability: achieving net zero while reducing natural resource consumption, improving human equity and enhancing corporate transparency. On the environmental front, along with ongoing decarbonization efforts, the industry must augment its focus on water stewardship, biodiversity protection and mitigation of air pollution. On the social front, companies should continue and even expand ongoing programmes that create value for all stakeholders—employees, suppliers and the community—by ensuring health and safety, respecting human rights, improving working conditions and increasing community engagement. Last but not least, the industry should aspire to adopt best-in-class corporate governance norms, use ethical business practices and leverage partnerships while undertaking its business operations.

6

Africa's Green Frontier

A Sustainable Agriculture Perspective

M.D. RAMESH

The logic

WHEN SUSTAINABILITY PRACTICES IN AGRICULTURE began gaining momentum about twenty-five years ago, the term started out as a buzzword. It quickly captured the attention of practitioners and soon became a necessary part of the storytelling by the sellers of the produce.

With more than 33 million small-scale farmers (SSF) in Africa, each typically working on around a hectare of land, the continent's slow adoption of cutting-edge farming methods has kept it behind on the global sustainability learning curve.

One of the earliest corporate success stories in Africa's agricultural value chain (and in parts of Asia) emerged in the late 1980s through a Singapore-listed entity. This African-born startup, rooted in Nigeria, set out to replace inefficient government parastatals by working closely with farming communities in some of the continent's more challenging rural regions. Its goal was to offer these communities far better and more sustainable services. As an early member of that team, I believe their story, shaped by a willingness to learn and adapt, shows how a commercially successful company can lead the way in sustainable agricultural practices in Africa. Over the past thirty years, I've had a front-row view to the industry. Time and again, I've watched short-term players fade away and those with a long-term vision have survived and flourished.

It's fair to say, then, that the logic behind sustainable practices has played a pivotal role in longevity of companies in this sector. Sustainability wasn't just a checkbox; it was integral to their long-term planning.

Several key factors helped shape, and in some cases compel, this mindset among the companies that proved resilient:

Partnering with farming communities

To ensure a steady, sustainable supply of tradeable and processable commodities of the right quality, companies needed to build strong, enduring relationships with farming communities, as expected by the shareholders. This required embedding sustainability into the business model through:

- Timely, appropriate and adequate financing
- Access to quality seeds
- Provision of subsidized agricultural inputs
- Training and upskilling farmers for effective, sustainable farming practices
- Guaranteed buy-back arrangements to ensure farmers gets the value for his sweat.

To our credit, we acted swiftly and effectively, devising and implementing practices to recruit the right people, install appropriate systems and structures, impart necessary skills and ensure efficient application. Decades later, I was invited by Harvard Business School's Dr Michael Porter to present our work as a case study in what he called the Shared Value practise. The concept captured the essence what we were doing: creating a mutual value-creating system in which the corporate and originator (farmer) shared the value the business partnership created. It was the foundation of a sustainable partnership.

Partnering with policymakers

By the early 90s there was growing awareness that African governments had begun to recognize that the dangers of relying heavily on food imports for their young economies. Companies like Olam, the Tropical General Investments Group, Export Trading Group and a few other forward-looking corporates in the sector saw this shift as an opportunity. They stepped in to support policymakers, who needed capable implementation partners to help establish a solid foundation for food security and agricultural self-reliance. In response, the African Union identified four major challenge areas—or buckets—that needed to be addressed in order to set Africa on its feet were:

- Food Security
- Employment
- Upskilling
- Import substitution

Clever private sector players realized that institutionalizing sustainable solutions to these challenges could also be a commercially powerful strategy. It became the defining mantra for how these developing nations could pull themselves out of the economic quagmire in which they were enmeshed.

With this shared understanding, the policymakers and the commercial businesses found themselves singing from the same hymn sheet. The policymakers gained efficient implementation partners, and the corporates embedded themselves through sustainable practises, fully leveraging the first-mover advantage the moment presented. It was full alignment.

Scale of the opportunity

It's logical to surmise that a successful and sustainable agrarian economy is the foundation upon which prosperous and durable commercial businesses can be built. The argument the African policymakers made to private-sector investors was simple and compelling: expand and invest by capitalizing on the continent's natural blessings:

- 60 per cent of the world's available arable land
- Adequate freshwater resources
- Abundant year-round sunlight
- An average population age of twenty
- 650 million Africans already involved and dependent on small-scale farming

These factors clearly pointed to enormous potential. Private sector players with the ambition and capacity to execute skilfully and sustainably stood to gain significantly. The scale of the opportunity and the audacity of the challenge proved intoxicating for the young and rapidly maturing private sector, eager to be unleashed. Africa was in many ways the final frontier—the forbidden apple waiting to be seized.

The Holy Grail: Yield

The question foremost in the minds of private-sector investors was how to pave the pathway to prosperity for their essential partner, the SSF. They knew this would be possible only by unlocking the holy grail of agriculture: higher per-hectare yield.

One key dataset that has since been widely discussed and analysed was:

Region	Percentage of Potential Yield Realized
East Asia	89
Southeast Asia	69
North America	65
Western Europe	62
South Asia	46
Sub-Saharan Africa	24

The ambitious view within the private sector was that the greatest upside lay in improving yields in Africa. No other region offered such headroom for growth. This meant long-term, sustainable practises were essential to establishing a beachhead, even if they required short-term costs, resource commitments and inevitably, losses.

Market changes

Private-sector players in food and agriculture have been under pressure to change their sourcing models and community engagement practices due to three compelling market forces, in the following sequence:

- **Buyers/businesses in developed markets:** Much of the pressure emanates from food retailers who must abide by the governing principles of the European Commission. The message is: align or die.
- **Positive reinforcement from buyers**
- **The gen-Z consumer:** The new, free-spending consumer of the chocolate bar and espresso shot is starting to flex its increasing consumer appetite. They typically ask three questions:
    - Is this product right for me?
    - Is it ethically produced and sourced?
    - Is it good for the planet?

This places serious pressure on the branded seller.

These forces have made sustainable agricultural practices and positive farmer engagement an operational imperative. Origination businesses are being called out, and there is an obvious commercial benefit to maintaining market relevance and profitability.

As a result:

- Markets are insisting on evidence/certification that farming methods support environmental health, producer profitability and social equity.
- Businesses increasingly need to seek alignment with SDG goals and provide evidence.

- Consumers, especially in the EU, expect evidence that sustainable practices reduce costs, such as through the shift from fossil fuels to electricity, or replacing plastic packaging with innovative, locally sourced materials (bamboo, husks, etc.).
- Demand for certifications across commodities (Rainforest Alliance, Fairtrade, etc.) is rising sharply, and will shape the conditions of agricultural practices. Those who fail to meet these requirements run the risk of losing buyers altogether.

By rewarding well-invested and durable originators through pricing, markets created incentives for them, and their farming community, to improve their practices. These commercial rewards were further supported by long-term commitments from blue-chip buyers, which facilitated liquidity for the originators.

Positive policy pressure

Africa's raw food import bill in 2021 stood at US $47 billion and is projected to reach US $100 billion by 2027. The question is: Where will the power to generate this level of funding and foreign exchange come from?

While positive policy support is still evolving and iterative, the policy environment is undoubtedly shifting in a favourable direction. Some examples of supportive policies include:

- **Import ban on essential food staples:** These bans have forced opportunistic private-sector players to invest in domestic growing and processing assets. Nigeria offers strong examples in rice and sugar, where the import ban has directly triggered significant private-sector investment in these sectors and led to dramatic increase in local production and processing capacity.

- **Mandates for value-added or processed exports of cash crops:** Through a mix of punitive and reward mechanisms, governments are increasingly requiring that cash crops be exported only after value addition. This brings about private-sector investment in processing assets investments after adding value to export products and automatically shifts pressure onto them to ensure that the supply chain of raw material is maintained. This fundamentally alters the short-term opportunistic trading mindset, which has led to large-scale imbalanced exploitation of the country's resources as well as unreliable relationships with the growing community.

  A good example of this kind of policy support is the scale of investment committed to value addition in the cocoa sector in the two largest producers in the world—Ghana and Ivory Coast—over the past decade. A telling sign that sustainable practices are taking hold is the manifold increase in local crop size.

- **Alignment to high international quality norms (RFA/Organic) for cash-crop exports:** Implementation of such policies has been immensely successful in installing:
  - Value-adding, crop-tending practices to ensure the output meets the norms. Corporates are attracted to countries with such standards since the revenues from these crops are higher, and they therefore willingly commit to assets and community partnerships to meet these norms. Examples of crops receiving full value under such norms include Rwandan coffee, Madagascan vanilla.
  - Much higher liquidity for these high-quality crops, attracting exporters/processors to invest and commit

to sustainable business practices, since the country's adherence to quality standards helps build a brand for its crops. Good examples are Ethiopian sesame and Benin cotton.

Countries where cash crops have not been guided by the above principle are, in fact, seeing the decline of those crops due to reverse market pressures. Increasingly, countries are therefore jumping onto this bandwagon to attract private-sector investment and improve the longevity of their crops through practices that meet international norms.

The reality

As discussed earlier, the sector in Africa has seen several compelling drivers for sustainable practices: commercial compulsions, the allure of the visible, scalable of opportunities and policy incentives nudging the private sector towards greener approaches. However, from my vantage point as an industry insider, I have also seen first-hand the formidable deterrents we faced in implementing sustainable practices. As early adopters with a proven track record of introducing cutting-edge, international sustainability norms at scale, we were among the first to encounter these barriers, often without any ready solutions at hand. Some of the key pushbacks we faced included:

Cost of installation: While most participants in the sector understood the value of sustainable practices, the issue, especially in the early days, lay in the significant upfront costs. Setting up community partnerships, adopting organic practices and the like. The expectation was that the customer would eventually cover these costs. But since the returns were long-term, most players took the shortcut and opted out early, cutting corners that ultimately led to their downfall.

Financial institutions, understandably, were averse to directly funding small-scale farmers, perceiving it as too risky. This created a need for a responsible, sustainable mid-level structures that could manage cash flow, coordinate crop collection and handle onward marketing. In the absence of such systems, only long-term players with higher appetite for risk and stronger working capital took on this responsibility, making sustainability part of an elite club.

Inadequate buy-in from community partners and service providers: Engaging the SSF and the service providers along the value chain was an enormous challenge. Many of them had been following the same practices for generations, and changing these behaviours was very tedious. It required reaching out to the vast spread of farming communities with patience and the ability to communicate in their language. Often, it meant the corporate had to allocate resources to demonstrate their commitment to driving meaningful change in practices.

Value expectation mismatch and buyers need for consistency: This was a persistent challenge. Buyers needed clear evidence of staying power, and most importantly, credibility and integrity in the processes adopted by the suppliers before they were willing to pay for products that were supposedly produced using the standards they demanded. Even acquiring internationally accepted certifications (like Rainforest Alliance or Organic) was a huge challenge, as these agencies were not readily available on the continent. Despite this, the buyer was slow to reward shippers, instead choosing to wait for a proven track record. Even when the

EU and US food processors and retailers began to acknowledge that a select few African players could deliver certifiably sustainable products, another challenge emerged: the financial and organizational capability needed to maintain consistent quality, certification and service delivery. In my experience, the buyers' fears were well founded. Yet the long-term stars showed resilience, persevered and adapted, ultimately setting up sustainable, world-class businesses.

Poor understanding of holistic picture by policymakers and patchy support: Implementing sustainable practices is a long-term endeavour. From the interface with the growers to retail partnerships, every stage must be set up, monitored and monetized to ensure the business remains sustainable. At various points in this value chain, policy support is essential. Policymakers must have a complete understanding of the value chain so that they can appreciate when and where intervention was required. In our experience, the government's commitment, in many cases, to engage with this holistic picture was weak, making the process of securing support even after pumping in millions of dollars as private investment tedious.

The investor's perspective

While our growth was mostly organic, we also developed an interest and capacity for making inorganic investment in the sector. Whenever we targeted acquisition targets, the presence of a sustainability mindset within the business was a critical starting point. As both investors and practitioners of sustainable agricultural practices, we believed:

- Integrating new businesses into our group would prove far easier if the incoming team shared a similar worldview about sustainability and long-term mindset.
- Replacing outdated practices with cutting-edge sustainable methods where we had proven expertise was possible but understandably frustrating and time-consuming. It also took a tangible toll on team dynamics, particularly among those who struggled to adapt.
- We were investing in businesses whose futures we intended to build and own. There was little point in buying dead-end businesses where this future was suspect.
- In our two decades of experience, businesses with a weak focus on sustainable practices had fragile relationships with both buyers and communities. We had no interest in backing such businesses or committing our resources.
- We had no wish to associate with businesses that failed to meet our standards for sustainable practices, as doing so would pose a risk to our reputation in the market.
- Our shareholders were blue-chip investors, guiding us to only engage with targets that clearly and stringently adhered to sustainability standards. A minimum threshold had to be met before discussions could even begin.

I believe the influx of corporate buyers and funders into African markets helped raise the sustainability performance standards across the industry. Any player seeking funding, whether equity or debt, was pushed to improve their practices.

One key difference between us and various other financial or strategic investors was our understanding of this sector. We had some of the most compact, detailed and effective audit frameworks. It was virtually impossible to bypass or mislead our assessments. In contrast, there was a noticeable amount of 'sustainability eyewash' taking place in other acquisitions. Several large private equity firms, for instance, learnt hard lessons when they underestimated the value of these audits.

In the end, it was the wise investors—those who actively motivated their investee businesses towards sustainable practices—who endured. They supported strategies aimed at increasing productivity through a variety of measures, including subsidizing or distributing improved seeds and agricultural inputs, providing capacity building on good agricultural practices, improving irrigation and enhancing market access. These were the investors who lasted the course.

The good news is that the African private sector, along with multinational corporations, has largely carried the flag in embracing sustainable practices. This has of course been driven by both commercial incentives and the desire to establish themselves as responsible corporate citizens. Encouragingly, these responsible footprints continue to grow. And with that, as Africa's opportunity begins to unfold fully, we can hope that its base will be built on sound practices and a distinctly green touch.

7

Fuelling the Future

A Policy Perspective on Biofuel

PRAVEEN GARG

INDIA IS ON A GROWTH trajectory. A Goldman Sachs report predicts that by 2075, India's GDP will reach $52.5 trillion, making it the second-largest economy globally, behind only China. This expansion is expected to be led by a rising working population and increasing capital expenditure.[1]

As India's economy expands, so too will its energy consumption. The Central Electricity Authority (CEA) projects that electricity demand will increase by 1.8 times between 2021 and 2031, with annual per capita electricity consumption reaching 1,700–1,800 units by 2031–32.[2]

The growing importance of energy in India's development was highlighted in the *India Energy Outlook 2021* report by the International Energy Agency (IEA), which estimates that since 2000, India's share in global energy demand has risen to 10 per cent. On a per capita basis, energy demand increased by 60 per cent between 2000 and 2020. India has also seen an increase in the number of vehicles over the last two decades. The fleet of two- and three-wheelers has grown to 200 million—five times the number of passenger cars. Freight activity has quadrupled in the same period, registering a thirteen-fold increase in the stock of heavy freight trucks.[3]

The following graph illustrates the increasing energy demand in India over the past twenty years, revealing consistent growth in demand across all energy sources.

Figure 1: India's energy demand[4]

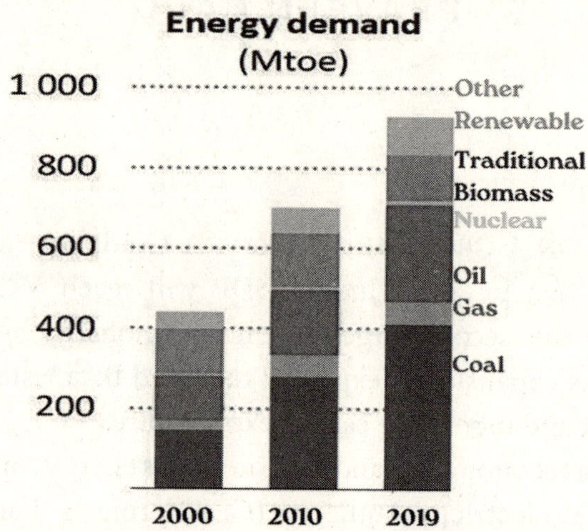

MTOE: million tonnes of oil equivalent

However, India's rising energy demands face significant constraints, with climate change posing the biggest challenge. While climate change is a global concern affecting every country, developing countries are far more vulnerable. This is due to the difficult balance they must strike between economic growth aspirations and the need to contain carbon emissions, a constraint that did not exist for the so-called developed countries when they were at a similar stage of economic development. As such, every economic action taken by a growing country like India must account for the limits imposed by our changing climate and degrading environment.

The ambitious Nationally Determined Contribution (NDC) recognizes this reality. India has pledged to reduce the emissions intensity of its GDP by 33 to 35 per cent by 2030 from 2005 levels. This will be achieved by increasing the share of electric power installed capacity from non-fossil fuel-based sources to 40 per cent, and by creating additional carbon sinks of 2.5 to 3 billion tonnes of CO2 equivalent.[5]

The Sub-Committee for the Assessment of Financial Requirements for Implementing India's Nationally Determined Contribution has estimated that India will need $206 billion (at 2014–15 prices) between 2015 and 2030 for climate change-related mitigation measures. The total requirement for meeting climate change actions, including resilience and disaster management, is estimated at $2.5 trillion by 2030.

Rising energy consumption and growing constraints on the use of traditional energy sources such as coal and oil mean that alternative methods are needed to support India's economic expansion. The government's increased push towards alternative energy reflects these contemporary challenges. Electricity generation from solar and wind saw a 15 per cent increase between 2015 and 2019, with a fivefold expansion of India's solar capacity during the same period. Solar photovoltaic (PV) capacity has grown at an annual rate of 60 per cent, primarily through various government-led initiatives like the Solar Park Scheme, Rooftop Solar Scheme and the National Solar Mission. However, this is not enough, and the search for other alternatives must continue to meet the country's rising energy demand.

Biofuels also have the potential to contribute to the development of alternative energy sources for India. They can address the growing needs of India's energy consumers while supporting the transportation sector by acting as a reliable alternative to liquid fuels such as diesel and petrol.

Efforts to promote alternatives to fossil fuels began in 2003. To reduce India's dependence on fossil fuel imports, the Ethanol Blended Petrol Programme and the National Mission on Biodiesel were launched, which aimed to increase the production and blending of bioethanol and biodiesel.

In 2018, the Government of India issued its National Policy on Biofuels (NPB), prepared by the Ministry of Petroleum and Natural Gas. This policy focuses on increasing domestic production, promoting the adoption of biofuels, improving energy efficiency norms, refining processes and encouraging demand substitution.

Biofuel blending is a core element of the policy. It has set the target of 20 per cent ethanol blending in petrol by 2025–26 and 5 per cent biodiesel blending by 2030. The policy envisions an increase in the use of biofuels prompted by greater availability of domestic feedstock and advancements in biofuel generation technologies. To achieve these targets, the Ethanol Blended Petrol Programme and the Biodiesel Blending Programme have been launched.

In India, the blending percentage of biodiesel in diesel has been very low—below 0.5 per cent—due to feedstock constraints, leading to an increase in biodiesel imports. The policy aims to address this by increasing feedstock availability, including through stringent norms against the diversion of used or waste cooking oil to edible streams.[6]

In 2018, ethanol blending in petrol stood at a meagre 2 per cent. The policy proposed to raise this to 20 per cent by 2030, an indicative target that was later shifted to 2025–26. Similarly, the target for biodiesel is set at 5 per cent blending by 2030.[7]

To address the shortfall in achieving targets, the government amended the policy in 2022 to expand the scope of permissible raw materials for both biodiesel and bioethanol. The new list includes C-heavy molasses, agro-food industry waste, damaged food grains such as broken rice, food grains unfit for human consumption, industrial waste and waste off-gases.

What are biofuels?

The concept of biofuels has been around for quite some time. During the Second World War, vegetable oil was used to make petroleum. In the 1970s, amid the oil embargo, alternatives to petroleum, such as biofuels, were explored. While there is no single, universally accepted definition, biofuels generally refer to various materials that can be used as fuel. These are hydrocarbon fuels produced over a short period from bio-based products. The National Biofuel Policy 2018 defines 'biofuels' as fuels produced from renewable resources and used in place of or in blend with, diesel, petrol or other fossil fuels for transport, stationary, portable and other applications.[8]

Biofuels have evolved over the years and are generally defined according to their stage of technological development: first generation (1-G), second generation (2-G), third generation (3-G) and fourth generation (4-G).[9]

The two prominent biofuels are:

- Bioethanol: Ethanol produced from sugar-containing materials
- Biodiesel: A methyl or ethyl ester of fatty acids produced from non-edible vegetable oils

Other types of biofuels include advanced biofuels, drop-in fuels and bio-CNG, amongst others. Some of the major crops used in biofuel production are sugarcane, sugar beet, sweet sorghum and jatropha. [10]

Why does India need biofuels?

India has been actively promoting the integration of biofuels, with an emphasis on increasing both their production and consumption. This is largely due to the country's changing energy profile and the energy security challenges triggered by fluctuations in global oil markets.

In 2022, mineral fuels, oils and distillation products were the largest category of India's imports, accounting for 38 per cent of total imports and valued at Rs 22,831 crore. According to the Petroleum Planning & Analysis Cell of the Ministry of Petroleum and Natural Gas, 85 per cent of the crude oil consumed in 2021–22 was imported. This figure rose to 87.3 per cent in 2022–23, primarily due to limited domestic fossil fuel resources.[11]

National oil production has not increased in the last two decades, while imports have almost doubled, rising from 2.1 million barrels per day in 2000 to 4.3 million barrels per day in 2019. A comparison of the production and imports of the three main fossil fuels in India's energy basket reveals that while coal and natural gas production have increased, oil production has stagnated at below 2 million barrels per day. This deficit in oil production has been met by increasing oil imports, which touched almost 4 million barrels per day in 2019, exposing Indian consumers to significant global price fluctuations. The volatility in crude oil prices is a significant macroeconomic threat to India; it increases the need to maintain large foreign exchange reserves and exposes consumers to international oil market uncertainties.

The inability of domestic crude oil production to meet India's growing demand raises concerns over energy security.

The growing Indian economy needs a reliable energy supply, as no economic system can expand without it. India's energy needs are rising rapidly. The energy demand for road transport alone is expected to double between 2020 and 2040, with diesel-based freight transport accounting for half of this growth and an additional 25 million trucks projected to join the Indian fleet by 2040.[12] Per capita energy demand has also increased, rising from 24 per cent to 37 per cent between 2000 and 2019. Similarly, per capita oil demand has grown by 12 per cent, fuelled by a rise in car ownership, which has increased from 7 per cent to 19 per cent over the last two decades.

Challenges to India's biofuel integration

a. Competing land use and crops

Globally, the transport biofuel market still depends on 1-G fuel sources and production methods. This means that to meet growing biofuel demand, significant amounts of land must be committed to the cultivation of biofuel crops such as sugarcane, corn and maize. In India, however, this is not possible, as most available land is primarily used for food crop cultivation.

Land-use statistics from 2018–19 show that 171 lakh hectares were barren and uncultivable, while cultivable wasteland accounted for 122 lakh hectares. Compared to this, the total net sown area of the country stood at 1393 lakh hectares in 2018–19, with food grains cultivated on 1269 lakh hectares in 2019–20 and sugarcane on 45 lakh hectares. Thus, it is clear that crop cultivation is heavily skewed towards food crops and increasing biofuel production would require significant land-use changes.[13]

The Expert Committee on the Roadmap for Ethanol Blending in India by 2025 has estimated that to meet its target of 20 per cent ethanol blending by 2025, India will require 13.5 billion litres of ethanol—6.8 billion litres from sugarcane and 6.6 billion litres from food grains. Research further suggests that achieving this target using molasses (a 1-G method of ethanol production) would require an additional 19 million hectares of land.[14] Achieving such a target solely through this method becomes a pipe dream considering the limited land availability.

Increasing biofuel production using 1-G feedstock is therefore daunting, as apart from being limited, land is already under pressure from competing demands such as food grain cultivation, horticulture and agroforestry. Moreover, the economic value of food grain production is much higher, which encourages land use for food crops rather than biofuel feedstock.

The limited number of crops that can be used for biofuel production is another challenge. The main crops used for ethanol production are sugarcane, rice and maize, but they have their own limitations. For example, rice is uneconomical for ethanol distillation as its economic cost is Rs 4,294 per quintal, more than twice the Rs 2000 price at which it is sold for ethanol. Substituting maize for rice would also require major land use changes, as an additional 4.82 million hectares of maize cultivation would be needed, which is half of India's current maize area of 9.42 million hectares.[15]

Furthermore, while promoting sugarcane juice for biofuel feedstock could help, it would increase India's sugarcane production. This is problematic because sugarcane is a water-intensive crop, and its expansion would lead to water stress in some regions, thereby adding to the woes of the 600 million Indians already facing extreme water stress.[16]

b. Skewed agricultural policy

India's agricultural policies and system of support prices have given rise to a political economy wherein farming communities exert significant influence on agricultural price policies. This poses a challenge for ethanol blending because, compared to the US, Brazil and Indonesia, the cost of ethanol feedstock per litre is significantly higher in India. These artificially high raw material prices could negatively affect the economic viability of ethanol blending.[17] The dominance of large and medium farmers in agricultural policy is starkly visible in the setting of the Minimum Support Price (MSP), a policy that often overlooks principles of economic efficiency in favour of trivial political gains.

c. Slow technological and scientific development

The absence of technological solutions and the limits to knowledge creation are restricting India's progress in biofuel integration. The dominance of 1-G biofuels has created a problem of technology lock-in, wherein innovative solutions are overlooked in favour of cheaper but inefficient methods such as sugarcane-based ethanol production. In its bid to achieve the blending target of 20 per cent by 2025, the government is focusing on 1-G raw materials, which makes a technology transition difficult. The promotion of food stock-based raw materials for biofuel production delays the switch to 2-G ingredients like cellulosic and lignocellulosic materials and also de-incentivizes the development of new technologies for 3-G biofuels.

Vehicle technology is another impediment to India's blending objectives. In order to increase the percentage of ethanol in petrol, vehicles would need to be reoriented. It is estimated that, to attain material compatibility, the current rubber and plastic components—designed for E10 fuels—would need to be improved for E20. This would increase the cost of E20-compatible vehicles[18] and consequently affect car sales, which has deterred automobile manufacturers from engaging in a full-scale technological transition.

Progress in the adoption of 2-G biofuels and scientific advancements in 3-G biofuel technologies have been minimal. There is a need to improve knowledge creation by investing in research and development (R&D). However, these remain largely proposals, and their materialization is yet to be seen. R&D is a long-term effort that requires sustained support and guidance. The assumption that technological solutions can improve biofuel integration and promote the transition to 3-G and 4-G biofuels overlooks the Indian reality of low R&D investment and the challenges that hinder technological advancements in educational institutions.

d. Acute policy limitations

The NPB 2018 is ambitious in scope but overlooks various governance challenges that will arise in its execution. Firstly, the policy seeks to make changes at all stages of the biofuel supply chain, from feedstock cultivation to blending technologies and engine retrofitting. The policy document outlines roles for eleven central government ministries, including the ministries of Petroleum and Natural Gas, Rural Development, Environment, Forest and Climate Change, and New and Renewable Energy, as well as departments such as Agriculture and Cooperation and Consumer Affairs. This will require a high level of coordination amongst various government agencies, which is difficult to achieve given the complexity of participating institutions and has not been realized so far.

Secondly, India's biofuel transition will need support through economic policy. This will involve managing market mechanisms using tools such as price policies, taxation and subsidies. This is a welcome step—so long as state involvement focuses on market creation and technological adoption. However, there is always a risk of regulatory capture of economic policy by vested interests that thrive on state protection and seek to perpetuate economic inefficiencies. Thus, the biofuel policy must recognize the limits of economic management and factor in this regulatory constraint when making long-term decisions.

e. Low ethanol blending

The supply of ethanol for blending in India has been increasing, but it remains insufficient. The current supply of 3.32 billion litres (332 crore litres) is far short of the NPB 2018 target of 13 billion litres.[19] To achieve the 20 per cent blending target, an estimated 13.5 billion litres of ethanol will be required by 2025, of which 6.8 billion litres would come from sugarcane and 6.7 billion litres from food grains. Both are 1-G raw materials that would require significant land-use changes, which may not be feasible given India's need for food grains.[20]

f. Abysmal biodiesel blending

In India, the blending percentage of biodiesel in diesel is very low. This is primarily due to feedstock constraints and the diversion of used/waste cooking oil (UCO) to edible streams. The Standing Committee on Petroleum and Natural Gas, in its 2021 report, noted that the blending level in 2019–20 stood at a miniscule 0.1 per cent, far from the indicative target of 5 per cent under NPB 2018. It further observed that biodiesel blending has 'not

[been] accorded due importance even though diesel is the most consumed fuel, and has a higher potential for curbing crude oil imports.'[21]

The National Mission on Biodiesel and the National Policy on Biofuels 2009 had emphasized the use of *Jatropha curcas*, a non-edible oilseed, for biodiesel production. However, despite significant government support, the output fell short of projections. The yield from Jatropha was 0.5-1.5 mg/ha (mean metric tonnes per hectare), much lower than the expected yield of 2-5 mg/ha. Thus, increasing production needed more land, which reduced farmers' profits.[22] The unsuccessful Jatropha initiative, along with the diversified nature of the biodiesel supply chain, has made it difficult to develop biodiesel as a viable industry in India.

Solutions and initiatives

a. Ethanol blending

The Ethanol Blended Petrol Programme faces many challenges, and it would make sense to explore alternative paths for achieving the policy's biofuel objectives. One path is the development and integration of 2-G ethanol, which involves using more advanced sources of ethanol and moving away from conventional molasses and sugarcane juice.

To increase ethanol supply, the government has permitted the procurement of ethanol from non-food feedstock such as cellulosic and lignocellulosic materials. Public sector oil marketing companies have also signed fifteen-year ethanol purchase agreements with 2-G ethanol suppliers, providing an assured market for producers and supporting 2-G ethanol development.

By July 2022, four commercial 2-G bioethanol projects had received financial assistance amounting to Rs 600 crores. These projects are in an advanced stage of construction and are expected to be commissioned from 2023 onwards.[23] This initiative is contributing to the evolution of India's ethanol industry and addresses the problems that have hindered the large-scale adoption of 2-G technology.

b. Biodiesel feedstock

To resolve the challenges faced in the integration of biodiesel in India, there is a need for active involvement of rural communities in enhancing feedstock through the plantation of non-edible oilseed-bearing trees and crops such as Karanja, Melia, *Jatropha curcas* and Simarouba. This could be undertaken by incentivizing farmers to grow these crops on rural wastelands and marginal lands, thereby increasing both feedstock and farmer income.

India will also need to augment its annual production capacity and shift from imported palm stearin to local sources like UCO. The role of UCO is particularly important in this regard, as domestically sourced UCO is a feedstock with large untapped potential. However, the lack of a robust supply chain has led to the under-utilization of this resource. There is also a need for stronger regulation of cooking oil disposal. The Food Safety and Standards Authority of India (FSSAI) estimates that 60 per cent of the 3 million tonnes of UCO is being reused instead of being diverted to biodiesel production. Establishing clear cooking oil disposal standards, along with the active involvement of Pollution Control Boards, could help in the productive diversion of UCO.

c. Financial incentives

The NPB 2018 proposes that oil extraction and processing units involved in biodiesel production, storage and distribution be categorized as a priority sector, which means that these enterprises would receive preferential treatment and favourable lending terms from development and commercial banks in India. Financial incentives such as viability gap funding, subsidies, and the creation of a National Biofuel Fund are suggested. The policy envisages the use of carbon financing mechanisms to improve fund flows to biofuel projects, along with automatic approval for 100 per cent foreign direct investment (FDI) in biofuel technologies.[24]

Implementing these incentives would require a realignment of the banking sector's priorities with government policy. India's Green Revolution in the 1980s was made possible through the integration of financial incentives and agricultural policy. The pre-existing infrastructure of rural banks, led by the National Bank for Agriculture and Rural Development (NABARD), can be utilized to streamline this incentive mechanism, support feedstock cultivation and aid the development of an agro-processing industry for biofuels.

d. Research and development

The success of biofuels in India is largely dependent on the effective development and integration of 2-G and 3-G biofuel sources, given the limited availability of arable land for cultivating 1-G feedstock. Technological progress and breakthroughs in scientific research alone can alleviate this problem. The policy recognizes this and includes several proposals, such as increased R&D activities for developing new raw materials, improving efficiency and innovating in biofuel production, processing and conversion technologies.

The proposal to develop a National Biomass Repository to assess the country's biomass resources is a positive step in this direction. The policy also emphasizes building knowledge infrastructure for biofuels, including the setting of specialized centres in high-technology areas and empowering institutions to conduct research on biofuels through national, bilateral and multilateral research programmes.

e. Economic policy support

The development of a robust biofuel market will initially require price support and trade protection. The NPB 2018 has proposed the use of administered prices through government institutions such as the Cabinet Committee on Economic Affairs, oil marketing companies and the National Biofuel Coordination Committee (NBCC). While the export of biofuels was previously prohibited, in 2022 the government allowed exports from special economic zones and export-oriented units for both fuel and non-fuel purposes, provided they are produced from imported feedstock.[25]

The economic management of biofuels will need to be supervised to ensure efficiency. Too often, vested interests benefiting from trade protection and artificial pricing want state support to continue. Thus, biofuel policy must account for the negative consequences of price controls and protection and develop appropriate mechanisms to deal with them.

The integration of biofuels is a welcome step, but the process is full of challenges. Whether these can be overcome through the proposed solutions remains to be seen. It is important for policymakers to recognize these realities and adopt measures that balance India's emerging energy needs with its green aspirations.

Conclusion

The complex policy issue of biofuels is being addressed in a linear way, in isolation, without integrating other equally—if not more—important concerns such as food security for a growing population and the increasing per capita consumption of food. Land resources are limited, and population density is high, creating a conundrum of competing pressures on land use. This approach overlooks the broader complexities of the problem and its interconnection with other pressing concerns.

These challenges can be addressed by the government through the establishment of an inter-ministerial group comprising the Ministry of Petroleum and Natural Gas, Ministry of New and Renewable Energy, Ministry of Agriculture & Farmers' Welfare and other relevant departments as deemed appropriate. This will help elevate decision-making and create a sense of urgency within the government to achieve biofuel integration.

It is high time that the government considers these competing policy interventions as a priority for development and governance. This would enable India to tap into its vast biofuel potential, reduce its carbon footprint and move closer to fulfilling its Nationally Determined Contributions.

Glossary

C-heavy molasses – The end by-product of sugar processing, which contains sucrose and is found in liquid form.

Cellulosic – An agricultural or wood feedstock primarily composed of cellulose, hemicellulose, lignin or a combination of these ingredients, grown on agricultural lands or harvested from timberlands.

Ethanol – A volatile, flammable, colourless liquid with a characteristic wine-like odour and pungent taste.

Ethyl ester – An ester that yields ethyl alcohol upon hydrolysis.

Jatropha curcas – A species of flowering plant in the spurge family (Euphorbiaceae), native to the American tropics, most likely Mexico and Central America.

Karanja – A fast-growing, multipurpose tree of the humid tropics. It is one of the few nitrogen-fixing trees that produce oilseeds.

Lignocellulosic – A natural resource derived from the stems and roots of trees and woody plants, consisting of brittle and fibrous tissues.

Methyl ester – Mono-alkyl esters of long-chain fatty acids derived from vegetable oils or animal fats.

Molasses – A viscous substance resulting from the refining of sugarcane or sugar beets into sugar.

Net sown area – The total area sown with crops and orchards.

Palm stearin – The solid fraction of palm oil produced by partial crystallization at a controlled temperature.

Simarouba glauca – A flowering tree used for industrial purposes, particularly for the production of biofuels.

Sweet sorghum – A grass whose stalks have a high sugar content.

8

Emerging Business Models for Environmental Change

The Catalysts

a. Circular Economy for Agri-waste

SUHAS BAXI

ON 14 FEBRUARY 2020, I had planned a lunch meeting. And no, this had nothing to do with Valentine's Day. I was scheduled to meet Ashwin Savé, co-founder and Chief Operating Officer of Biofuel, to discuss a business idea that had been occupying my thoughts for some time.

For many of us, 'how things work' is a daily brain teaser. For me, trying to understand industry structures, history, people, processes, investments and their wider impact on society has often filled my 'me time'. Another habit that developed as I moved through multiple industries and roles was a desire to connect seemingly unrelated dots and cross-fertilize ideas from different experiences.

For some time, I had been thinking about three disconnected experiences from my professional journey, searching for a connection between alternative fuels, organized commodity markets and bioenergy opportunities in India. From 'how things work', the teaser changed to 'why things don't work'.

Some twenty years ago, Ashwin and I had worked together on a dream, and I had a feeling we could find an answer. So, while enjoying organic delicacies at Fab Café, we brainstormed, and the idea quickly transformed into a shared belief.

The opportunity

India ranks amongst the top three countries in crop production. While every harvest produces food crops, it also generates crop residue. Traditionally, this crop residue has been used primarily as fodder. Today, however, India generates a minimum of 700 million MT of crop residue annually, of which around 60 per cent goes towards cattle feed. This leaves up to 235 million MT of surplus agricultural waste available on farms each year.

The bioenergy industry has the potential to use this vast annual feedstock. Solid, liquid and gaseous biofuels can replace coal as industrial fuel, be blended with petrol and diesel, and replace fossil fuels entirely in industries such as aviation. Harnessing agri-residue biomass can potentially meet more than 17 per cent of India's annual energy needs—equivalent to 125 million MT of coal or 600 million barrels of crude oil.

This is, quite literally, a 'waste-to-wealth' opportunity for the world's third-largest economy. Agri-residue-based bioenergy is a carbon-neutral energy source that promises to accelerate the journey towards net zero.

The bottlenecks

Unlike solar and wind energy, which in recent years have attracted investors and built capacity across the world, biomass as a renewable energy source has yet to achieve its potential.

Solar and wind do not depend on a supply chain. Bioenergy, however, has a supply chain that touches the lives of people. At the heart of this chain is the farmer, who is the (accidental) producer of agri-waste. In many cases, the actual economic realization from biomass is lower than the farmer's cost and effort. The easier approach adopted, therefore, is to burn the waste. While this saves the farmer both time and money, it takes a toll on soil nutrients and the environment.

An average Indian farmer holds about two acres of land and generates roughly 4 tons of agri-waste each season. Aggregating 235 million tons of biomass annually may therefore involve collecting it from 25 million farmers. Participation of farmers and rural service providers in evacuation, transportation, storage, supply and payments at this scale needs a structure. The absence of such a structure is both a bottleneck and an opportunity.

Assuming that one can solve the problem of farmer participation, an equally enormous challenge lies in distribution. An efficient distribution mechanism will need an extensive network of rural biomass businesses. Access to capital, working capital and markets for these small rural enterprises is once again a bottleneck and an opportunity.

Meanwhile, existing and emerging bioenergy technologies are seeking big investments. The feasibility of these investments can be guaranteed only if the biomass supply chain can assure supply visibility, price predictability, quality and delivery reliability—everything one expects from a typical industrial supply chain. This, too, is both a challenge and an opportunity.

The idea

Ashwin and I settled on a concept that could broadly be described as a three-sided marketplace—one that brought together three distinct threads.

The first thread ran along the lines of what commodity exchanges do worldwide. Rural businesses, biomass processors and industrial buyers could access the marketplace to buy and sell biomass. The platform would support spot deals, term deals, auctions and other B2B transaction tools. Over time, such a mechanism would create visibility for demand, supply and pricing, enabling the kind of decision-support framework familiar to any industrial supply chain.

The second thread focused on services that could elevate the buying and selling experience. Vendor development, logistics, quality assurance, working capital and warehousing are all services that both buyers and sellers seek. Adding these to the marketplace could create an all-new customer experience, a trust framework.

The third thread was our model for rural engagement. We envisioned digitally enabled rural franchisees for biomass collection, and encouraging farmers to participate through a simple mobile app. By setting up 1500 rural franchisees, each connecting with 1000 farmers, we could potentially harness biomass from 1.5 million farmers.

We wove these threads together to create an entirely new business. The first year was a breeze, from initial ideation in February 2020 to functional architecture in June 2020, and finally to an alpha product in January 2021. Most of this time was spent behind locked doors thanks to the COVID-driven lockdowns, but it was an extremely productive period.

Two soon became four when Tushar and Jacob came on board, and before we knew it, we were a team of twelve believers by the end of 2020.

Likely impact

While our initial goal was to create a marketplace mechanism with an eye on the end-user industrial businesses, we quickly realized that our model could help unlock several interconnected opportunities.

One of the positive outcomes has been rural financing. On a transparent platform, lenders can assess underlying assets and risks associated with businesses that need both capital and working capital support. This opens the door to making competitive lending rates a reality for small rural businesses.

Our model for rural biomass franchisees has the potential to create a strong economic and environmental impact through a circular economy. A single franchisee can supply 10,000 MT of biomass annually. This small step could increase income by up to 20 per cent for 1000 farmers, secure employment for approximately thirty and stimulate indirect economic activities around transport.

The rural franchisee network not only generates employment but also acts as a conduit to bring bioenergy by-products, such as bio-fertilizers and green bricks, back to rural areas for end-use.

At scale, this model could impact the lives of 1.5 million farmers, create 50,000 rural jobs and help reduce 15 million tons of CO2 emissions annually.

Rural challenge

The success of our business model depends on the success of rural enterprises. India's Milk Revolution has already demonstrated that rural collectives are indeed a good business idea. Our concept of rural biomass enterprises also aims to use this proven model.

Over the last ten years, agencies such as the National Bank for Agriculture and Rural Development (NABARD) have focused on creating farmer-owned collectives known as Farmer Producer Companies. These collectives aim to enhance the efficiency and competitiveness of farmers' businesses. We have targeted farmer collectives in biomass catchment areas for setting up rural biomass franchisees. A typical franchisee can operate within one of four standardized business templates, which can be set up with an investment ranging from Rs 5 lakh to Rs 1 crore.

Another interesting aspect of our model is the utilization of idle transport capacity in rural areas. Tractor owners, for instance, can rent out their vehicles during lean seasons to transport biomass from rural areas to nearby industrial areas.

We have established twenty rural biomass franchisees so far, and their success gives us the confidence to replicate this model across the country.

Our belief and passion

The prevailing industrial policy, environmental norms, the government's determination to empower rural businesses, and India's commitment to net zero targets were all in sync with the business segment we wished to influence. India's bioenergy policy is being shaped with the vision of becoming a global leader in this space. Businesses in the bioenergy domain are working on cutting-edge technology to achieve significant breakthroughs, and Indian companies have the perfect opportunity to be global leaders in the industry.

Our discussions with policymakers and industry professionals convinced us that the environment was both enabling and empowering, further strengthening our belief in our business idea.

While we did not have first-hand experience with rural businesses, our interactions with foundations and people working in rural economies deepened our conviction and fuelled our passion to build a business that could have a positive social and environmental impact.

Team and alliances

A typical start-up environment is full of people with high energy, bold dreams and infectious enthusiasm. We added to this a bigger-than-usual dose of experience and maturity.

Our business brings together industrial users of bioenergy, small rural businesses and farmers to create a symbiotic relationship. Using modern technology, we aim to disrupt the way industries buy and sell biomass. To achieve this, we have built an enthusiastic team of about fifty people, with experience ranging from rural markets to bioenergy, all of whom share our passion and vision. We have also been fortunate to be based in a city with a strong talent pool.

Alongside our team, our alliances with agriculture-focused foundations have helped accelerate our path from idea to implementation. One of our most important partnerships is with a seventy-year-old non-profit institution dedicated to creating rural livelihoods through technology-driven interventions. Their experience, insight and credibility have added necessary heft to our idea and vision. The non-profit's leadership team views biomass franchisees as a socially relevant business model that helps create sustainable livelihoods without depending on aid or charity.

While we knew that our idea could have a social impact, the nature and form of this impact have exceeded our initial expectations.

Our first interaction with officers at the Ministry of New and Renewable Energy was aimed at understanding policy disposition. What we did not anticipate was the active encouragement we would receive. The ministry is at the forefront of creating a conducive business environment for the bioenergy industry. Global agencies such as GIZ (Deutsche Gesellschaft für Internationale Zusammenarbeit, or German Society for International Cooperation—Germany's primary development agency) are leading ground-level projects to drive circular economy initiatives through rural intervention.

Our first twenty biomass franchisee projects are being supported by GIZ. Their organizational support has helped our business take flight. Over the past three years, we have seen strong stakeholder momentum as we continue to build an organized supply chain for India's bioenergy sector.

Scale up

The net-zero ambition is driving nations to create incentives and disincentives aimed at reducing their carbon footprint. In India, this policy push is working at multiple levels. The use of biomass and its derivatives as both industrial and automotive fuel is the central theme of these policies. Key objectives include encouraging end users to adapt, driving investments in the sector, and creating an incentive framework.

In the next three to five years, we are likely to see an energy transition that could be led by the co-firing of biomass in thermal power plants, the Ethanol Blending Programme and sustainable alternatives for transportation. Additionally, an incentive programme for investment in the biomass supply chain targeting small rural businesses is being rolled out.

A behavioural shift is also being encouraged through the promotion of green credits. Certification and monetization of these credits through an organized market are now being facilitated by the newly announced Green Credits Policy. This framework could further incentivize investors and biomass supply chain participants.

The bioenergy sector in India is projected to exceed $40 billion by 2030. This could pave the way for 70 per cent of agricultural residue to be used for clean energy. Given the industry's scale, we are no longer alone in our efforts to create a reliable supply chain. Multinational corporations with an interest in clean energy are investing in biomass supply chains. Angel investors and venture capitalists are seeking to invest in innovative business models in the sector, and more aspirants with solutions ranging from conventional to digital are vying to enter this space.

While the shape of this new energy industry is still evolving, we believe the proverbial 'invisible hand' is making the right things happen.

Our belief in our idea remains as strong as ever. More importantly, we have been able to create a business model that promises to transform a rural and unorganized supply chain. In just twenty-one months of operations, we have added 850 subscribers to our platform, connected over 12,000 farmers to help deliver 1,75,000 MT of biomass to replace coal and reduced 2,30,000 MT of carbon emissions.

We expect to quadruple our impact in the next twelve months.

Ashwin and I strongly believe we are on the right path to creating a socially conscious business that not only accelerates the bioenergy supply chain but also contributes to India's net-zero ambition.

b. AI and Satellite data for Climate Adaptation

PRATEEP BASU

> 'The Earth is the only world known so far to harbor life. There is nowhere else, at least in the near future, to which our species could migrate. Visit, yes. Settle, not yet. Like it or not, for the moment the Earth is where we make our stand.'
>
> —CARL SAGAN, *The Pale Blue Dot*

While space offers exciting and endless possibilities for exploring the mysteries of our universe, it is also the only means of capturing data about our own planet, Earth, at scale. Among the many ways in which data from space benefits mankind, enabling climate action by providing actionable climate data and extracting land-cover information ranks among the top uses of satellites in geostationary and low Earth orbits.

It is often said that one cannot manage what one does not measure. Satellite remote sensing provides a cost-effective way to measure and monitor our planet's climate and natural resources. However, its potential is only now being realized, as the number of Earth observation satellites has increased exponentially in the last decade, generating more data than we could ever process or analyse. Advances in computing, artificial intelligence and machine learning are now making it possible to identify patterns within this vast amount of satellite data and derive meaningful inferences.

Recognizing these trends, I founded a space data analytics company in 2017 with a vision to enable better decision-making for climate adaptation across businesses and policymakers. Given my background in space technology, I felt a strong drive to create impact using data. However, I soon realized that the awareness gap among target users was extremely high. Despite India having the fifth-largest space programme globally by budget-to-GDP ratio[1] and an impressive track record of sending probes to the Moon and Mars, there was limited understanding of how satellites could help in climate adaptation and the move to sustainability.

While satellite remote sensing has applications across urban planning, natural resource monitoring, and the security and energy sectors, in the context of climate action and adaptation, several key use cases stand out:

- **Enabling local climate action:** Satellites provide decades of data on climate variables such as temperature, precipitation, vegetation and sea surface conditions. Using AI on this data helps identify climate change patterns, forecast extreme weather events, and provide early warnings to vulnerable communities. Despite the global scale of satellite data, its impact is often local, as it provides provincial and city-level policymakers with tools that enable effective, data-driven decision-making. Satellite imagery is now commonly used by first responders during floods or earthquakes as well as to manage natural resources better by assessing land cover changes, deforestation rates, and water availability.
- **Measuring carbon sequestration:** As satellites collect data across multiple parts of the electromagnetic spectrum, it is possible to measure changes in carbon sequestration from forests and agricultural lands, which could be a game changer in sustainability initiatives. The biggest roadblock to scaling carbon markets is the absence of a reliable measurement, reporting and verification (MRV) system. Many emerging companies are addressing this challenge using satellite data

combined with AI and ML. By offering financial incentives to farmers, carbon trading increases the likelihood of transitioning to sustainable agricultural practices.

- **Preserving food systems:** Agriculture is among the sectors most affected by climate change, with unseasonal rains and droughts reducing yields and threatening farmer livelihoods. Satellite remote sensing has become a de-facto source of data for farmers, agribusinesses, financial services and governments to plan climate adaptation. Using AI and satellite imagery, one can predict crop yields, estimate water deficits at the farm level and assess soil health. Such insights can be tailored from the continental scale down to the small farm level, demonstrating the power of this technology.
- **Conservation of biodiversity:** Understanding and monitoring changes in the quality and condition of biodiversity, forests and the atmosphere are essential to assess their health. Evidence-based conservation practices and policymaking require the analysis of high-quality and high-frequency data to validate intervention strategies and inform decision-makers. Satellite data, in conjunction with species models and AI, plays a major role in biodiversity conservation. It not only enhances our understanding of current and emerging pressures on biodiversity but also helps build predictive knowledge of species distribution.

While there are many more use cases of satellite data for climate adaptation and preserving our natural ecosystems, limited awareness in this area led us to focus our business model on financial services in agriculture and government actors. A key factor in determining a business's success is achieving product-market fit. For use cases where policies and systems that create a conducive business environment don't exist, entrepreneurial focus shifts to where they do, leaving, in this instance, vitally important areas like climate adaptation and preservation of natural ecosystems unaddressed.

Agriculture was the first market we targeted, as our team saw strong political will to try new technologies. The opportunity to positively impact over 100 million farmers was a meaningful challenge. We successfully developed and demonstrated the impact of field interventions such as better crop contingency planning, harvest procurement intelligence from farmers at Minimum Support Prices (MSP), improved crop yield estimates, rapid crop damage assessment for getting insurance claims and large-scale crop health monitoring.

The government's interest in agriculture also had a direct spillover effect on the financial services sector, which became our second market of interest due to the scale and magnitude of the challenges—only 38 per cent of farmers receive institutional credit, while high levels of non-performing assets (NPAs), low insurance penetration and poor confidence are persistent issues. What excited us most was the potential to use data to improve risk perception, reduce costs for farmers, and make financial services available to them despite the risks posed by climate change. Today, we have enabled over a million loans and claims.

However, not every sector was receptive to the use of satellite data. For example, while the world was enthusiastically exploring the use of satellite data for environmental, social and governance (ESG) reporting, India lacked policy guidelines for such applications. Similarly, areas such as climate hazard assessment, infrastructure vulnerabilities analysis and biodiversity conservation showed a low willingness to adopt satellite data analysis. This hesitation stemmed from well-placed concerns around achieving outcomes, as it required skill sets not typically taught in Indian colleges.

For example, sectoral knowledge must first be translated into product requirements, which are then converted into technical specifications. This requires policymakers, climate scientists, remote sensing analysts, data scientists and software engineers to come together and speak in a common language. Unfortunately, our education system is not flexible enough to allow such fluidity in language—data scientists rarely understand remote sensing, and remote sensing specialist often do not understand software engineering.

Thus, the absence of awareness, policy guidelines, appropriate skill sets and sector-specific incentives (unlike those in agriculture and financial services) has limited the potential for satellite data and AI/ML to protect and preserve our planet, and the opportunity could be lost. In my opinion, these are solvable problems that just need the attention of the right people. For example, the issue of talent gaps could be addressed by redesigning curricula in geo-informatics, climate studies and data science to include interdisciplinary components. Similarly, financial incentives (or penalties) for organizations on ESG reporting could help create greater awareness on this subject.

Today, the convergence of satellite data, AI/ML and high-performance cloud computing presents an opportunity to build resilient infrastructure, improve disaster response and protect vulnerable populations. It also offers an excellent opportunity for entrepreneurs to innovate, monetize and deliver a positive societal impact. Beyond policy and regulation, raising awareness and developing talent is essential to changing this dynamic and enabling us to adapt to climate change in better-informed ways, ultimately building a better future for the generations to come.

9

What Works, What Doesn't

SUTAPA BANERJEE

THIS CHAPTER IS NOT A summary of the chapters in each section. The contributors—domain experts and business practitioners—draw on their knowledge and experience to make each section rich with diverse viewpoints that invite personal engagement from the reader. Many will likely come away with insights that go well beyond those highlighted here.

In this piece, I outline a few approaches, models and regulations that merit deeper study to scale their impact and assess their applicability across other sectors, geographies and domains. In some instances, I expand on the contributors' views and examples; in others, I offer suggestions of my own.

Entrepreneurial zeal

Pioneering entrepreneurs identify and seize opportunities where gaps in ecosystems or markets can be addressed through business models, technologies, approaches or practices not previously applied. They act as catalysts and, when successful, gain first-mover advantage while drawing attention to the space and encouraging others to enter. This section focuses on two such examples.

In the first, an entrepreneur deploys an internet-based marketplace model to transform a fragmented biofuel supply structure into a more organized and sustainable supply chain, while also generating wider social benefits.

In the second, the business proposition uses artificial intelligence (AI) and machine learning (ML) to make data gathered by geo-satellites accessible to policymakers and businesses, improving decision-making for climate adaptation. While the entrepreneur has focused on financial services in the agricultural sector—reflecting the readiness of both the market and the policy environment—many high-impact use cases, including biodiversity conservation and climate hazard management, remain untapped.

It is worth examining in depth the conditions that enabled entrepreneurial activity in these sectors to help scale the impact of existing business models and use cases, and to build the necessary ecosystem of incentives, skilling and collaboration to unlock the many opportunities yet to be realized. The nature of skilling and collaboration, discussed in the 'Multi-stakeholder collaboration' sub-section below, requires both urgent and sustained attention.

Regulations

From the National Voluntary Guidelines in 2011 to the National Guidelines for Responsible Business Conduct in 2019;[1] from Business Responsibility Reporting in 2012 to Business Responsibility and Sustainability Reporting in 2021;[2] followed by Reasonable Assurance on core key performance indicators (KPIs) in 2023, value chain disclosures on core KPIs in 2024, and limited assurance on value chain disclosures on core KPIs in 2025, the regulatory 'glide path'[3] has steadily pushed the corporate sector to move from viewing responsible business practices as a 'nice to have' to a 'must have', with mandated board oversight in several areas.

This trajectory will continue to drive innovation across corporate value chains and accelerate the adoption of responsible business practices, including environmental sustainability.

Multi-stakeholder collaboration

Collaboration—whether inter-ministerial, within a sector, across sectors or involving government and regulators—is imperative for solving complex problems. While this may seem self-evident, what is often less clear is how to forge effective alliances, how to involve government and regulators, how to select appropriate pilots when testing new approaches, and how to use scientific research and data to scale impact.

Among the many initiatives highlighted in the preceding chapters, one noteworthy example is Responsible Care, a global voluntary programme in which large players in the chemical industry came together to improve health, safety and environmental performance. Although the industry's association with disasters—particularly in the aftermath of the Bhopal gas tragedy—may have catalysed its formation, the programme's global achievements and its implementation in India are worth close examination.

Peer pressure and mutual assistance played a critical role in its success, with state regulatory bodies granting faster project clearances to signatories. This created both the 'push' and the 'pull' for companies to commit to higher health, safety and environmental standards. The role of Trustea in the plantations sector, discussed in the same chapter, offers similar lessons.

In the same vein, the Build Ahead Coalition, launched by the advisory firm Xynteo, 'aims to bring together multiple stakeholders from the construction value chain including producers, consumers, financiers and technology providers to accelerate the use of low carbon building materials, with the goal to support India achieving its net zero targets by 2070'.[4]

One of the most compelling examples, referenced across several chapters, is the Emissions Trading Scheme (ETS) in Gujarat, which brings together private industry, regulators, a private trading platform and leading research partners to implement a cutting-edge policy instrument.

A pioneering market-based mechanism to curb air pollution, the ETS was piloted in Surat in 2019 as the world's first pollution market for particulate matter. It 'achieved the rare win-win of reducing industries cost and decreasing pollution emissions, fostering faster economic growth and clean air'.[5] Its success in Surat, along with the depth of research it yielded on environmental policy, led to its adoption in Ahmedabad in September 2023.

The scheme was implemented by the Gujarat Pollution Control Board (GPCB), in collaboration with affiliates and researchers from the Economic Growth Centre at Yale University, with support from the Energy Policy Institute at the University of Chicago (EPIC) and the Abdul Latif Jameel Poverty Action Lab (J-PAL) South Asia. It is now cited internationally as a leading example of evidence-based policymaking.[6]

While these examples illustrate successful collaboration in traditional industries, emerging domains such as space data analytics face a pressing need for policymakers, climate scientists, remote-sensing analysts, data scientists and software engineers to come together and develop a shared language. This is crucial for creating a supportive ecosystem of policies, incentives and interdisciplinary learning formats—eloquently articulated in the relevant chapter—that can spur high-impact use cases in this domain.

Reward and amplify success stories and best practices

If, as the saying goes, nothing succeeds like success, awards can help amplify the success stories manifold. For the many media-sponsored awards given with great fanfare to businesses and business leaders, responsible business practices—including environmental sustainability—should not be confined to one category. Instead, they should form a key criterion with significant weightage used in the selection of every award category. Just as entities must weave environmental sustainability into the very fabric of doing business for it to be meaningful, every award category should integrate responsible business practices as a critical qualifying metric in its evaluation process.

PART III

Equity and Economic Participation

10

Being a Good Ancestor

MANISH SABHARWAL

INDIA'S POLICY THOUGHT WORLD IS shifting from an over-reliance on fiscal and monetary measures to a focus on raising productivity. This will create the high-paying jobs needed for mass prosperity by India@100. Jonas Salk, the inventor of the polio vaccine, once said that our most significant duty is to be 'good ancestors'.[1] This long-term view of success recognizes that anything valuable takes decades to build, that stakeholders must be balanced rather than ranked and that weather-of-the-moment difficulties, while painful, are less critical for our destiny than we often believe.

The stress on the job market caused by the COVID-19 pandemic was a passing storm, not a reflection of climate change. However, geopolitics suggests that economic climate change is underway, with most large and wealthy countries turning on trade, offering subsidies in a resurgence of industrial policy, and slowing foreign investment flows. These changes matter because India's two primary labour market shock absorbers—farm employment and self-employment—which have historically kept unemployment between 4 and 9 per cent since 1947, are no longer acceptable to today's youth, who want decent work with a decent income. My thesis is that India's problem is not a lack of jobs but the issue of wages. Let's look at the challenges and opportunities in raising productivity.

Recent debates about current labour market data—high-frequency changes in unemployment—have become needlessly controversial as all models and surveys remain incomplete. Our massive underinvestment in statistics—the Rs 78 crore budget of the Central Statistical Office and the Rs 529 crore budget of the National Sample Survey Organization—must be reversed. Until better data becomes available, we can accept three broad truths about our labour market: first, increasing the size of our economy requires changing its shape; second, widespread employed poverty means wages are a bigger challenge than jobs; and third, narrowing the productivity gap between our regions, firms and individuals is as important as raising levels.

I make the case that the inability of many Indians to find decent work with a decent income is rooted in six historical imbalances that must be reversed.

The first imbalance, between the three pillars of Team India—public, private and non-profit—arose from the 1955 Avadi resolution. It constrained the private sector while placing the government in charge of running hotels, airlines and liquor stores, and even building scooters, steel and bread. Things are now changing: the Air India sale and privatization programme, the unicorn and venture capital explosion, and the civil society response during the COVID-19 pandemic are all signs of a shift. Hopefully, this lane driving becomes a template because the private sector has a trust deficit, the government has an execution deficit and non-profits have a scale deficit. Neither is more critical or capable; each is unique and necessary.

The second imbalance is between the next quarter and the quarter-century. Populism often tempts politicians to fund the welfare state by borrowing—or stealing—from future generations. While few disagree that a modern state is a welfare state, the key is financing it with borrowings or expanding the tax base through higher productivity of our states, cities, sectors, firms and individuals. We all want to end poverty in the next quarter, but it will take a quarter-century plan for India@100 that transforms the productivity of our regions (Karnataka and Uttar Pradesh have the same GDP with a 300 per cent population difference); our cities (if every city had the productivity of Bangalore, then our country's GDP would exceed China's); our firms (our largest manufacturing firms are twenty-four times more productive than the smallest); our sectors (software employs only 1 per cent of the labour force but contributes 8 per cent of GDP); and our individuals (graduates with the same age and qualifications often see a fivefold difference in starting salaries based on skills).

The third imbalance lies between education and employability. In 1938, Gandhiji proposed 'Nayi Taalim', the massification and vocationalization of education. However, the 1948 Radhakrishnan Committee, the 1968 Kothari Committee, and the 1986 New Education Policy did not end the false conflict between 'learning for living' and 'learning for earning'. The National Education Policy (NEP) 2020 recognizes the trade-offs between quantity, quality, cost and employability and blurs the boundaries. It has a fifteen-year glide path for implementation that must be reduced to five years because human capital is the most scalable and renewable resource any country has in the twenty-first century.

The fourth imbalance is between the central and state governments. The 299 remarkable people who drafted our constitution flipped their decentralized view of governance to a strong centre after Partition. Indira Gandhi once said that strong states lead to a weak nation, while the chief minister of Andhra Pradesh, N.T. Rama Rao, countered that the central government was a conceptual myth. However, cooperative and competitive federalism is the only choice for a country like India. For the first seventy years of independence, the central government's budget was larger than that of all state governments. Only in the past five years has the devolution of funds, functions and functionaries begun to make the twenty-nine chief ministers matter more than one prime minister. One hundred mayors matter more than twenty-nine chief ministers, but unfortunately, the lack of power for that position has left cities as policy orphans. Tellingly, the combined budget of India's 2.5 lakh municipalities and panchayats amounts to only 5 per cent of total government spending across all three levels—centre, state and local.

The fifth imbalance is between men and women. Women's workforce participation in rural India is higher than in urban India, but this is deceptive, as it ignores productivity and income. Capital is an important driver of women's low productivity in self-employment or small entrepreneurship; According to the RBI, women-owned MSMEs accounted for only about 7 per cent of outstanding MSME credit in scheduled commercial banks, despite nearly 40 per cent of MSMEs being women-owned. Women are also hurt by the low productivity of India's informal sector: our 63 million enterprises only translate to 22,500 companies with a paid-up capital of more than Rs 10 crore.

Other laws matter too. The tax wedge can be larger for second earners and single parents and is particularly relevant for women's labour force participation rates. India's colossal farm employment not only produces limited GDP (condemning most farmers to poverty) but is only made possible by the massive self-exploitation of women. Just as the only way to help farmers is to have less of them, the best way to help women is to move them into formal, non-farm activities with higher productivity (and therefore higher incomes).

While India has greatly improved girls' enrolment and completion rates in primary education, secondary enrolment has declined. The lack of a uniform civil code also sabotages equal inheritance rights. Moreover, action must be mindful of unintended consequences that hurt the people we are trying to help. For example, research by Professors Sofia Bapna and Russel Funk at the University of Minnesota[2] '*The Unintended Consequences of Maternity Leave Policy*' suggests that the Maternity Benefit Act of 2017 may have discouraged some employers from hiring women of certain ages.

On a more encouraging note, flexibility or hybrid work is a positive development. COVID-driven digitization has created an unimaginable global experiment in work-from-home, work-from-anywhere and asynchronous work—showing promising results. Estimates suggest that flexible wage work could rise from 5 per cent pre-pandemic to 25 per cent. Flexibility matters because it transforms the traditional 'child break' from an irreconcilable conflict into personal choices and trade-offs.

India also offers some upside surprises. Women gained the right to vote in 1947, whereas Switzerland granted universal suffrage only in 1972. India's Medical Termination Act of 1971 offers more freedom than restrictive laws such as the Texas Healthcare Act of 2021 tackling abortion. However, India also has a legacy of rules that create powerful men. For instance, our invention of chess as *Chaturanga*—Sanskrit for 'four divisions of the army': elephants, chariots, cavalry and infantry—had a weak queen. Some historians suggest the queen only became the most powerful piece in chess after Isabella became Queen of Spain in 1479.

There remain several gender justice challenges such as infant mortality, paid leave, paternal leave, sexist family laws, unequal property rights, differential education, early marriage for girls (According to the United Nations Population Fund 2024, around one in five women globally are married before 18[3]), patrilocal marriage, polygamy, dowry, son preference, violence against women and legal indulgence.

The sixth imbalance is between cities and villages. Cities are engines of productivity, but India can't take jobs to people—it must take people to jobs. In China, a four-day weekend in February sees 250 million people buying train or plane tickets to head home. In contrast, India has nothing of this kind on Diwali, Eid or Christmas because we have 6,00,000 villages (of which 2,00,000 have less than 200 people), and around sixty-five cities with populations over one million (China has 141).

This poor urbanization has created a painful divergence between real and nominal wages. India needs at least 300 cities with populations exceeding one million. Yet cities remain policy orphans with poor governance, weak resources and problematic incentives. The future of India lies in its cities, but today even our job magnets suffer enormous challenges. I live in Bangalore, where the average taxi speed is 13.9 kilometres per hour (most people can walk that fast).

While progress has been made in devolving funds from Delhi to state capitals, the next priority must be the devolution of money from state governments to city governments.

How should we fix these imbalances? Policy has three tools: fiscal, monetary and structural. Fiscal spending matters, but no country would be poor if fiscal deficits could make nations rich. After past fiscal indiscipline and COVID, we are already approaching the limits of public debt to GDP (not counting the irresponsible noises from some state governments about restoring index-linked defined benefit pensions for civil servants).

Monetary policy matters to financial markets, but even there, it is unclear whether it functions as a placebo, painkiller or steroid. The chaos of quantitative tightening on global markets and banks (Credit Suisse and Silicon Valley Bank) suggests that quantitative easing was a bad idea if you consider the unintended consequences.

This leaves us with structural reform. India does not have a shortage of the three factors of production—land, labour and capital. You could give every Indian household half an acre, and they would fit in Rajasthan and Haryana. About 40 per cent of our labour force is *vela* or underemployed. We can attract capital when we deserve it; more than 50 per cent of India's foreign direct investment since 1947 has come in the last five years.

The real challenge for India is not land, labour or capital but how they combine, or the fourth factor of production of entrepreneurship, innovation and productivity. We face a drought in what economists call total factor productivity. While others in this book cover many areas of structural reform, I focus on three human capital reforms and one meta-reform.

School education reform

There is a new world of education: lifelong learning matters more than knowing because Google knows everything; soft skills matter more than hard skills; curiosity matters more than intelligence; and Stanford psychologist Carol Dweck's 'growth mindset' (people who believe that capabilities are like muscles) matters more than a fixed mindset (the belief that capabilities are like shoe size or height).

If anything should be free in a country, it should be quality education. Only 4 per cent of children in Japan and 15 per cent in the US attend private schools, while in India, the number is an embarrassing 55 per cent. We have wasted time and money debating class sizes, teacher qualifications and teacher salaries. These matter, but they do not move the needle on learning outcomes. What is needed is tackling the complex governance issues—allocation of decision rights on funds, functions and functionaries—and performance management that create both a fear of falling and a hope of rising in government schools.

Higher education reform

The most crucial change in higher education over the next two decades will be the number of employed learners crossing full-time learners. This shift requires regulatory changes that allow multimodal learning (online, in-office, on-the-job and on-campus) and create qualification corridors between certificates, diplomas, advanced diplomas and degrees.

To achieve this, five regulatory changes are essential. First, modify clause 22, Section 3 of the University Grants Commission (UGC) Act, 1956, to recognize and legitimize degree apprenticeships for all accredited universities.

Second, remove clauses 4(1)(i), 4(1)(ii), 4(1)(iii), and 6 of the UGC Online Regulations 2018, which restrict licensing and prescribe a discretionary approval process, and replace them with provisions authorizing all accredited universities to design, develop and deliver their own online programmes.

Third, amend clause 4(2) of the UGC Online Regulations 2018 to allow innovation, flexibility and relevance in online curricula, enabling universities to work closely with industries on their list of courses and ensure integrity of purpose.

Fourth, modify clause 7(3)(viii) of the UGC Online Regulations to allow rolling admissions.

And finally, replace clause 7(2)(vi) with clause 4(4)(iv) in the UGC Online Regulations to allow technology-driven, on-demand and credible online assessments.

Skill and apprenticeship reform

Mahatma Gandhi articulated Nayi Taalim in 1938 at Wardha as a vision for experiential and vocational education. However, this was not embedded in the 1948 Radhakrishnan Committee Report, the 1968 Kothari Committee Report, or the 1986 New Policy on Education.

We should re-architect our skill system based on five design principles: learning while earning, learning by doing, learning with modularity, learning with flexibility, and learning with signalling value. We must also complete the transition from multiple labour laws to unified labour codes and truly embrace degree apprenticeships. Expanding our current 4 lakh apprentices to 50 lakh requires four changes by four regulators [the Ministry of Skill Development and Entrepreneurship (MSDE), the Central Apprenticeship Council, the Ministry of Education and the UGC].

1. MSDE introduced the definition of degree apprenticeship in 2019. These rules must also include 'University' in their definition. The university should become the third party in the apprenticeship contract, alongside the 'Employer' and 'Apprentice', to protect the interests of students engaged as apprentices. This is possible under Section 8(2) of the Apprentices Act.
2. The role of universities and the processes they must follow in running apprenticeship-embedded degree

courses should be clearly outlined in guidelines issued by the UGC under Section 22(3) of the UGC Act. Current UGC guidelines do not even mention MSDE, despite the fact that it is responsible for implementing apprenticeships in India. Obviously, this needs to change, and the guidelines should be redrafted after genuine (not hurried or insincere) consultation with MSDE, industry associations, higher education institutions, sector skill councils and other stakeholders.

3. The UGC Regulations issued under Section 26(1), read with Section 2(f) of the UGC Act, should be amended to create space for 'skills universities'.
4. While doing so, a parallel set of guidelines for skills universities should be framed, which may require changes to the UGC Regulations for Teachers (2018), UGC Online Regulations (2018), and the Internal Quality Assurance Cell (IQAC) guidelines. Similarly, UGC rules regarding the fitness of universities must be amended to introduce a new category of skills universities, as has been done in the case of agricultural, technical and open universities.

Civil service reform

India's so-called 'steel-frame' has become a 'steel cage'. Our current civil service sabotages permissionless innovation with its mentality of 'prohibited till permitted', writes laws for the thief and is mainly staffed by generalists who are too big for small things but too small for big things. The clearest manifestation of this is the regulatory cholesterol for employers—69,000+ compliance requirements, 6,000+ filings and 25,000+ jail provisions.

Better human capital and more high-wage employment for India require civil service reform that reduces the number of central ministries; replicates the 'Agniveer' programme for all civil services hiring to allow differential exit ages; restores the organizational structure from a cylinder to a pyramid by reducing top-heaviness (for example, there should be twenty-five Secretaries to the Government of India in Delhi instead of 250+); creates differentiation through specialization; and adopts a performance management system that recognizes performers—if you treat a *gadha* (donkey) and *ghoda* (horse) as equals, it is the *gadha* who celebrates and the *ghoda* who gets frustrated.

While Swaraj means independence to most, Gandhiji reminded India of its original meaning: *swa-raj,* or 'self-rule'. Our political Swaraj since 1947 hasn't always translated into individual economic swa-raj. Driven by the wrong tone from the top and codified in the Avadi Resolution of 1955, our economy became inadequately formalized, industrialized, urbanized, financialized and skilled. Gandhiji's vision of individual self-reliance recognized poverty as the worst form of violence.

Let us be good ancestors and end the imbalances that sabotage our national prosperity, inclusiveness and power by creating high-wage jobs for every Indian who seeks employment.

11

Building India's Digital Job Marketplace

The Genesis of Naukri

SANJEEV BIKHCHANDANI

THE IDEA OF 'NAUKRI.COM', AN online Indian portal that connects job seekers with employers across various industries, came from a couple of seemingly simple observations. Yet embedded within them were profound customer and market insights.

The first dates to 1989, when I was working in the marketing team at HMM Ltd (now GlaxoSmithKline). My colleagues and I would invariably read the fortnightly magazine *Business India* from the back. In those days, the magazine carried thirty to forty pages of appointment advertisements at the end. Often, my colleagues barely glanced at the editorial content and passed on the magazine after reading only the recruitment ads.

It wasn't that they were actively looking for jobs. They were working at a good company and doing well in their careers. Back in 1989, if you wanted to work in marketing (not sales) at a multinational fast-moving consumer goods (FMCG) company headquartered in Delhi, then you were already in the best possible place. In the pre-liberalization era, there were only two or three such companies in Delhi, and they did not hire from each other.

My colleagues were simply interested in staying abreast of what was happening in the job market. They were competitive and wanted to know whether they were missing out on any opportunities or what the current market benchmarks were. Today, we might call this behaviour the fear of missing out, or FOMO.

This practice led to the realization that information about jobs was of great interest to working professionals—even if they weren't looking to switch, they still wanted to review job listings.

Another observation was that every week, two or three head-hunters would call one or another of my colleagues. We all sat in an open hall, so I often overheard one side of the conversation. Over time, I noticed a pattern: each call came from a different head-hunter about a different job at a different company. And none of these jobs was advertised in any magazine or newspaper.

This led to another insight: many vacancies across hundreds, perhaps thousands, of companies were never advertised at all. What appeared in print was merely the tip of the iceberg. Beneath it there was a much larger job market where information was fragmented and not easily accessible to the public.

Armed with these two insights, I concluded that if someone could aggregate information about all available jobs across companies, it would create a highly valuable database. Of course, there were many hurdles and several unanswered questions: How would we gather job data and keep it current? How would we make this information available to the public? How would the platform be funded, and would companies even pay for such a service?

The idea seemed promising, but I could not answer these key questions satisfactorily. So, it became one of those file-and-forget ideas. I eventually quit my job and moved on to conducting salary surveys, followed by a series of small ventures over the next several years.

Then, in 1993, the Department of Telecom (DoT) placed a large advertisement in the Delhi newspapers announcing the launch of a Videotex service in the city. The concept was simple: a central server housed at a telephone exchange would host a series of databases, and fifty public-access terminals across the city would allow people to use these databases for a fee. The advertisement invited applications from Private Information Providers (PIPs)—organizations that would create and maintain databases on the server, with revenue shared between the DoT and the PIP.

We applied to build a jobs database on the Videotex server. Our proposal was accepted, and we began work. Before we could complete the project, however, it was cancelled. Although we had developed the concept and the plan, we had no idea what to do with it in 1993. So, once again, we filed it away and forgot about it.

In 1996, I attended the IT Asia expo at Pragati Maidan in Delhi, where I saw the internet for the first time. At the time, there were only 14,000 internet accounts in the country—a number that, to me, seemed very large. That was the moment the penny dropped: a job site on the internet would be a good idea.

We revived our old plan and product concept and quickly moved to implementation. Our approach was to aggregate job listings from newspapers and magazines across the country and upload them to the internet. Almost immediately, the site began to attract traffic, and Naukri.com saw early success.

Over the years, Naukri grew steadily, and we eventually tasted financial success as well. The company went public in 2006, and the platform made a remarkable impact. We effectively organized the Indian market for white-collar jobs in the organized private sector. Today, over 1,00,000 organizations recruit through Naukri, and over seventy million job seekers use the site.

Then we decided to launch a platform for blue-collar jobs—JobHai.com—as Naukri was not well suited to the needs of blue-collar workers. This market operates differently: it is hyperlocal, lacks detailed CVs, relies more on voice interaction over mobile than text or email, depends heavily on walk-in-interviews and frequently requires communication in the vernacular.

Job Hai is seeing initial success. The widespread penetration of mobile data has made this market viable in recent years, whereas earlier attempts by other players struggled to gain traction.

Mobile phones and internet access have made it possible to create a unified market and bring underserved segments of the workforce into the mainstream. This includes enabling more women to join the workforce. But this will be a gradual process. While the technology now exists, social attitudes will take time to change. In many families, women are still discouraged, or not permitted, to work, even if job information is readily available online. Many jobs also require women from smaller towns and villages to relocate to cities, a step that is far easier for men than for women. Educational qualification can also be a barrier for certain jobs. And even in households with mobile phones, the device is often controlled by the man in the house and not the woman.

Clearly, the biggest impediment to increasing women's economic participation is social norms. In a heterogeneous country like India breaking these barriers will entail taking significant, coordinated efforts across multiple fronts, and in tandem rather than isolated measures.

12

Show Me the Money

Addressing Gender Bias in Corporate Spaces

PREETI REDDY

Addressing gender bias in corporate spaces

GENDER INEQUALITY REMAINS A PRESSING global issue in today's corporate world. It has ramifications not only for the lives and livelihoods of women but also affects human development and GDP growth.

Companies are powerful drivers of social change. They have a captive set of people dependent on them for their livelihood. Their structures tend to be hierarchical, with instructions flowing from the top down. They have a large number of teams, so social impact initiatives can create a ripple effect.

Progress being made

The corporate world—both globally and in India—has ostensibly embraced the mission of calling out and removing gender stereotypes and promoting women's participation in the workforce and in leadership roles. Many companies have committed to becoming more diverse and have long been engaged in efforts to make their workforces and communities more diverse, equitable and inclusive. These efforts combine regulatory compliance with a focus on long-term mindset change as well as embedding cultural change into the fabric of their organizations. Initiatives include professional development programmes, unconscious bias training, the promotion of inclusive behaviours at the individual level, the creation of support groups, and adherence to compliance standards.

At the global level, the Parity.Org Best Companies for Women to Advance list recognizes organizations that foster the culture and conditions for women to thrive, with best practices that fall into three categories: equality, inclusion and representation.[1]

Some companies that made it onto the list include:

- **PepsiCo:** Provides on-site or near-site childcare in various office locations, enhanced maternity leave policies, flexible working, well-being programmes and dedicated mother's rooms. Offers back-up child and elder care services, as well as a 'Ready to Return' programme in New York to support employees re-entering the workforce after taking time off to care for a loved one.
- **Best Buy:** Maintains significant female representation in executive roles, with 60 per cent of board directors being women. Offers family benefits such as back-up childcare, paid caregiver leave, and adoption, infertility and surrogacy support. Provides peer support through its Women's Employee Resource Group, which focuses on networking, mentoring, professional development and leadership

opportunities. Inspires young women to pursue tech-reliant careers through all-girl Geek Squad Academy camps and over 100 Best Buy Teen Tech Centers around the country. Requires at least one qualified female candidate to be interviewed for every open position at the vice president level and above.

- **BehaVR:** Offers work-from-home and telecommute options as well as flexible working hours, provides equal paid family leave for men and women, reports regularly on gender parity to the executive ream, encourages men to take their full family leave, and has a zero-tolerance policy for harassment.

Indian companies are also increasingly taking cognisance of global trends by advancing their diversity and inclusion (D&I) efforts. For example, the India Diversity Forum voted BCG, Sodexo and TCS as the top three companies for D&I practices in 2021–22. Their initiatives include, but are not restricted to:

- Recruitment and integration of talent from diverse gender backgrounds
- Mentorship and affiliation for both professional and personal guidance
- Part-time and flexible working arrangements
- Internal well-being and transformation initiatives through support groups, employee assistance programmes, and inclusive policies on maternity, return-to-work and child and elder caregiving responsibilities
- High senior-level involvement in D&I efforts

Many other companies are similarly working towards creating more equitable and inclusive workplaces.

The numbers tell a different story

On 25 May 2020, George Floyd, a forty-six-year-old Black American man, was killed in Minneapolis, Minnesota, during an arrest by police officers. A bystander's video showed Officer Derek Chauvin kneeling on Floyd's neck for over nine minutes, despite Floyd repeatedly saying, 'I can't breathe.' The video spread globally within hours, triggering massive outrage. The incident became a symbol of racial injustice, systemic racism and police brutality in the United States and beyond.[2] Following the murder of George Floyd in 2020, companies ramped up their diversity, equity and inclusion (DEI) efforts, and the world saw an unprecedented explosion of corporate DEI commitments.[3]

Since then, however, the pace of commitments has slowed. Business leaders, employees and other stakeholders have expressed frustration with the lack of significant progress on well-intentioned DEI pledges.[4] Recent developments in DEI efforts across major U.S. companies reveal a significant shift—many are scaling back or restructuring their initiatives in 2025. President Donald Trump's administration has issued executive orders that restrict race- and gender-based DEI programs. Companies are adjusting to avoid legal risk. Major companies scaling back DEI efforts include IBM, Meta, Amazon, Target and Disney. Some firms are reframing DEI language to emphasize 'inclusive culture' or 'belonging' rather than equity or diversity, aiming to stay within legal boundaries. Critics argue these rollbacks undermine trust and question whether past DEI efforts were genuine. Consequently, gender parity in workplace advancement remains elusive. McKinsey's 2024 Women in the Workplace research, conducted with LeanIn.org, showed that for every 100 men promoted from entry-level to manager positions, only 81 women are promoted. The same research also revealed that women leaders, particularly women of colour, leave companies at a much higher rate than white men.[5]

Top five countries by percentage of board seats and CEO positions held by women[6]					
Percentage of board seats held by women			**Percentage of CEO roles held by women**		
Country	**Percentage**	**Per cent change from 2021**	**Country**	**Percentage**	**Per cent change from 2021**
France	44.0	+0.9	Poland	13.5	10.3
Norway	43.5	+1.1	Sweden	12.3	-0.1
Italy	40.4	+3.8	Philippines	12.0	5.8
Belgium	38.0	+3.2	Singapore	11.9	-1.2
New Zealand	36.3	+4.4	Thailand	11.9	0.3

In 2021, in India, women:

- were CEOs in 4.7 per cent of firms[7]
- were CFOs in 3.9 per cent of firms
- held 17.9 per cent of board seats
- earned 65.5 per cent of their male colleagues[8]

Clearly, across the world, and more so in India, we are still struggling to make significant progress in these areas. We have not been able to instigate the behavioural and cultural changes required to achieve equitable outcomes.

It is not that companies are not trying. Most companies do take a systematic approach to their D&I strategies. They establish a baseline, determine the interventions needed most, and set aspirational (but achievable) goals linked to the company's overall strategy. They mobilize resources and develop a plan to deliver on the D&I initiatives. They monitor progress over time. People are held accountable for desired outcomes and for course correction.

Yet progress has been slow. The eighth edition of Deloitte Global's *Women in the Boardroom* report shows that the worldwide average of women on boards now sits at 23.3 per cent, an increase of just 3.6 percentage points since the previous edition. However, the presence of more women does not mean they are reaching top leadership positions. Although nearly one-quarter of board seats are held by women, only 8.4 per cent of board chairs are women. Female CEOs are even rarer, at 6 per cent globally in 2023.

In India, as of 2025:[9]

- 97 per cent of NSE-listed companies now have at least one-woman director.
- 48 per cent of these companies have two or more women on their boards.

However, many women directors are promoter-affiliated, raising concerns about tokenism rather than true inclusion. And executive roles remain elusive: fewer than 5 per cent of women serve as MDs or CEOs, and only 10 per cent as executive directors. India's board diversity is improving, but deeper structural changes are needed to ensure women not only join boards but lead them.

What accounts for the shortfall in progress?

Deep-seated biases that hold women back continue to prevail, especially among those who are in positions to make a difference.

The findings in this section are based on *The Gender Equality Attitudes Study* conducted under the leadership of UN Women, in partnership with five organizations—AT&T, Johnson & Johnson, Kantar, Procter & Gamble and Unilever.[10]

The pilot study was conducted in 2018 across ten countries. The second iteration of the study was done in 2020 with the scope expanded to include ten additional countries. The countries were: India, United States, United Kingdom, Brazil, Mexico, Argentina, South Africa, Nigeria, Kenya, Egypt, Turkey, Russia, China, Japan, South Korea, Indonesia, Thailand, Philippines, Australia and Germany

Interviews were online, face-to-face, or a mix, as appropriate for each country. Approximately 1000 interviews were conducted in each country. The respondents included:

- Women and men (fifty-fifty split)
- Individuals between the ages of sixteen and fifty-five (nationally representative quotas)
- Urban and rural participants (nationally representative quotas)
- A range of income and socio-economic groups (nationally representative quotas)

The study explores how people perceive gender equality in leadership, education, employment and media. Typically, women face gender inequality across all areas of life, and those in power are least likely to recognize this. The findings reveal both the momentum and resistance faced in building a truly equal world. Key findings reveal that:

- The gender gap is relatively lower in education (4 percentage points), but men's education is still more likely to be prioritized.
- More significant gaps are observed in personal and economic empowerment (12 and 14 percentage points, respectively), with the largest gender disparity found in politics (26 percentage points).
- While all cohorts are aware of this power imbalance, men over the age of thirty-five are the least likely to recognize it. This highlights a key challenge: women are under-represented where policy decisions are made, and men who are in power don't acknowledge the extent of the problem.
- When it comes to gender roles and responsibilities, men are more likely than women to endorse gender stereotypes. However, women themselves subscribe almost as strongly to these biases: 46 per cent of women agree that women should work less and devote more time to caring for their families (versus 51 per cent of men), and 31 per cent of women agree that a man's job is to earn money while a woman's job is to look after the house and the family (versus 40 per cent of men).

Companies tend to follow a 'carrot' approach to addressing gender biases

Efforts in the corporate world have largely been directed at changing mindsets and culture—through engagement, interventions, resource groups and equality targets—to build more equal companies and a better world. This is the proverbial 'carrot' approach. While this is a necessary and a laudable goal, mindsets take time to change. The carrot approach is inherently soft, relying on 'thinking', or a more cerebral, moral approach to change. However, when biases are strong, what is needed is a push to adopt behaviours that will lead to change.

Companies also often fail to establish a business case for the one factor that could lead to more rapid change—the return on investment (ROI) on diversity. They neglect to point out that diversity is desirable not only because it is the right thing to do, but also because it makes economic sense. For example, McKinsey's Global Institute (MGI), in its 2015 report *The Power of Parity*, found that:

- Narrowing the global gender gap in work could double the contribution of women to global GDP growth between 2014 and 2025. In a 'full-potential' scenario, where women participate in the economy on par with men, global GDP in 2025 could be $28 trillion—or 26 per cent—higher than in a business-as-usual scenario. This impact is roughly equivalent to the combined size of the US and Chinese economies today.
- Both advanced and developing countries stand to gain. In forty-six of the ninety-five countries analysed, the best-in-region outcome could increase annual GDP in 2025 by more than 10 per cent compared to the business-as-usual case, with the highest relative boost in India and Latin America.
- There is, expectedly, a strong link between gender equality in society, prevailing attitudes and beliefs about the role of women, and gender equality in the workplace. The latter cannot be achieved without the former two elements. MGI

found virtually no examples of countries with high social gender equality but low workplace gender equality

Similar evidence-based arguments need to be built at a corporate level to demonstrate that women in the workplace add hard, economic value, not just diversity and colour.

It is time to put the carrot on a stick

Data and evidence, however, take time to build. Their veracity may itself depend on the speed and earnestness with which an organization adopts its diversity agenda. Progress towards equality is slow and not guaranteed.

It is time, therefore, to put some teeth into our D&I strategies by mandating behaviours and through more definitive affirmative action. Significant social change needs a stronger impetus than the feel-good notion of simply 'doing the right thing'.

- In India, the percentage of women directors rose after the Companies Act, 2013 made it mandatory to appoint at least one female director as a board member in certain types of companies. The 2023 edition of Deloitte Global's *Women in the Boardroom* report (data collected in early 2023) revealed that women held 18.3 per cent of board seats in India—an increase of 10.6 percentage points from the 2014 edition.
- The French consortium that funded the Kochi Metro mandated that 70 per cent of employees must be women. Today, Kochi Metro is 100 per cent run by women.
- Nasdaq had introduced rules requiring its listed companies to have or explain gaps in having at least two 'diverse' directors—including one woman and one who identifies as a minority or LGBTQ+, depending on the listing tier

and board size. However, those rules were struck down in **December 2024** by the U.S. Court of Appeals for the Fifth Circuit, which found they exceeded the Securities and Exchange Commission's authority.[11]

As of the 2023 Sustainability Report, Nasdaq's own workforce is **35.8 per cent female globally**.[12] Adena Friedman remains the president and CEO of Nasdaq (she became CEO in 2017), making her among the first women to lead a major global exchange.

- Google is known to refuse meetings with partners who do not come with diverse teams.
- Norway has closed more than 87 per cent of its overall gender gap and continues to make steady progress, largely as a result of gender quotas enforced by legislation.
- Some companies in India have mandated women's participation in jobs traditionally viewed as male bastions. For example:
    - **Tata Steel** became the first company in India to deploy women in all shifts in mines, including for functions such as mining, electrical/mechanical maintenance and beneficiation. Subsequently, a similar initiative to induct women in all three shifts as Heavy Earth Moving Machinery operators was also introduced at the company's coal mines in the West Bokaro division.
    - **Godrej and Boyce** created an enabling work culture and processes for women to work in shop floor operations—approximately 40 per cent of the workers on the shop floor in its locks factory are women.

Gender equality must be seen as relevant to everyone, not just women—men should stand as allies

Men don't feel as strongly about gender equality as women. According to Kantar's GEA study, only 60 per cent of men believe that more respect for women's rights is 'completely important', compared to 74 per cent of women. This suggests that men are less likely to have the conviction to support change and highlights the importance of actively involving men in discussions about gender equality.

We need political will

Women continue to be underrepresented at all levels of decision-making worldwide, particularly in politics. Despite a general acknowledgement that creating more opportunities for women in politics is important—and even with increased agreement compared to 2018—it is still not widely regarded as essential. Only one in two respondents consider it 'completely important', significantly fewer than the number who believe equal pay for equal work is important (70 per cent).[13]

Globally, only:[14]

- 22.9 per cent of government ministers are women
- 27.2 per cent of national parliamentarians are women
- 35.5 per cent of elected members in local deliberative bodies are women
- In the 2024 Lok Sabha elections, **74 women** were elected out of 543 seats, which is **13.6 per cent** of the Lower House.[15] This is a slight decline from 2019, when **78 women** (about **14.3 per cent**) secured seats.[16]

- Rajya Sabha: about **17 per cent** of the members are women.[17]
- State Legislative Assemblies: women hold about **10 per cent** of the seats on average.[18]

Multiple barriers block women's entry into politics. Men are often perceived as better political leaders, and there are gendered expectations for women to balance work and family duties. Other barriers include limited funding, a lack of female role models and mentors, and the reality that the few women leaders who do succeed will likely be held accountable to different standards as compared to their male counterparts.

While individual women have overcome these obstacles, more frequent and consistent representation will be needed if women are to be seen as equally suited to holding office. Even in Denmark, where two of the last three prime ministers have been women, women are still not considered equal to men in their suitability to lead. Without fair representation in elected office, public policymaking and leadership roles, the pace of change across all areas of society will remain slow.

Women need more role models

Organizations that have women leaders tend to be more diverse. The most diverse boards are often found at companies led by women at the executive or board levels. For example, companies with women CEOs have significantly more gender-balanced boards on average than those led by men: 35.3 per cent women versus 23 per cent.[19]

My experience as the female CEO of a leading global consumer insights agency in South Asia reinforced this. As an industry, market research is women-friendly. It is non-hierarchical; skills and expertise are valued as much as length of experience; and working hours are flexible, with the option to work from home. The company also has a strong gender diversity programme to encourage women to join, stay and aspire for leadership positions.

Yet, despite all these initiatives, time and again, our female team members would tell us that having a female CEO and women in senior leadership positions was one of the strongest reassurances: 'I can also make it, it can be done'.

The next generation of women are strong advocates for change. They expect equality and are not afraid to voice this demand. They need our support to drive change and to remove structural and social barriers. Who can do this better than other women?

13

The 'Accidental' Company, the Informal Economy and Diversity

A Business View

DEEPINDER GOYAL

ZOMATO IS AN 'ACCIDENTAL COMPANY'. I never, even in my wildest dreams, thought there was money to be made from this when I started it as a passion project in 2008, on my twenty-fifth birthday. There was no intention of turning it into the business it is today.

I had noticed that many of my colleagues at Bain Capital would queue up at the pantry in the afternoons and late evenings to look for menus to order food. It baffled me that they were willing to stand in line day after day for such a time-consuming process—and that too for a limited selection of food. That observation got me thinking: how could this experience be improved?

One weekend, I went around town, collected every takeaway menu I could find and put them on a website, largely to help my colleagues and others around me. That is how Zomato began, and it is the same spirit of service that has shaped the company ever since.

Zomato was never meant to be a company, which is why I call it an 'accidental company'. Its purpose was to serve the community; over time, it also became a business. This is what we tell all Zomans—our employees—on their first day: we don't build products and services to make money. We make money to build products and services so we can serve our communities better.

In fact, Zomato did not even pioneer food delivery in India. We were primarily a restaurant discovery and menu-listing platform across twenty-two countries and pivoted to food delivery only in 2015, entering as the second player in India in response to competition. That experience taught me that first-mover advantage is often given more credit than it deserves. Entering a business second or even third can work, as long as the product you offer is significantly better.

We have done this by staying true to our origins. The purpose of our work is to help people live happier, healthier and more fulfilling lives—whether through convenience, nourishment or simply a moment of joy. In our case, this is more complex still, because we serve three key partners.

1. Customers

They are Zomato's heart and soul. When we say 'customer first', we mean it. Every application feature, every design tweak and every policy is aimed at making the customer's journey smoother and tastier. We are not just delivering food; we are delivering experiences. And because we were the second player to enter the business, we had to be more paranoid than anyone else about creating a truly superior customer experience. That obsession hasn't changed. If anything, it has only deepened as our customers' expectations of us have risen.

2. Restaurant partners

They are the beating heart of our platform. Over the years, we have helped millions of restaurants and brands get discovered, grow their businesses and reach new customers. Our platform allows stand-alone and small business owners, often with less capital, to compete with larger brands that enjoy greater capital and brand equity.

We enable business owners to focus on what they do best: making great food and building great brands. Early in our journey, we realized that there was little value in featuring only a handful of well-known restaurants on Zomato. Our biggest edge is, and always will be, variety. A core pillar of any marketplace's success is a broad assortment, and for us that means supporting local food businesses of every size.

We support businesses by giving them discoverability and lowering the cost of starting a restaurant, including through Hyperpure, our B2B company that supplies fresh groceries, staples and other essentials to restaurants and cloud kitchens.

From day one, Zomato has stood for the small guy. We strive to be a trusted partner to everyone in the food business by providing a level playing field. That's why we launched Zomato Food Trends, a free, publicly available platform, in 2023. We share analysis from data collected over millions of transactions across hundreds of cities in India. Existing and aspiring restaurateurs need to make crucial decisions on location, cuisine, menu design, pricing and more. Zomato Food Trends provides that information, locality by locality and dish by dish. This data compares demand and supply for all cuisines and is also used extensively to set menu pricing.

Consider India's most popular food item: biryani. Year after year, it is the most ordered dish on Zomato. In 2022 alone, we delivered 186 portions of biryani every minute. Below is a table I drew from Zomato Food Trends while writing this chapter. This can provide incredibly valuable insights for restaurateurs. What you see here is the pan-India trend, but we also have information for neighbourhoods within neighbourhoods. Restaurants can use this data to evolve and innovate constantly.

Price bucket (Rs)	Per cent orders: Chicken biryani
0–100	2.56
100–200	29.92
200–300	39.68
300–400	18.11
400–500	4.09
500+	5.63

Account managers and data analysts at Zomato team up to help our restaurant partners arrive at decisions that can be best for their business. When a restaurant's business grows, so does ours. It's a win-win situation.

Take biryani again: we can get even more granular, and tell you, for example, if customers in a particular area prefer it spicier, or advise adding a 'Gucchi pulao' because consumers in a locality are searching for it. They say data is the new oil—and we use it to guide restaurateurs on whether there's an appetite for a 'meal for one in a bowl' in a subzone, if they should offer a combo of tandoori rotis with daal or whether to avoid opening a cloud kitchen for pizza in a locality that's already oversaturated.

Traditional cuisines like Mughlai or Chinese now coexist with an increasing demand for artisanal pizzas, gourmet burgers and authentic regional Indian cuisines. The Indian food entrepreneur excels at spotting trends, identifying gaps and innovating to fill them. At Zomato, we understand this journey and look for ways to support both current and budding restaurant partners in their endeavours.

3. Delivery partners

These incredible folks form the backbone of our food delivery service. Imagine this: nearly 3 lakh delivery partners weaving through the city streets every day, determined to bring you your favourite dishes. They are the unsung heroes who ensure your biryani arrives fragrant and your desserts remain as sweet as ever. We didn't start with this vast fleet—it grew as our delivery services did.

Zomato's model relies on lakhs of partners voluntarily signing up to deliver for us. This means we must focus on their needs: flexible work slots and on-time payments that are deposited straight into their bank accounts every week. More than 60 per cent of our delivery partners log in for about six hours a day.

Tips also play an important role in boosting their earnings. Unlike weekly payouts, we transfer tips as soon as they are received. Fun fact: nearly 80 per cent of tips reach delivery partners' bank accounts within sixty minutes of being paid. The rest, if delayed due to various issues, are always eventually transferred in full.

I would like to categorically deny something I often read on social media: that Zomato withholds a portion of tips. This is absolutely false. Delivery partners receive 100 per cent of every tip, and we even absorb payment gateway and administrative and convenience fees to ensure the full amount goes to them.

When I ask our delivery partners why they've chosen this line of work, I'm always in awe of their reasons and their determination to succeed.

Shiv Kumar, one of our delivery partners in Delhi, works in an office during the day and delivers for Zomato at night. This extra income helps him cover his ailing father's medical expenses and his children's education. Few part-time earning options are available at night, which is when he has the time. Deliveries have helped him avoid taking on costly informal loans.

Khadrvalli, from the holy town of Tirupathi, shared that he had once worked in IT but joined Zomato for the flexibility it offered, enabling him to be there for his family. He also finds our weekly digital payouts more suited to his spending requirements.

Stories like these reinforce how platforms like ours play a pivotal role in increasing and improving earning opportunities for India's enormous workforce.

And to bust some popular myths about delivery partners, as of March 2023, Zomato had approximately 2000 active female delivery partners. One of them, Aparna Bhatia from Jalandhar, became Punjab's first female delivery partner during the COVID-19 pandemic. People would cheer her on with a thumbs-up when they saw her riding past. As a single mother, she wanted work that would allow her to spend enough time with her son, while also covering her financial needs.

In August 2023, we had over 160 differently-abled delivery partners who had collectively delivered approximately 39,000 orders. Their incredible achievement was powered by our unique partnership with NeoMotion, a start-up that converts wheelchairs into road-worthy electric scooters. For many of these partners, such as cricket aficionado Shivaji from Pune, delivery offers not just financial empowerment but also a renewed sense of confidence and the resolve to pursue their dreams. By December 2023, we aim to help 300 differently-abled partners stand on their own feet.

The people we help create livelihoods for—like our delivery partners—don't just work for themselves; they work to provide their children with access to better opportunities. Their commitment inspired me to start the Zomato Future Foundation, a public trust dedicated to funding the education of our delivery partners' children. I have committed a significant part of my vested employee stock options (ESOPs) to this foundation. Based on Zomato's average share price in April 2022—when we launched the foundation—these ESOPs will be worth approximately Rs 700 crore.

One of the foundation's first initiatives is the Sibling Project, a mentorship programme where volunteers, starting with Zomans, can chose to become lifelong mentors, or siblings in spirit, to a delivery partner's child.

I have faith that the ecosystem we are building will, in just a couple of decades, enable Zomato as well as many other platforms to massively empower India's next generation.

Areas ripe for social and technological innovation

All our delivery partners work remotely, which means they often lack the face time with supervisors and the sense of community that traditional office-goers enjoy. In fact, it's usually only after their fiftieth delivery that most partners feel truly comfortable with the work, and many drop-off before reaching that point. I believe the most common issues can be addressed with empathy from all stakeholders in society, along with a bit of support from technology to help our partners feel more included.

We are already using technology to solve for those who want to work in delivery, but don't own vehicles. We recently launched a digital electric vehicle (EV) rental marketplace on our delivery partner app to seamlessly connect people who want to work as delivery partners. We have already helped over 900 cyclists increase their earnings.

Another major issue is the lack of respect for service providers in India, and the harassment they often face from security guards, restaurant staff and even customers. At Zomato, we mandate that everyone undertake deliveries as a principal. On a recent delivery run, a senior colleague in Delhi discovered that his bike tyres had been deflated by mall security.

We recognize that delivery partners face multiple challenges on the job, from navigating traffic to delivering orders in inclement weather. In line with our commitment to their welfare, we launched the Shelter Project, an initiative to build public infrastructure (called Rest Points) to support not just Zomato partners but the entire gig economy.

Every day, hundreds of delivery partners from different companies use our rest points. These spaces are more than just a place to take a break between deliveries. They offer clean drinking water, phone-charging stations, washroom access, high-speed Internet, a 24×7 helpdesk and first-aid support. We believe that by providing a space for delivery partners to rest, recharge and take a moment for themselves, we can create a better environment that promotes their physical and mental well-being.

We are thankful to see that these rest points have been warmly welcomed by not just Zomato partners but also by delivery workers across multiple last-mile platforms.

If there is one change I wish to see in my lifetime, it is for delivery partners to be treated with respect and gratitude. Their role as ambassadors of the Zomato brand is why I launched the Spirit of Service Awards, which recognize delivery partners who have gone above and beyond their regular responsibilities. These awards are presented on the same platform where we recognize our employees—the Zomato town hall.

Another area I am passionate about is cognitive diversity. Research shows that innovation thrives when cognitively diverse people come together. More than 50 per cent of our board is female—gender diversity was our baseline, not our north star. Today, it makes me truly happy to share that our board members come from different occupational backgrounds, bringing diverse cognitive skills and perspectives to the table.

Many companies start with a diverse employee base at the entry level, but this diversity tends to reduce significantly over time, and at senior levels. We decided to turn this paradigm on its head by introducing diversity at the top, with our board of directors. We're hoping this is another small step towards building a truly lasting organizational culture where everyone belongs and everyone thrives. It is the only way for an organization to be truly enduring.

14

The Migrant Workforce

A Construction Sector Perspective

PIROJSHA GODREJ

THE CONSTRUCTION SECTOR CONTRIBUTES APPROXIMATELY 9 per cent of India's GDP and employs nearly 57 million workers—around 50 million men and 7 million women—according to government data. A significant proportion of these workers are unskilled, seasonal migrants from India's heartland, searching for livelihoods in larger cities and metropolitan areas. Despite this large workforce, the industry often faces seasonal labour shortages, leading to delays in delivery and escalating costs. There is an acute shortage of skilled construction workers in the country, which is exacerbated by the demands for such talent in the booming Middle Eastern markets.

The industry is also not very inclusive, particularly along gender lines, where it does not provide a level playing field. Employed in the lowest-paying, often hazardous and labour-intensive jobs, women workers are typically marginalized and unrecognized. Gender-specific data on women's migration and actual participation remains limited. Opportunities for women to earn equal wages or access skilling opportunities are scarce. Women are also almost entirely absent from specialized roles such as supervisors, contractors or surveyors, and even semi-skilled jobs such as crane operators, carpenters, plumbers, painters or masons. The majority of the limited women workers are typically unskilled, including brick kiln and quarry workers, load carriers or assistants.

As India's workforce evolves to meet demand, reliability, skilling, inclusivity and retention of migrant workers will be a critical pillar for the construction industry's growth. From a business standpoint, we have found that worker strength on project sites is one of the key proxies for productivity, timely project completion, and, in turn, revenue collection and profit margins. Many real estate companies now track such data to monitor progress.

Skilling and technology adoption are also key to making the industry more efficient and a profession of choice in the coming years. However, we must first get the foundation right in order to transform construction work from an occupation of distress to one of choice for our workers.

The construction industry is a challenging one, where daily jobs can pose numerous unaccounted risks for workers. Unfortunately, the complexity of the labour supply value chain often places 'principal employers' at a distance from the workforce. As a result, workers are often not covered under formal company policies that would typically ensure the payment of minimum wages, safe working and living conditions, access to food, healthcare and other basic services.

While workers are hired by contractor partners, it remains the responsibility of the principal employer to ensure that their working and living conditions uphold human dignity. From an industry perspective, investing in both skilled and unskilled construction workers to strengthen their capabilities and income potential can help build a future-ready workforce.

In such a complex value chain, our business has found that contractual mechanisms—such as integrating applicable labour laws for the informal workforce within general contract conditions and instituting robust mechanisms to audit these across sites—have proven to be useful. These measures allow us to ensure that worker welfare moves from being a 'good to have' to a 'must have' on our sites. We also found it helpful to integrate worker welfare metrics into external certification systems. For example, certifying sites under ISO 45001 (occupational health and safety management systems), which involves external audits, helps maintain a strong focus on working conditions. Similarly, ISO 14001 (environmental management systems; EMS) is internal governance-based and not prescriptive, allowing businesses to identify key impact areas and work on continuous improvement. In our case, we focused on worker welfare and its impact on productivity and presenteeism, integrating initiatives such as labour camps, creches and access to schooling for workers' children into our EMS, enabling systemic changes across sites.

During the past several years, corporate social responsibility (CSR) programmes across the industry have focused on skilling, but with limited success. For these programmes to be truly effective, the sector must be seen as an employer of choice. At present, for many workers, migration for economic opportunities tends to be driven by distress.

This reality was underscored during the pandemic-induced lockdown and its impact on the migrant workers' community. We believe that enabling access to entitlements and social protection can address gaps in this ecosystem and transform the sector from a secondary source of income to a primary employment of choice. While there are government policies backed by strong legal and compliance frameworks to assist workers, these often fall short in implementation, regulation and follow-through owing to several challenges.

A key example is the Building and Other Construction Workers (BOCW) Act, 1996, a progressive scheme intended to ensure basic entitlements, protection and worker well-being. Under this Act, employers contribute a fixed percentage of a project's cost of construction—typically 1 per cent—as a cess, which can be utilized for the welfare of workers as entitlements. However, our studies found that while a significant amount of cess has been collected since the inception of the policy, there is severe under-utilization in terms of actual disbursements. As of June 2020, 62 per cent of the cess funds collected remained unutilized, including the emergency aid provided at the onset of the COVID-19 pandemic. According to the Ministry of Labour and Employment's annual report (FY 2021–22), Rs 78,521.24 crore (cumulative) has been collected as BOCW cess by state governments and union territories, yet Rs 43,121.84 crore (cumulative) remained idle with state welfare boards. The ministry further noted that many workers could not avail of direct benefit transfers (DBTs) during the pandemic as they did not have Aadhaar cards or bank accounts.

Educating workers on their rights to government entitlements and social protection programmes is therefore amongst the first steps towards building a robust foundation. The industry can come together to facilitate BOCW registrations for workers, enabling them to access cash incentives through government benefit schemes.

Each BOCW-registered worker has the potential to unlock approximately Rs 12.41 lakh in government benefits, with this number expected to increase, as new schemes—such as housing access—have been announced recently. We can collectively commit to registering active workers across the ecosystem within the next five years. Given that short-term migrant workers form a major part of the construction workforce, our registration efforts must also extend to daily-wage workers.

We identified several key challenges that need to be addressed to enable and facilitate these entitlements. For example, there is currently no uniformity in the structure of state BOCW boards. Each state board operates independently, and a BOCW card issued in one state is not valid in another.

Previously, BOCW registration required a ninety-day work certificate from the contractor, who was often reluctant to provide it due to concerns about attracting provident fund and other compliance requirements. However, through continuous engagement with our NGO partners, the registration and renewal process has become more streamlined. A ninety-day work certificate can now also be issued by the labour department after physical verification of a worker's self-declaration. That said, this process has been facing delays due to staffing challenges in labour departments.

Other practical challenges include the requirement for mobile numbers to be linked to Aadhaar cards for registration verification. In our experience across geographies, we have found that many workers still do not own a mobile phone. Biometric verification has now been recommended for Aadhaar card verification.

In our journey, we have worked with our NGO partners to provide complete support including documentation and verification. We have helped facilitate over 79,000 BOCW welfare registrations and positively impacted the lives and livelihoods of 24,382 construction workers by enabling access cash incentives through government benefit schemes. We have also committed to registering 5,00,000 workers across the ecosystem by 2026, with a specific goal of achieving a 100 per cent BOCW-registered workforce on our sites by 2026.

As our industry prepares to adopt environmental, social and governance (ESG) performance metrics—due to growing investor focus and government mandates for risk identification and non-financial disclosures—the social parameter, particularly the construction workforce, needs greater attention.

Several sector-specific benchmarks, such as the GRESB for real estate, are helping companies establish ESG strategies and demonstrate consistent improvement. In real estate specifically, there has been a shift in investor focus towards asset classes such as commercial and office realty. ESG performance in increasingly treated as baseline hygiene by foreign direct investors, institutional investors and the like during due diligence before capital deployment. Expanding the assessment of company performance beyond financial returns to include ESG parameters allows for a more holistic assessment of sustainable business growth. Incorporating ESG goals into the business value chain is the right and responsible thing to do. This does not contradict business viability, rather, it sustains and enhances it in the longer term.

The CRISIL ESG India Report 2021 observed that the Nifty ESG 100 Index surpassed the Nifty 100 Index for all periods analysed between April 2011 and March 2021, demonstrating that sustainable Indian businesses have shown better financial performance than their peers. The same report indicates that companies are increasingly focusing on the 'social' component of ESG, especially in the aftermath of the pandemic, which brought many critical issues into sharp focus. The social dimension of ESG evaluation has a strong bearing on employee rights being extended to cover all workers, workplace safety, inclusion and diversity, the treatment of families, compliance with laws, access to entitlements, social protection, alignment across the supply chain and the well-being of worker communities, among other factors.

Our view suggests that any such journey begins with a belief that a socially responsible business is a successful one, and that workers are a big part of that responsibility. Any established code of conduct, company values and policies should therefore be aimed at ensuring implementation of human rights at all levels of operation. Responsible businesses should make conscious efforts to maintain a safe and supportive environment for the entire workforce across sites and provide equal opportunities, fair and competitive compensation and decent working hours across the extended workforce.

The lockdown and its impact on the migrant worker community underscored the need for us as an industry to better understand the fault lines that allowed a crisis of this scale to occur. It was a call to action for all stakeholders across the value chain to identify and bridge these systemic barriers to ensure that such a crisis does not happen again. As the government plays its part in safeguarding workers' rights and providing social protection, business leaders can equally shoulder the responsibility for the future and well-being of our workforce. Industry associations can help champion the cause of workers' welfare to create a level playing field for responsible businesses, while non-profit organizations can provide critical impetus to this movement through their work on the ground. Together, industry and philanthropy can offer additional resources to address the most distressed communities that not only provide labour to the sector but also require support for skilling, development, growth and well-being. Human-centric outcomes that increase productivity result in a win for all stakeholders.

We hope our experience will provide some insights into what business can do for this critical workforce. Our journey was predicated on a report we commissioned with Dasra, a leading Indian strategic philanthropy-focused NGO, to highlight the realities of informally engaged workers in the construction sector. The report, titled *Inclusive by Design: Cementing the future for informal workers in India's construction sector*, offers actionable insights on the systemic barriers that heighten the vulnerability of workers employed in this sector.

We took away five key points of advice from this exercise, which highlight the significance of convergence between multiple stakeholders:

- **Improve data collection and integration across workers' migration corridors and value chains to enable greater visibility and security**

The biggest hurdle in addressing the needs of informal workers in government and business policies has been the lack of a comprehensive database that captures their numbers by industry, migration patterns and demographic profiles. Even for available data, there are gaps in timely updating and disaggregation. Only 50 per cent of workers registered under BOCW are eligible for benefits, as the rest do not have updated profiles.

- **Enable financial, social and legal protection by securing requisite identity proof and worker registration**

Less than 35 million workers are registered with state welfare boards under the BOCW. Many workers are either unaware of or lack easy access to entitlements or redressal mechanisms, especially with respect to registration under BOCW, banking and Aadhaar. At the onset of the pandemic, 64 per cent of the workforce was unable to avail Direct Benefit Transfers, finding themselves in dire conditions without essentials such as food.

- **Create expectation alignment for workers through a channel informed by industry demand**

Employment is the reason approximately 10 million workers in India undertake rural–urban migration. Of these, less than 14 per cent have formal skills or education. The low barriers to entry in the construction sector act as a pull factor for unskilled workers, many of whom leave their homes without being aware of the nature of work, wages or living arrangements at their destination. Their journeys are fraught with challenges due to lack of seamless support or opportunities for upskilling.

- **Ensure gender equity in opportunities, working conditions and wages through inclusive policies and practices**

Women are most affected by informal employment and are more likely to be engaged in low-paying, unskilled work, perpetuating inequity. Responsibilities of care and domestic work further add to their burden. In India, women spend 84 per cent of their working hours on unpaid activities, while men spend 80 per cent of their working hours on paid work. Not only are women likely to be paid 30 to 40 per cent less than their male counterparts, but they were also 1.8 times more vulnerable to job loss during the pandemic.

- **Empower construction workers' families and communities by providing access to diverse livelihood opportunities to prevent distress-led entry into the sector**

The choice of work undertaken by the vast demographic of informal workers is often driven by financial distress. Entire families and communities rarely have opportunities that allow them to break away from the intergenerational cycle of poverty. There is a paucity of viable livelihood options at source, fragmented services for building individual capacities at destination, and limited access to market-led training across locations. This pushes children and youth to follow the same occupation as their families and elders.

The report also highlighted key actionable areas for industry-level focus:

- **Improve on-site responsibility:** Undertake greater oversight of working conditions on-site, including routine visits and reporting to senior management, to ensure workplace safety and a healthy environment.
- **Promote digital modes of payment:** Enable payments through bank accounts as the first step towards financial inclusion, eventually leading to economic security, access to formal credit and the use of products such as insurance.
- **Institutionalize measures to create gender equity:** Enforce policies of equal pay for equal work, implement targeted behaviour change communication on gender equity and champion it within supply chains, and address the practical needs of women to boost their participation in the workforce.
- **Introduce robust and stringent subcontracting policies:** Establish stronger checks and balances when hiring contractors to ensure compliance with prescribed standards on minimum wages (including timely payments), fair treatment, and health and safety measures.
- **Support implementation of government measures:** Mandate registration of all workers on-site, facilitated through awareness programmes, enable access to entitlements and aid in decoding legal processes and requirements.

- **Facilitate data collection:** Create and share worker databases with peers in the same region or geography to build a repository of profiles that can be used to facilitate registrations, match workers with future opportunities, and build legitimate work histories that enable upward mobility.
- **Create a level playing field:** Leverage the voice and influence of industry associations and bodies to enable systemic improvements that incentivize the adoption of better worker practices across the ecosystem to ensure that responsible businesses continue to thrive.

In our experience, multi-stakeholder initiatives that bring together industry organizations and associations, non-profits, experts and civil society can help drive more socially sustainable practices across business value chains. The Social Compact is one such initiative that provides a framework for companies to identify potential gaps and blind spots in worker practices. Social Compact standards, spanning six core themes and thirty impact areas, help identify priority areas for worker welfare. To facilitate adoption by a wider set of industry peers, these standards are mapped to both Indian legal requirements and global ESG frameworks.

Participation in such industry-led initiatives can help highlight both areas of strength and opportunities for intervention. In our experience, such assessments have provided insights for setting up targeted programmes—for example, we benefitted from bifurcating workers into those residing in our labour camps and daily workers, recognizing that each cohort had specific requirements that needed to be addressed.

These standards also encourage data capture, including labour participation, attendance records and BOCW registrations by gender, allowing on-ground teams to question biases, improve gender-based participation and ensure equity for women workers.

The task before us is ambitious. It calls for systemic government support, on-ground insights, a coalition of industry peers, a network of non-profits and the patience of philanthropic and CSR capital to join forces. Most importantly, it calls upon us—the employers of this 57-million-strong workforce—to champion this aspiration. As business leaders, we must take greater responsibility for worker practices in our ecosystem.

It also calls upon industry bodies to acknowledge the critical importance of this workforce and to uphold higher standards of worker well-being in a way that enables socially responsible businesses to remain both viable and successful.

As we emerge from the pandemic, India's real estate and construction industries face a choice: to rebuild as before, or to reset the foundation to one that befits an industry of the future that places worker well-being at the core of resilient and sustainable business. In these challenging times, the onus lies with us to chart a future where workers join out of aspiration rather than distress.

15

Hiring People with Disabilities

A Global Call Centre View

SANDIP SEN

Staggering numbers

ACCORDING TO THE OFFICE OF the Chief Commissioner for Persons with Disabilities, Government of India, based on the 2011 Census (the last census carried out in India), 2.21 per cent of India's population has some form of disability. This translates to approximately 2.68 crore people—a massive number. The World Health Organization (WHO) goes further, estimating that 16 per cent of the world's population lives with some form of disability. That is one-seventh of humanity.

The competitive advantage

Juxtapose this with the fact—seen all over the world, and India is no exception—that people with disabilities have much lower rates of employment than the general population. This is primarily due to negative prejudices and perceptions among employers, who often believe that people with disabilities cannot perform as efficiently as non-disabled workers. These fixed patterns of thinking and entrenched corporate cultures unfortunately prevail in most industries. It is this bias, not only among corporate decision-makers but also line managers, that creates disadvantages not just for job seekers but also for employers themselves.

It is indeed ironic because people with disabilities exemplify qualities that employers seek, such as adaptability and resourcefulness. They have been solving problems their entire lives and bring that problem-solving mindset to the workplace. In my experience, they also bring uncommon tenacity to their roles. Moreover, because they often have to find new ways to get things done, they approach their work with out-of-the-box thinking. Having encountered obstacles and challenges in their personal lives, they are well suited to devising solutions to complex problems. Their perspective not only fosters a diverse company culture but also improves innovation and creativity.

In my experience in the business process outsourcing (BPO) industry, I have found that people with intellectual disabilities often work with greater concentration and perform repetitive tasks better. Workers with disabilities possess skills and experiences that can offer employers a competitive edge. For example, research shows that many adults with autism possess higher-than-average abilities in pattern recognition, attention to detail, memory and mathematics—highly sought-after skills in the information technology (IT) field and many other sectors.[1] The Swiss IT company, Asperger Informatik AG, for example, prefers to employ people with Asperger's syndrome, a mild form of autism.

It has also been observed that employees with disabilities display higher levels of motivation than the average workforce. One reason for this is that it is often significantly more difficult for them to get a job. As a result, they are grateful for the opportunity and motivated to exceed expectations. They also tend to seek more stable jobs and have higher retention rates. For example, in the IT and BPO sectors, people with disabilities have lower employee turnover and absenteeism rates. Their motivation is also due to the fact that, many a time, managers and co-workers place less confidence in them, which drives them to prove that they are every bit as capable as their peers.

Having people with disabilities in the workforce creates and promotes an inclusive work environment. It encourages empathy among employees, which is particularly important when interacting with customers and partners. Inclusion improves a company's brand perception. To the wider public, it communicates social responsibility and a commitment to broader social issues. Inclusion also has an impact on how employees feel about a company. Studies have shown that in companies that value inclusion and diversity, employees are far more likely to hold favourable opinions about their organization.

As we have seen, the number of people with disabilities is growing, and they are becoming an important target segment. For many companies, employing people with disabilities in various functions enables a far better understanding of consumers with disabilities—a large and growing market. Losing this opportunity can create a competitive disadvantage and may result in lower revenue growth and market share.

A success story

I would like to illustrate my broad argument with the example of a BPO I headed for several years. The company in question was a global outsourcing organization with the goal of positively impacting our clients' businesses by enhancing their customers' experience across all touch points and channels. Between 2005 and 2015, we experienced rapid growth and soon had centres in over fifty locations across nine countries, with a workforce of over 50,000 people.

The company felt the need for diversity and inclusion to address our globally diverse client base, encourage innovation and out-of-the box thinking, enhance our brand image, and position the organization as an employer of choice. Our model of diversity included gender inclusivity, hiring from socially disadvantaged segments, and recruiting mature-age people. A key pillar was hiring people with disabilities.

To ensure that this was not just a tick-the-box initiative, diversity and inclusion became a strategic priority for the company, fully endorsed by our leadership team. We developed measurable goals for the organization and communicated them across the company, particularly to our hiring managers. We also educated them on why hiring people with disabilities benefits the organization, the skills such workers bring to the workplace, and how specific disabilities can make candidates more suitable for certain roles.

We met our hiring goals but soon realized that employees with disabilities could not be truly comfortable or productive unless their co-workers treated them with respect. Therefore, we implemented disability inclusion training programmes and cultural sensitization workshops. A key aim was to remove both conscious and unconscious bias.

We developed dedicated 'Diversity Champions' in each of our locations. To monitor this programme, we created a diversity scorecard through which all facets of diversity were monitored and presented to top management. We worked with our administration and facilities departments to ensure workplace infrastructure improved accessibility and convenience. This included installing wheelchair ramps in appropriate areas, elevators with grab handles, wide doorways and passageways for wheelchair movement, auxiliary aids and accessible restrooms. We also provided specific skill-building programmes for employees with disabilities. More importantly, we established mentoring programmes to help nurture their career.

Additionally, we partnered with several non-governmental organizations (NGOs), such as Sarthak Education Trust, which played a pivotal role in promoting the employment of people with disabilities.

For us, hiring people with disabilities was not merely a 'nice to have' initiative but a business necessity, one that helped create a more diverse and innovative organization, fostered a better workplace, and above all, enhanced our competitive advantage in the global market.

Scaling it up

As recently as a few years ago, in India, only about a dozen Nifty companies were employing almost 90 per cent of people with disabilities. So, how can this be scaled across large and small companies in multiple sectors? Legislation certainly helps. In the US, the Americans with Disabilities Act (ADA) prohibits employment discrimination based on disability. Similarly, Section 503 of the Rehabilitation Act requires affirmative action and advancement of people with disabilities by federal contractors and subcontractors with contracts exceeding $10,000.

In India, the Rights of Persons with Disabilities Act, 2016, mandates that there be no discrimination against employees with disabilities in the workplace. The Government of India has also reserved 3 per cent of posts in some categories for people with disabilities in central government ministries, public sector undertakings and banks. The Act also provides companies with an additional avenue for fulfilling their corporate social responsibility (CSR) obligations. Firms can deploy more financial resources towards mandatory schemes by providing benefits for persons with disabilities.

However, beyond legislation, Indian companies that have taken significant steps towards inclusion must evangelize the benefits they have realized. Organizations such as Startek, Lemon Tree Hotels, Capgemini, Wipro, Accenture and SAP Labs India have done yeoman service in this regard. For example, Lemon Tree Hotels have been recruiting differently abled people since 2007 and have seen excellent results in areas such as housekeeping.

Industry bodies like the Confederation of Indian Industry (CII), which has worked extensively to promote inclusion in India, can aggressively partner with companies to mainstream people with disabilities in the workplace and facilitate their employment across different sectors. Other bodies such as the Federation of Indian Chambers of Commerce and Industry (FICCI), the Associated Chambers of Commerce and Industry of India (ASSOCHAM) and the National Association of Software and Service Companies (NASSCOM) should also step up their efforts in this direction.

Professor Dr Thomas Aichner, formerly Associate Professor at John Cabot University, Rome, has succinctly explained the economic rationale for employing people with disabilities in his model (below).

The economic model of hiring[2]

Moral perspective

Legal perspective

Economic perspective

Characteristics of people with disabilities

- Higher motivation to work
- Very loyal towards their employer
- Friendlier dealings with customers
- Score higher in job satisfaction
- Perform more consistently
- Better ability to identify creative solutions
- Higher willingness to experiment
- Superior problem-solving skills

Advantages of hiring people with disabilities

- Lower absenteeism rates
- Lower employee turnover
- Higher ROI in training and development
- Overall more positive work environment
- Increased productivity
- Higher levels of innovation
- Increased business performance, market share, and shareholder value

To sum up, apart from the moral and legal imperatives of hiring people with disabilities, there is a sound economic logic that companies must take note of. A 2018 study by Accenture found that businesses that actively hire people with disabilities reported higher net incomes and profit margins compared to those that did not.[3] Companies that fail to do so risk placing themselves at a competitive disadvantage, missing the opportunity to become an employer of choice, weakening their progressive and socially responsible brand image, stifling innovation and lateral thinking, and ultimately losing market share and profits.

16

Women as Economic Actors and Decision-Makers

An Investor Perspective

MARY ELLEN ISKENDERIAN AND CHRISTINA JUHASZ

THROUGHOUT HISTORY AND AROUND THE world, women have been excluded from full engagement in commerce and formal economic activity. This enduring exclusion is detrimental not only to women, but also to the businesses that exclude them and the economies in which they operate. While often seen as merely a social equity issue, fully including women at every level of society and economy is essential for the healthy growth of economies and communities.

The potential gains from fully integrating women into the economy are well-documented. A 2020 McKinsey Global Institute study found that advancing gender equality and opening economic pathways for women could add $13 trillion to the global gross domestic product (GDP) by 2030, strengthening social and economic growth for all.[1] Similarly, a 2020 report from

Oliver Wyman estimated that financial services firms are missing at least $700 billion in annual revenue by not fully addressing the needs of women customers.[2]

At the workforce level, gender diversity in both employee bases and management teams brings diverse perspectives for better decision-making, higher creativity and innovation, greater productivity and superior customer insights and outreach—especially in reaching women customers. Research from Morgan Stanley shows that global companies adopting a holistic approach to equal gender representation have outperformed their more homogenous peers by 3.1 per cent annually.[3] Similarly, companies in the S&P Composite 1500 with women in top management generate, on average, $40 million more in economic value.

These insights—recognizing women as powerful economic actors rather than mere beneficiaries—present a compelling investment opportunity, one whose potential is particularly recognized by women investors. However, given the relative dearth of women in investment leadership, tapping into this opportunity does not form a significant part of current investing strategies.

With men comprising the vast majority of senior investment executives, most investments also go to companies led by men.[4] A 2019 report from Oliver Wyman, RockCreek and the International Finance Corporation (IFC) found that nearly 70 per cent of senior GP investment teams are entirely male, with only 15 per cent being gender balanced. The study also found that for portfolio companies, female entrepreneurs in emerging markets receive only about 7 per cent of investment capital, and less than 20 per cent of senior leadership teams that receive capital are gender balanced.[5] This represents a missed opportunity to invest in women as economic actors and thereby capture the outsized business and economic growth opportunity their inclusion represents. It is also a missed opportunity to build more vibrant, safe, socially responsible and inclusive societies.

To capture this opportunity, investment companies must increase their commitment to gender lens investing, placing gender equity and women's inclusion at the centre of their investment strategies. Applying a gender lens to investment is not limited to merely selecting companies with female founders and leadership—though that strategy does have merit. Rather, it is a holistic approach aimed at identifying portfolio companies that are (or can become) intentional about: i) designing and marketing products that effectively reach women purchasers; and ii) building organizations that are inclusive of women at every level of their workforces.

Gender-focused investors also aid their portfolio companies in achieving these goals and hold them accountable for success.

This is the strategy we follow at the organizations we lead: an NGO dedicated to expanding women's financial inclusion, and its investment arm, which focuses on gender lens investing in innovative financial inclusion companies across emerging markets.

'If you want to change the world, start with yourself.'

—Mohandas Gandhi

Our gender lens investing strategy begins with a look inward. We are conscientious about building a gender-diverse investment team, ensuring balanced female and male voices at the decision-making table. We heed the advice of a 2022 Vanguard research study, which found that funds managed by single-gender teams underperformed their benchmarks by an average of 12 basis points (bps), while those managed by mixed-gender teams outperformed their benchmarks by an average of 10 bps.[6]

The study encourages anyone involved in investment management to approach team diversity with the same rigour they would apply to portfolio diversification, recognizing the meaningful impact both have on fund performance. Just as importantly, equal representation of women on our investment team allows us to invest better in our women-focused strategy.

As Forbes has noted, one of the main reasons most woman-owned businesses do not receive venture capital funding is the presence of conscious and unconscious gender bias.[7] Men tend to invest in men. Evidence of bias among female investors is weaker, which suggests that increasing the number of female investors may be imperative to supporting more women entrepreneurs and advancing gender lens investing overall.[8]

Our gender lens value creation strategy for our funds under management is based on five key pillars:

1. Target companies that are willing and able to intentionally build for gender parity in their employee and customer bases in order to achieve investment outperformance.
2. Secure gender commitments from portfolio companies in the investment documentation or Articles of Association to ensure ongoing prioritization of gender fairness.
3. Invest in market research to understand the context and opportunity for each portfolio company to attract more women in its workforce and as its customers.
4. Use management targets and incentives to hold them accountable for gender results.
5. Measure and report results to understand underlying gender dynamics and validate whether initiatives are delivering the desired results.

In the follow sections, we explain how these pillars have proven effective in achieving both our social and investment goals.

1. Target companies that are willing and able to intentionally build for gender parity in their employee and customer bases to achieve investment outperformance.

In our own portfolio, we have seen that companies with more than 50 per cent women customers experienced higher asset growth (2.1x), higher revenue growth (1.5x) and higher return on equity (2.1x) compared to those with less than 50 per cent women clients.[9]

However, it is not enough to view women customers as a single aggregate group. We must look at them in every product category. For example, in the case of Indian microfinance organizations, we often see nearly 100 per cent female clients in the group lending portfolio, but almost 100 per cent male clients in the still-smaller—but higher-value—individual or small business lending portfolio. This gap leaves women-owned businesses underserved, even by women-focused lenders,[10] and in turn limits economic growth.

A 2018 study of over 350 start-ups by Mass Challenge and BCG found that businesses founded by women deliver higher revenue—over twice as much per dollar invested—than those founded by men, likely because only the very best secure any funding at all. But at this point in the small business funding journey, women-owned companies are likely to be better investments for financial backers.[11] The World Bank estimates that the global economy could gain between $5 trillion and $6 trillion if women started and scaled new businesses at the same rate as men.[12]

Because business-as-usual cannot change market dynamics that overlook women, there is much heavy lifting to be done to achieve different outcomes. We have found that one of the keys to increasing gender diversity in customer bases is to improve it within employee bases—especially in customer-facing roles. In our portfolio, we see a positive correlation between the number of women in customer-facing positions and the number of women customers.[13] Put simply, to attract women customers, a good first step is to hire women staff.

While customer-facing roles can be demanding, much can be done to improve working conditions to make them more women-friendly. For example, two of our Indian portfolio companies—a rural-based microfinance lender and a woman-focused affordable housing lender—have invested in: improving branch infrastructure, installing women's washrooms, adding CCTV systems, implementing evening branch closures, and providing late-night car services. These measures improve the comfort and safety of women employees (and, indeed, all employees). The return on these investments extends beyond simply attracting more women customers. We also see higher retention rates among women employees across our portfolio companies, which translate into lower talent acquisition costs, quickly offsetting the infrastructure investment.

While women in customer-facing roles are highly impactful, we also need women at senior leadership levels to assure effective outreach to women customers. As McKinsey's *Diversity Matters* research[14] repeatedly demonstrates, gender-diverse leadership teams are more likely to understand female customers' needs and preferences and develop products and services that meet those needs. Moreover, senior women leaders serve as role models and mentors for younger women employees.

Achieving gender diversity is not easy, however, especially given where it stands today. Therefore, it must be prioritized and incentivized. To support this, we set out gender diversity goals as commitments in investment documentation, provide relevant market research, use incentives and measure results.

2. Secure gender commitments from portfolio companies in the investment documentation or Articles of Association to ensure ongoing prioritization of gender fairness.

Private equity and venture investors are in a position to ask for commitments to gender diversity in exchange for their valuable capital investment. This is an opportunity that should not be squandered. These gender commitments can include, among others: increasing the percentage of women in executive, P&L management and customer-facing roles over a certain time frame; working towards targeted representation of women across the customer portfolio; adopting a gender equality policy for all staff and client activities; and committing to gender-disaggregated reporting to track progress and efficacy of interventions.

Enshrining gender commitments in investment documentation or Articles of Association serves several purposes. For one, it elevates gender diversity objectives to the same priority as governance, business and performance objectives. Without this elevation, gender diversity often takes a back seat to more immediately identifiable operational challenges that appear more directly tied to results, despite its proven role as a driver of business performance. Too often, gender diversity is relegated to 'nice-to-have' over 'need-to-have' when other operational challenges arise. Moreover, problem-solving for these challenges does not consider the gender angle—even though there is almost always one. How could there not be, when both customer and talent acquisition are the cornerstones of business success?

By enshrining these moral and legal commitments to gender in investment documentation, which all shareholders agree to, the investor is in a position to bring the gender perspective to the table whenever other business priorities are being discussed. Some examples of our success in doing so are described below.

Indian Microfinance Company A: Shortly before our investment in Company A in 2012, the company engaged our team for a women's market study to determine how it could better serve its women clients. We identified turnaround time as the biggest pain point for women—it simply took too long to receive a loan from the time of application. We also found that the longer a woman waited for her loan approval, the more she delayed her repayments.

On the back of that study, the company decided to go all-in on shortening turnaround time. It invested in a digital document management system, decentralized credit decision-making, rolled out handheld devices to loan officers for data entry in the field, and invested in real-time connectivity to Indian credit bureaus (all practices that have since been widely adopted across the industry). The company reduced turnaround time from fourteen days to three, becoming the industry leader on this measure within a year, while simultaneously improving repayment rates. Its customer base grew exponentially and its valuations grew linearly in subsequent private equity rounds. It was among the first group of microfinance institutions in India to receive a small bank licence and achieve an IPO (2015).

Tanzanian Retail Bank B: For Bank B, mobilizing deposits had been a key operational focus in recent years, as it was highly dependent on low-cost deposit funding. Shortly after our investment, a change in government policy resulted in the loss of a substantial amount of government deposits. Bank B had to pivot quickly to a retail deposit mobilization strategy. As part of this strategy, our team helped the bank design, pilot and roll out a youth savings programme in conjunction with school curricula to encourage young women and girls to open savings accounts. In addition to mobilizing a small but meaningful amount of savings directly, this programme became a pillar of the bank's longer-term strategy to develop a savings culture in Tanzania and to build trust and long-term relationships with a new client segment and their parents. Together with other strategies to mobilize savings, this initiative helped Bank B regain its position as the largest bank by deposits in the country and achieve the highest net income in Tanzania's banking history in 2020, despite the challenges of the COVID-19 pandemic

Indian Microfinance Company C: Another microfinance lender, Company C, was struggling with competitors poaching its branch managers. Because our investment arm had been collecting gender-disaggregated date for several years, we knew that Company C's women staff had higher retention rates than its male staff, making them less vulnerable to poaching. We also knew there was a dearth of women branch managers.

Company C committed to a gender policy to address the barriers preventing women from becoming branch managers—ranging from changing a rotational policy (which kept branch managers far from home and constantly relocating) to installing women's bathrooms in all the branches—and introduced mentoring and career planning for women. These measures, combined with other initiatives to improve compensation and retention, made gender diversity an important component of the solution. Moreover, improving the attractiveness of the job for women improved it for everyone.

As a result, poaching is no longer a problem. During the COVID-19 pandemic, Company C raised a record-setting $100 million in new equity.

The incorporation of gender terms in an investment offer also serves to align all shareholders around clear gender objectives, making gender diversity and inclusion a core priority for them. Likewise, documented commitments create accountability for management to deliver on gender objectives.

3. Invest in market research to understand the context and opportunity to attract more women in the workforce and as customers.

To effectively bring women into their workforces and customer bases, companies must understand the economic landscape and social context in which these women operate. Investors and management teams must be willing to invest in market research; otherwise, companies are left to guess at the barriers they face, and often, they guess incorrectly. It is very difficult to design solutions for women without incorporating their voices.

For example, an affordable housing finance company in India that we invested in had gender balance at its headquarters but very limited representation of women in field roles. Through a deep-dive market research study, we found that the company's staff had divergent views on women's representation in the company. Men—who were largely responsible for recruiting—commonly believed that field officer roles were unsuitable for women due to long hours, family pressures and safety concerns, and that women generally couldn't perform well in these roles. On the other hand, women who held these roles reported high job satisfaction, felt quite safe and were confident in their ability to succeed.

We also conducted a quantitative analysis of loan officer performance and found that women loan officers had higher loan approval rates than their male counterparts. Women customers also expressed a preference for interacting with women loan officers. While they were generally satisfied with male officers, they often deferred to their husbands to manage the interaction, weakening company–customer connection and losing the message of the value proposition for women customers.

Finally, the research revealed valuable insights from women employees on improving their workplace experience, such as installing female washrooms, adding CCTVs in branches and deploying technology to reduce time and travel requirements to visit customers in person. Proper market research and listening to the voices of women enabled the company to separate fact from fiction and address its real pain points and opportunities.

In another example of the power of market research, we worked with a large public sector bank in India following the launch of the government's Pradhan Mantri Jan Dhan Yojana (PMJDY)—a financial inclusion initiative that has provided millions of Indians with their first-ever bank accounts. We have long recognized that access is not the same as usage, and noted that among the bank's customers—who represented 15 to 20 per cent of all Jan Dhan accounts in the country—most were using their accounts only to withdraw money, not to save it. This was a missed opportunity for both the bank and its customers. Furthermore, women transacted 44 per cent less than men, and their total deposits were 35 per cent lower.

Our goal with the bank was to increase account usage and cross-sell multiple financial products to drive profitability at the bank while improving quality of life for women customers. We began with customer behavioural research to identify the needs, behaviours and barriers preventing customers, particularly women, from actively using their accounts. Once the barriers had been identified through direct interviews and focus groups, the bank was in a position to properly ideate, prototype and user-test solutions that addressed them. Together with the bank, we designed Jan Dhan Plus, a product that helps women build consistent saving habits and use their accounts to access credit, insurance and other financial products.

After successfully launching Jan Dhan Plus with rural clients in Uttar Pradesh, 3,96,000 women improved their engagement with formal financial products, and the bank enrolled over 28,000 new women customers. In one region where the programme was rolled out to all customers, women's balances increased by 51 per cent, compared to 34 per cent for men. Women also outpaced men in cross-purchasing financial products, with a 46 per cent increase in life insurance (vs 36 per cent for men), a 119 per cent increase in pension purchases (vs 87 per cent for men), and a 24 per cent increase in accident insurance purchases, on par with men. The solution was replicated with two additional Indian banks and later exported to four banks in Nigeria.[15]

4. Use incentives to drive results

One of the most powerful tools shareholders have to influence results is management performance metrics and incentive compensation. Managers can be charged with achieving certain gender results along with business results. Incentive compensation, such as bonus payments, should include the achievement of gender targets. Stock option programmes can be structured with goal-based rather than time-based vesting and can include desired gender diversity outcomes.

Gender metrics need to be clearly articulated and achievable. Good managers are results-oriented, and we have witnessed creative and committed problem-solving from senior teams when they are rewarded for their efforts through incentive compensation.

For example, we structured the bonus payment of the CEO of a small business lender in the Middle East to be tied, among other factors, to the hiring of a certain number of female loan officers. Initially, the CEO was frustrated by his inability to recruit women with credit experience, as such experienced women were uncommon in his market and were highly sought after by banks, making them difficult to hire at an appropriate price point. Where another CEO may have thrown up his hands and called it mission impossible, this CEO—with a monetary award at stake—became creative. He rethought the job requirements and determined that a woman with sales experience and a head for numbers could be trained to perform credit analysis. He recruited two women from the e-commerce industry and is now growing his own credit talent—securing his bonus in the process.

5. Measure and report results to hold companies accountable and to determine whether initiatives are delivering the desired outcomes.

Companies should measure and report detailed gender-disaggregated data periodically to understand what is happening within their own organizations. The data should go beyond simply measuring the number of women among clients and staff—it should reflect what the company is trying to learn and achieve. For example, Indian microfinance companies often report that upwards of 80 per cent of their clients are women. However, what this statistic conceals is that while 100 per cent of group loan clients are often women, they are nearly absent from higher-value products such as individual or small business loans. It is important to look at gender within every product a company offers, and then not just at the number of women but also other metrics such as gender-disaggregated average loan sizes (in the case of a lending company), repayment rates, retention rates, and cross-sell rates by gender. These should be tracked over time to determine whether improvements are being made.

Similarly, on the workforce side, it is important to track gender data for every level of the workforce and for different roles. Too often, women are clustered in back-office or support functions, limiting their participation in revenue-producing roles that lead to executive management. It is also important to monitor indicators such as hiring rates, promotion rates, retention rates and pay parity. Access to such data over time provides valuable and actionable management intelligence. For example, recognizing higher retention rates among women staff becomes an element in the defence against poaching. Such data will also reveal whether efforts to increase gender diversity among staff and clients are actually working. This allows management to stop investing in solutions that don't address the problem and redeploy resources towards more effective solutions.

A final benefit of measuring gender-disaggregated data is the simple truth that you achieve what you measure.

What changes in the ecosystem can facilitate these approaches and drive adoption?

More data, more cases

While there are clear actions investors and companies can take to facilitate gender lens investing, examples and case studies can be uniquely influential. Increasing the number and breadth of studies and success stories, and ensuring their dissemination, is critical to inspiring replication among other investors and driving the adoption of gender-based investment approaches. Achieving this will require an expansion in results-based measurement and analysis, as well as the publication of findings that demonstrate the two-fold promise of full gender inclusion: economic value and social justice.

Enlightened regulation

Similarly, the role of governments and policymakers cannot be understated. There is no harm in mandating some of these approaches while we wait for evangelization and inspiration to take hold. Since we know that key metrics are needed to drive gender diversity, regulators could make collection of gender-disaggregated data mandatory. Such data, in turn, would enable investors and policymakers to use business success stories to convince companies to improve gender diversity in their organizations and promote the most effective solutions.

Extensive research shows that gender diversity on boards and senior management teams leads to good business and social outcomes. Regulators could therefore also mandate board and senior management diversity. More than a dozen countries already maintain some form of quota for women on the boards of listed companies, and these requirements have resulted in significant increases in board diversity. However, their impact has largely been limited to the largest, publicly traded companies.

To create system-level change that also benefits smaller companies, policymakers should consider other incentives within their control. For example, offering incentives—such as lower interest rates or guarantee fees for loans—to companies that demonstrate greater gender diversity would be a powerful tool to drive action on gender diversity. Likewise, requiring more localized surveys and gender information reporting from large and small companies can provide policymakers with a more nuanced picture of the state of women's participation in their economies—data that is essential to improving their economic standing on a global level.

Maintaining active data collection related to the products being used by different demographic groups, how they are accessed, and the role of various providers in supporting access will enable policymakers to create more informed and effective policy interventions for economic inclusion. These interventions could include the expansion of quotas and baselines, which in turn will improve overall access and representation across the economy.

Finally, increased diversity within government agencies themselves is a powerful way to push for women's economic growth and inclusion. As discussed above, there are clear connections between having women represented in the leadership and governance of financial institutions and higher portfolio quality and profitability. In the case of regulatory bodies, more gender-diverse leadership and governance can have a system-wide impact on financial stability.

To conclude, achieving gender equity and inclusion for women at all levels is critical for the social and financial well-being of all.

The business case for increasing women's roles as both leaders and stakeholders is clear—at the corporate level, the start-up level and the investment level. And yet, women continue to be excluded from full economic participation. To drive progress, we must steadily increase women's representation across all levels of the economy, gather comprehensive and actionable gender data and case studies that showcase the powerful benefits of inclusion and pursue committed and enlightened government regulation and role modelling to drive adoption of best practices by all economic actors.

17

Bringing Threads Together Using Evidence-Based Tools

SUTAPA BANERJEE

THE THEMES OF UNDEREMPLOYMENT, FORMALIZATION, workplace flexibility, technology and the participation of women (or lack thereof) in the workforce have been covered in interesting ways in the preceding chapters.

With regard to workers at the bottom of the pyramid, one company in the construction sector, as a principal employer, has set a target of 2026 to ensure 100 per cent of its construction workers are registered for benefits under the Building and Other Construction Workers (BOCW) scheme. One wonders why the government can't mandate this across the sector, especially given that 62 per cent of the BOCW funds collected for workers remain unutilized.

When it comes to women's inclusion in the workforce, India is at alarmingly low levels, ranking just above countries such as Pakistan and Iran. Improving India's ranking in the Gender Development Index must be a high priority for the country.[1]

As mentioned in one of the chapters, several social ills—such as dowry, early marriage of girls and sexist inheritance and property laws—continue to hold women back from participating in the workforce. Even where legislation exists, it alone cannot eradicate these challenges.

A 2017 World Bank report stated that 'conventional approaches ... such as education and skills and legal provisions will be insufficient. Policies should focus on promoting the acceptability of female employment'.[2]

Deeply entrenched social norms remain the biggest barrier preventing women from joining the workforce, both at the bottom of the pyramid and in the upper echelons of the organized sector.

When it comes to women workers in the construction sector, the statistics cited in one of the chapters are a telling comment on the power of social norms. Unpaid work accounts for 84 per cent of the working hours of women, in sharp contrast to 80 per cent of men's working hours being spent on paid work.[3]

There is an urgent need for policies that make women key decision-makers rather than passive beneficiaries across all social strata. Such policies, coupled with appropriate incentives and behavioural insights (tools and techniques drawn from empirical studies in the behavioural sciences), will make it possible to reshape social norms. As stated by a renowned behavioural economist in the very first chapter of this book, 'behaviour is a function of context', implying that appropriate change in context is likely to elicit the desired change in behaviour.

Empirical studies illustrate what this can achieve: 'In the 1990s, in a few randomly selected villages, three years of recruitment services to BPOs were provided to women. This not only increased the employment of women, [but] girls in these villages experienced greater improvements in health and were more likely to be in school.'[4]

'The Panchayati Raj amendments introducing reservation for women were implemented in the early 1990s by choosing villages at random, making it a "natural experiment" studied widely. In West Bengal, villagers, including men who were against voting for women when the quota was first introduced, overcame their longstanding bias and rated male and female leaders equally after being exposed to two female chiefs. This also induced them to invest in their daughters' higher education, make them spend less time on household chores and defer their marriage. A simple behavioural insight—salience—just seeing women in power normalised it and induced behaviour change in people with traditional mindsets.'[5]

These are only two of several examples from the research on reshaping societal norms.

Unfortunately, policies—both from the government and within the corporate world—have sometimes unwittingly reinforced the entrenched belief that women are primarily homemakers while men are breadwinners. The well-intentioned six-month maternity benefits legislation introduced in India in 2016 is a case in point. Though it was ostensibly designed to improve women's economic participation, it has, unsurprisingly, proved detrimental to women joining the workforce.[6]

What could have helped instead is a combination of maternity and paternity leave on a use-It-or-it-lapses basis, as in the Nordic countries.

The business case for increasing women's representation at all levels, particularly in senior leadership and on boards, has been clear for years, with research consistently showing a correlation between higher female representation and better business performance. However, recognition of this fact has not led to significant improvement. Two key factors may be contributing to this lack of progress:

a) The belief that a 'no discrimination policy' alone will ensure merit.

b) Women-centric policies that empirical evidence has shown to be counterproductive.

The first factor betrays a lack of understanding of the implicit biases that arise from the historical norm of men as primary earners and women as homemakers. The second demonstrates how even progressive companies can mistake affirmative action for seemingly empathetic women-centric policies that tend to backfire.

Evidence shows that policies such as work-from-home or flexi-time arrangements only for women create a backlash, resulting in women being overlooked for key P&L and business head roles, thereby exacerbating the existing occupational bias.[7] Similarly, very long maternity breaks (sometimes running into years) with extensive flexibility, while seemingly supportive of women, reinforce the stereotype of women as primary caregivers. The simple solution is to provide paternity leave for men, and make flexible work policies, such as work-from-home and flexi-time (where appropriate), available to all.

However, to change a norm, it isn't enough to simply create policies. For policies to work, the use of evidence-based research is key. In the case of paternity leave, encouraging a few high-performing men to avail themselves of the leave and then celebrating it in company townhalls, on the intranet and in newsletters, could be helpful. This visibly demonstrates the behaviour the company values and makes other men more likely to take the leave—even if their personal beliefs are not fully aligned. This is one of many examples where, counterintuitively, a change in behaviour precedes a change in beliefs, hastening the reset of norms within the company.

Useful examples from the preceding chapters include the need for more women in senior leadership, who can serve as role models and attract more women to the sector. Inclusion must be treated as part of the key strategic agenda, driven by the CEO with key performance indicators (KPIs) cascading down to business heads, rather than being relegated to a peripheral initiative driven solely by the HR function. Likewise, institutional investors need to accord it the same priority as governance and financial results to propel management in this direction.

This approach of making it the key strategic agenda may help create more success stories in inclusion (as cited in a chapter) or addressing data (paraphrasing from a chapter) that shows men above thirty-five years tend to underestimate both the underrepresentation of women in the workforce and the reasons it persists. Another interesting example, cited in the last chapter, is of a company in the Middle East where all credit officers were male. By tying the CEO's incentives to hiring female credit officers, the investor encouraged the CEO to think 'out of the box' and successfully recruit women credit officers despite their limited availability in the market.

Turning the existing paradigm on its head by hiring more women in predominantly male P&L, business head and sales roles; ensuring equal representation of women on boards rather than appointing a lone woman director to comply with regulations; collecting and making salient gender-disaggregated data in all people practices—recruitment, promotion, rewards and exit; and using that data along with empirical evidence from the behavioural sciences to pilot initiatives and policies—these are the approaches that work, according to empirical research.

By contrast, gender sensitization and 'unconscious bias' training, though often conducted with great fanfare in organizations, have barely any empirical data backing their effectiveness. Rigorous use of data and evidence-based practices in people management remains critical but is, sadly, still missing even in many well-regarded progressive companies.

The examples in this section of affirmative action demonstrate that measures that help break stereotypes are far from being concessionary or lowering the bar; in fact, they level the playing field for all. Finally, just as with environmental sustainability, diversity needs to be built into the fabric of doing business and decision-making, not treated as a side agenda.

PART IV

Reshaping Social Norms and Breaking Stereotypes

18

Artificial Intelligence

A Perspective on Bias and Inclusion

SRIKANTH VELAMAKANNI

IN THE EARLY DAYS OF building Fractal as an Artificial Intelligence (AI) company, we were tasked with automating the lending process for a leading bank. As we examined the details of consumer loan processes, we discovered deep-rooted prejudices and biases.

Back in 2001, credit lending operated on unwritten rules that would make us cringe today—no loans for lawyers, filmmakers or politicians; specific neighbourhoods excluded because residents were deemed unlikely to repay, or considered 'uncollectible'; and policies to exclude entire communities—insert prejudice of your choice.

This archaic and often biased approach to lending began to change with technology. As the digital age ushered in new possibilities, the financial sector saw a pivotal shift.

The first glimpse of data analytics in lending came in the form of underwriting models. Underwriting involves a detailed examination of a person's financial situation, payment history, and other relevant factors used to evaluate a loan application. As loan volumes grew, the manual process became overwhelming, paving the way for models to streamline the entire process.

These underwriting models used computer algorithms to analyse vast amounts of data. By identifying patterns and trends, they predicted the risk associated with a loan. They became the gatekeepers of financial access, which meant they also wielded the power to either perpetuate discrimination or usher in a new era of democratized lending.

As their use became widespread, however, these models proved to be double-edged swords, often reinforcing existing biases under the guise of risk management. Now, with the advent of AI, a seismic shift is underway, amplifying their capabilities to unprecedented levels.

It only takes opening YouTube in incognito mode to experience the power of models. A product designed for individual preferences (personalization) transforms into an unwieldy, generic platform (generalization), presenting a stream of unrelated, unpredictable, and often unhelpful content. This simple change demonstrates how AI-powered models shape our digital experiences.

In business, the dichotomy between personalization and generalization reflects the broader challenge in harnessing AI's power: will it become a tool for inclusive customization, or an inadvertent amplifier of existing biases?

The best AI algorithms find a middle ground between two key approaches: exploration and exploitation. Exploration is about trying new, untested methods, while exploitation involves using known, effective methods that have worked before. Striking this balance allows AI to both discover new things and improve on what has already been proven to work. However, achieving this balance is challenging.

Take Amazon's recruiting tool (2018), which infamously perpetuated gender biases. It stands as a stark example of the unintended consequences of purely algorithmic decision-making. Designed to streamline and automate the hiring process, the AI-driven system ended up disproportionately favouring male candidates. The tool was trained on resumes submitted to Amazon over a ten-year period, a time that reflected historical gender imbalances in the tech industry. Consequently, the algorithm learned to reward certain keywords and experiences that were prevalent in applications from male candidates.[1]

Recognizing these pitfalls is only the first step. AI's evolution is not just about rectifying past mistakes, but about unlocking its potential to become a responsible and revolutionary force across various sectors.

As we embrace this transformative phase, AI is stepping into a new era marked by widespread adoption and impact. This shift is not merely a continuation of past trends; it represents a significant leap forward in how we interact with and benefit from AI technologies.

The new breed of AI

Sundar Pichai declared Google an 'AI-first' company in 2016.[2] Since the launch of ChatGPT in November 2022, AI has entered a phase of mass adoption. While AI models have been improving our lives for several years (consider our reliance on Google Maps for directions), the release of ChatGPT and other generative AI tools has made the magic of AI immediate, palpable and accessible for a wide range of everyday activities.

This new breed of AI is game-changing in three ways:

1. **For the first time in history, we have a technology that aims to understand us.** With every new technology,

humans were expected to learn how it worked in order to use it better—for example, learning how to drive a car. However, the new generation of AI (ChatGPT, MidJourney V6) is different. It welcomes our half-formed thoughts, incomplete sentences and misspelled words, understanding our intent and answering our questions. This a game changer and a great equalizer. Technical expertise is no longer necessary to get started.

2. **It is super-responsive to our needs.** AI systems are now meticulously programmed to cater specifically to human preferences and needs. Techniques such as learning and improving based on feedback (RLHF—reinforcement learning from human feedback) have ensured that these systems generate responses that are both satisfying and useful. When given feedback, they learn quickly—even within the space of a single conversation—to provide more relevant, better answers.
3. **It is more knowledgeable than ever before.** Think of the new AI systems as a library containing all the books ever written. Traditional search engines function like a library's index card system, helping you find books based on specific titles (keywords). In contrast, AI models like GPTs are akin to a librarian who understands not only your question but also its context and intent. Rather than simply pointing you to a shelf, the librarian offers you excerpts or summaries of exactly what you are looking for. This level of sophistication and comprehension is a significant leap in how we access and utilize the vast reservoirs of human knowledge.

Moreover, AI continues to improve across these capabilities, as evidenced by the steady stream of breakthroughs. Regardless of one's belief or scepticism, the influence of AI extends beyond mere rhetoric, manifesting tangibly in sectors that significantly impact our lives.

From the moment we wake up to the time we go to bed, AI influences various aspects of our experiences. This power is what makes it both a transformative force, revolutionizing how we interact with the world, as well as a source of ethical dilemmas that require scrutiny and responsible governance on its influence on our every decision. Recognizing these profound implications, it's important to explore how AI is already reshaping critical sectors, making them more accessible and effective.

AI: The universal tool

AI in education and healthcare is already enhancing accessibility. Platforms like Khan Academy and Duolingo use adaptive algorithms to cater to individual learning needs and break language barriers, making education more inclusive.[3] Similarly, in healthcare, AI tools like Qure.ai are improving diagnostic accuracy in medical imaging, particularly benefiting regions with limited access to medical specialists. These advancements ensure timely medical interventions and democratize learning, underscoring AI's role in making essential services more accessible and efficient. [4]

AI is also becoming a transformative force for individuals with disabilities. 'Seeing AI', developed by Microsoft, is an AI-powered application designed to assist individuals with visual impairments.[5] The app uses computer vision to narrate the world to users through their smartphone cameras. It can recognize and describe objects, read text aloud and even identify people, enabling those with visual disabilities to better navigate and comprehend their surroundings.[6]

Umang, a comprehensive government services platform, empowers Indian citizens to access a wide array of e-government services, bridging the gap between government and people, saving a considerable amount of time.

Another initiative, Bashini, enables citizens to easily access the Internet and digital services in their own language, while expanding digital content in Indian languages. In a country as linguistically rich as India, this is not merely a technological advancement but a catalyst for democratizing the digital landscape, turning the challenge of linguistic diversity into an opportunity.

These advancements are more than just technological feats; they are stepping stones towards a more inclusive, equitable society. As we appreciate the wide-reaching implications of AI in modern society, it becomes clear that the core of its impact lies in how we interpret and use data. This is a fundamental principle behind some of the most pivotal moments in history.

Data: The starting point

During World War II, a team of statisticians led by Abraham Wald (Nobel Laureate Milton Friedman was considered only the fourth smartest person in this group) took on the challenge of figuring out how to make American bomber planes more likely to survive their missions. Observing the bullet-ridden planes returning from missions, the initial conclusion was to reinforce the most damaged areas of the aircraft.

Wald, however, realized this approach was based on a biased sample: the data only included planes that had returned. These planes had managed to endure the damage, whereas those that did not return were not a part of the dataset. Wald understood that the undamaged areas on the returning planes were likely the most vulnerable—hits on those spots would have brought the aircraft down. He advocated reinforcing the undamaged areas, understanding they were crucial to a plane's survival.[7]

This finding not only saved countless lives but also holds a profound lesson for the modern world of artificial intelligence. AI, with its powerful algorithms and vast datasets, can analyse and make predictions based on the data on which it is trained. It is limited by what it can see—and it cannot see what's missing. When data is incomplete, voices remain unheard and perspectives go unrepresented.

The limitations of data are a common problem facing many organizations. They are often unable to leverage its full potential because of the complexity of their datasets. Frequently, the data is messy and convoluted, presenting a considerable challenge to AI systems. It could be incomplete, outdated or riddled with errors and inconsistencies. Different departments within companies collect data in varying formats, leading to data silos that hinder the flow of information across an organization. To add to this, the data—as we saw in the Amazon example—can carry implicit biases, reflecting historical imbalances in how it has been collected and curated. This messiness often forces AI algorithms to grapple with disparate, sometimes contradictory, and unreliable data.

The challenge involves not only managing structured data but also unstructured data such as text, images and multimedia content, which often require advanced techniques in natural language processing and computer vision. Algorithms and AI systems can go awry for a multitude of reasons. For example, the incorrect framing of a problem, where the underlying issue is not clearly defined, can lead to algorithms attempting to solve the wrong challenges.

We must acknowledge that AI, for all its capabilities, operates within the boundaries of the information it is given. It is up to us to ensure that the data it receives is representative and unbiased.

Responsible AI is one such undertaking towards that future.

Using AI responsibly

Responsible AI emerged as a response to growing concerns over the unchecked and opaque use of AI technologies. The concept gained traction as major global tech companies faced fines, public backlash and government scrutiny over unethical AI practices.[8]

This led to a collective realization within the industry: without ethical guidelines, AI's potential could be overshadowed by its risks. Responsible AI is underpinned by core principles such as explainability, fairness and auditability:

1. Explainability ensures AI decisions are transparent and understandable to users, addressing the 'black box' nature of complex algorithms.
2. Fairness involves designing AI systems that are unbiased and equitable, preventing discriminatory outcomes.
3. Auditability allows for the ongoing evaluation of AI systems to ensure compliance with ethical standards.

These principles are not just lofty ideals but are being systematically integrated into frameworks established by leading AI players. They represent a concerted effort to align AI development with societal values and ethical norms, shaping AI into a force for good.[9]

The European Union's provisional agreement on the AI Act represents a landmark step in establishing the world's first comprehensive legal framework for AI, setting a global precedent much like the General Data Protection Regulation (GDPR). This act categorizes AI applications based on risk, emphasizing transparency and accountability, and is expected to influence global AI practices.[10] Meanwhile, countries like China and the United Kingdom are advancing their own AI strategies,[11] focusing on development and governance, indicating a growing global momentum towards balancing AI innovation with ethical and responsible use.

To hasten the global—and particularly Indian—adoption of Responsible AI, a multifaceted approach is required:

1. Firstly, fostering public-private partnerships can accelerate the development of ethical AI frameworks by leveraging both government oversight and industry expertise. In India, this could involve collaborations between tech giants and government bodies to create tailored guidelines reflecting the country's unique socio-cultural dynamics.
2. Secondly, offering incentives such as tax benefits or grants to companies for adopting Responsible AI practices could serve as a powerful motivator. Alongside, educational efforts and awareness campaigns are essential to embed an understanding of Responsible AI principles within India's business leadership and workforce. To amplify these efforts, incorporating Responsible AI topics into the curricula of universities and academic institutions, and encouraging research in this area, will be instrumental.
3. Lastly, establishing a national-level AI ethics committee in India, similar to the European Union's AI regulatory body, would provide a centralized framework and set a clear benchmark for companies to strive towards, creating a cohesive and accountable AI ecosystem.

Regulation in the realm of AI should not only enforce compliance but also encourage the adoption of responsible practices. Such regulation is vital to prevent misuse and foster an environment where AI can be developed and used for the greater good, while maintaining public trust and confidence in these rapidly advancing technologies.

However, it is equally important to ensure that AI regulation is balanced, targeting meaningful, practical applications while preserving the creativity and exploratory drive that fuels technological advancement.

A call for balance

Regulating AI stems from the recognition that when powerful and consequential decisions are entrusted to machines, a framework of oversight becomes imperative. Unlike research and development (R&D), where innovation thrives on experimentation, the regulation of AI focuses on the deployment of products in real-world scenarios. The distinction lies in not burdening the regulatory landscape with inconsequential decisions, but rather channelling efforts towards instances where the impact is substantial.

While human errors are part of the natural course of decision-making, errors made by machines can have amplified consequences due to their ability to scale rapidly and widely. This necessitates a higher degree of responsibility in machine-based systems, as their failures can potentially affect a larger audience.

Just as architects balance aesthetics with structural integrity, AI developers must factor ethical considerations into the foundational design of their systems. This means embedding principles of fairness, transparency and accountability right from the initial stages of AI development.

Continuous learning and adaptation should be integral to AI systems. AI systems must be designed to learn and evolve over time. Continuous learning mechanisms within AI systems can help identify and rectify biases, adapt to new data and respond to feedback, ensuring these systems remain beneficial and fair for all users.

The governance of AI should draw inspiration from the interdisciplinary approach used in climate change governance. Just as panels of climate experts comprise scientists, policymakers and activists, AI development should be overseen by committees that bring together ethicists, sociologists, technologists and end-users.

In India, organizations such as The National Association of Software and Service Companies (NASSCOM) are contributing to shaping responsible AI by providing frameworks and guidelines. The decision-making process involves leveraging information from diverse sources, including expert opinions, ethical considerations and data-driven insights, ensuring a comprehensive and informed approach to the development and deployment of AI technologies.[12]

As we navigate the burgeoning landscape of artificial intelligence, it is increasingly clear that the responsibility for regulation goes beyond mere compliance with rules and legislation. Companies are at the forefront of this challenge, and their actions can set precedents for responsible AI usage.

Here are just three actionable measures to get us started:

1. **Develop a responsible AI framework.** While this has been covered in detail earlier, developing a Responsible AI framework requires companies to embed ethical considerations throughout their AI journey, from data collection to algorithm design, ensuring fairness, transparency and privacy. Additionally, establishing a

governance body with diverse expertise is essential for adherence to this framework.

2. **Ensure equitable and inclusive AI solutions.** It is crucial for businesses to ensure that their AI solutions are accessible and cater to the needs of diverse groups. This entails continuously assessing AI's impact on various demographics, including marginalized communities. Companies should actively collaborate with community stakeholders to integrate their perspectives and insights, ensuring AI tools are designed with inclusivity in mind.
3. **Integrate sustainability and policy advocacy in AI development.** Companies should focus on enhancing energy efficiency in data centres and utilizing more efficient hardware. Additionally, engaging in AI policy development is imperative to ensure diverse and equitable governance, aligning AI advancements with global needs and ethical standards.

The journey towards AI in businesses is influenced by a complex interplay of internal motivations and external pressures. On one hand, forward-thinking companies recognize that adopting responsible AI practices is not just ethically sound but also strategically beneficial in the long term. They understand that ethical AI fosters trust, sustains customer loyalty and aligns with evolving regulatory landscapes, thus safeguarding their future.

On the other hand, businesses resistant to change can face mounting pressures. These pressures come in various forms: stringent regulatory requirements, public scrutiny and the growing demand for ethical practices from stakeholders. Governments and international bodies are increasingly imposing fines and sanctions on companies that fail to adhere to ethical AI standards, acting as a strong deterrent against irresponsible practices.

Furthermore, the rise of socially conscious investors and consumers who prioritize ethics in their decision-making compels businesses to reevaluate their stance on AI. This evolving ecosystem creates a compelling case for businesses to proactively embrace the ethical use of AI, balancing profitability with social responsibility.

AI for all

The archaic, biased lending models that once excluded entire communities and professions have gradually evolved into more equitable, AI-driven systems. Today, AI plays a pivotal role in democratizing financial access, employing sophisticated algorithms that go beyond traditional prejudices to assess creditworthiness. While there is still some way to go, this shift reflects a broader trend in AI's evolution: a move from reinforcing existing biases to actively challenging and correcting them.

As AI continues to evolve, its potential will extend beyond current applications, promising transformative changes in global socio-economic landscapes. Future innovations could see AI further democratizing education, making advanced learning accessible in remote areas, and revolutionizing healthcare with predictive analytics for preventive medicine.

Alongside these developments, there is growing concern around AI displacing jobs. However, this is not the complete picture. In fact, it is more likely that individuals who fail to embrace and integrate AI into their work will find themselves outpaced by those who adeptly utilize AI technologies. This further underscores the critical need for AI to be accessible and inclusive, ensuring that a diverse range of individuals can engage with and benefit from its advancements, thereby mitigating the risk of a digital divide in the workforce.

A business, at its most evolved, transcends the narrow pursuit of profit and shareholder interests. It serves all stakeholders, a collective that encompasses employees, customers and society at large. AI's role in ethical decision-making and sustainable practices represents a new frontier, aligning corporate strategies with global welfare goals.

The ongoing challenge is to ensure AI is developed equitably, so that its benefits reach all social strata, bridging the digital divide. This vision necessitates continued collaboration between governments, businesses and communities to responsibly harness AI's full potential and foster a more inclusive, sustainable world.

19

Diversity in Boardroom Decision-Making

SAMIR KUMAR BARUA

The regulatory push for board diversity

REGULATIONS ACROSS THE WORLD ATTEMPT to nudge companies towards more diverse board compositions to reduce biases in decision-making and thereby improve corporate governance. In the Indian context, the corporate governance requirements specified in the Securities and Exchange Board of India's (SEBI's) Listing Obligations and Disclosure Requirements (LODR) mandate the Nomination and Remuneration Committee (NRC) of a company to articulate a policy on board diversity (Regulation 19(4) read with Part D (A) (3) of Schedule II of the SEBI (Listing Obligations and Disclosure Requirements) Regulations, 2015). These regulations specify the inclusion of a minimum percentage of non-executive independent directors (NIDs) on the boards of listed companies, to both enhance board diversity and improve the functional independence of the board. Since 2015, the regulations have also required that the boards of listed companies include at least one woman director, thereby ensuring a minimum level of gender diversity (Regulation 17(1)(a) of the Securities and Exchange Board of India (Listing Obligations and Disclosure Requirements) Regulations, 2015).

Board diversity is measured by the dissimilarities in the profiles of directors on a variety of attributes, such as academic background, skills, competencies, experience, economic status, gender, race, ethnicity, nationality and sexual orientation. The regulatory push for diversifying board composition arises from the belief that such diversity enhances the quality of governance by introducing a multiplicity of views during board deliberations.

Diversity as a foundation, not a guarantee, for good governance

However, compositional diversity of boards is merely a prerequisite for achieving good governance. Effective corporate governance also requires constructive conversations in the boardroom that can integrate often disparate views into a cogent decision. This, in turn, demands a collegial atmosphere during board discussions and a sincere commitment by board members to their fiduciary responsibilities to the company.

The extant regulations in India nudge NIDs to play such a role by holding them accountable on par with executive directors. There is no immunity from penalties for abstaining from a board decision (an act of omission) if that decision is later found to contravene extant regulations and laws. By removing the safety net often provided for inaction or neutrality, NIDs are encouraged (or shall we say, compelled) to participate with commitment in board discussions.

The regulation specifying timelines for sending information to the board, including setting the agenda and providing all relevant documents, is primarily covered under the Secretarial Standard-1 (SS-1) on Meetings of the Board of Directors issued by the Institute of Company Secretaries of India (ICSI). These requirements are aligned with Section 173(3) of the Companies Act, 2013, and the Companies (Meetings of Board and its Powers) Rules, 2014. While such detailed timelines prima facie may appear to be a regulatory overreach, these provisions provide ammunition to board members to insist on compliance if management regularly flouts them.

In sum, Indian regulations push NIDs to take an active and independent stance on issues placed before the board. The penal provisions ensure that NIDs recognize the prudence of recording their dissent when they disagree with a majority decision, particularly if they believe the decision to be questionable.

The Indian reality: Dominant shareholders and weak enforcement

Despite the regulatory provisions that strengthen compositional diversity and director accountability, good corporate governance continues to be elusive in India. The primary reason lies in the ownership structure of Indian companies. There are very few companies with widely dispersed shareholding, that is, without an identifiable dominant shareholder in control. In most cases, whether it is the government or a family/group, the dominant shareholder controls both the board composition and the board processes. As a result, boards of Indian companies often function as groups of 'nodding heads', with the direction of the nods dictated by the wishes of the dominant shareholder.

While India's corporate governance regulations are excellent on paper, the main shortcoming has been in their observance. SEBI has largely failed to penalize boards that have flouted governance requirements. A significant reason for this is the non-compliance of listed public sector enterprises (PSEs). As the government is the controlling shareholder in these companies, SEBI has been either unable or reluctant to hold their boards accountable for violations.

Recognizing the challenge posed by concentrated ownership, the regulations were amended to further empower NIDs. Earlier, the regulations required NIDs—like executive directors—to periodically seek shareholders' approval for their continuance on the board. This allowed the dominant shareholder to orchestrate the ouster of 'inconvenient' directors within the ambit of the law. This requirement has since been done away with. Under the revised regulations, NIDs are appointed for a fixed term, free from the Damocles' sword of being voted out by the shareholders before their term ends.

However, despite this improved security of tenure, NIDs in India remain hostage to the whims and fancies of the dominant shareholder. In a way, the regulatory change has proved counterproductive, as the inability to remove a board member once appointed has made dominant shareholders even more cautious about whom they appoint in the first place. As a result, individuals who are a priori deemed to be 'manageable' are selected as board members. This has eroded the independence and effectiveness of boards over time.

Challenges to independent decision-making and board dynamics

The potential for friction between the dominant shareholder and the NIDs arises in situations where there is a possible conflict between the interests of the dominant shareholder and those of the minority shareholders or the larger interests of the company. An illustrative list of areas where such divergence of views or perspectives may occur includes investment proposals or capital deployment—particularly in cases involving acquisitions, selection of suppliers or contractors, recruitment of executives for key positions, compensation for top management, pricing of options issued to the dominant shareholder and the choice of new board members to replace retiring ones.

Mistrust or misunderstanding often arises from the beliefs and biases held on both sides. The dominant shareholder may believe that NIDs form their views based on a cursory or incorrect understanding of the day-to-day challenges faced by executive management. Conversely, NIDs often suspect that proposals from the management are dictated by private benefits to the dominant shareholder, rather than by the overall interests of the company.

The way to mitigate such biases and suspicions is by clearly specifying the criteria and processes for decision-making. However, business decisions can rarely be fully automated, with rules that lead to unambiguous choices in all scenarios. Trade-offs and judgement calls are invariably required, and it is in such situations that biases come into play. In the absence of mutual trust regarding each other's motivation, competence and fiduciary commitment, open discussion and honest articulation to find an agreeable solution often become difficult.

Such impasses are particularly hard to resolve in boards with CEO duality, that is, where the CEO also serves as the chair of the board. Without this duality, a non-executive chair could play the role of a non-partisan arbiter, helping to negotiate a solution. Recognizing the importance of having a non-executive board chair, SEBI initially mandated through Regulation 17(1B) of the SEBI (Listing Obligations and Disclosure Requirements) Regulations, 2015, that from April 1, 2020, the chairperson of the board of the top 500 listed entities must be a non-executive director (NED) and should not be related to the managing director or CEO as defined under the Companies Act, 2013. After deferring the requirement to April 2022, SEBI omitted Regulation 17(1B) in 2022, making the separation of roles of chairperson and MD or CEO voluntary rather than mandatory. As a result, CEO duality continues to prevail in many listed public sector enterprises (PSEs), where government as the controlling shareholder has chosen not to comply with SEBI's suggestion. There are other such regulations as well that the government has chosen not to adhere to. SEBI's inability (or reluctance) to enforce compliance has significantly dented its credibility and damaged the cause of good corporate governance in India.

Another category of board directors—the non-executive nominee directors, who represent institutions with substantial shareholding—can play the role of mediators in addressing differences in views arising from bias, particularly on boards with CEO duality. However, nominee directors of Indian institutions have largely failed to play this critical role of independent, unbiased arbiters. As most institutional investors in India are government-owned and controlled entities (many of which are now listed PSEs), their nominees are often unable to take an independent and unbiased view, even when the concerned companies are not PSEs, thereby detracting from good governance principles.

Conceptually, there is an alternative, less favourable view on board diversity. The complexity of communication dynamics in compositionally diverse boards is sometimes cited as a reason to limit the extent of diversity. Effective communication, which is essential during board discussions, can be significantly compromised due to diversity. Members of a diverse board may lack the skills or a common language to make themselves understood, or to understand the viewpoints of others.

In such cases, the role of the chair becomes even more critical. A competent board chair is essential for moderating discussions, clarifying misunderstandings arising from miscommunication, and reconciling views that may initially appear irreconcilable. The greater the board diversity, the higher the board entropy, and the greater the need for an effective chair who can ensure the business of the board is conducted efficiently and effectively. Unfortunately, there is no guarantee that a board will have such a capable chair.

The way forward: Making diversity work

Does that mean board diversity is simply a utopian solution for reducing the influence of biases in decision making—and thereby improving governance? The answer may lie in the Indian fable, 'The Six Blind Men and the Elephant'. In the story, each blind man describes the elephant based on the part of its body he touches. Each man is individually correct, and yet collectively they are hopelessly off the mark. The complete and correct conception of the elephant emerges only when a wise man weaves together the individual descriptions into a comprehensive picture.

The story teaches us that a well-functioning board requires both: the availability of diverse individual perspectives, as well as the ability to pool these perspectives together wisely to form a comprehensive understanding of the issue at hand. This requires not only the chair but also the board members to operate with sagacity, fulfilling their fiduciary duty to act in the best interests of the company.

In conclusion, while board diversity is desirable, it delivers benefits only when all members work together to make that diversity effective. Of all the different metrics of diversity, perhaps the easiest to understand is gender diversity. By one reckoning, about one-third of senior executives in Indian companies are women.[1] To begin with, therefore, let us use this statistic to correct gender representation on company boards by reducing the presence of men to, say, less than 75 per cent, to align the gender composition in company boards with the gender representation among senior management. Shall we?

20

Men and Money

Behavioural Insights on Mitigating Gender Stereotypes

SUTAPA BANERJEE

THE TRADING DESKS IN THE dealing rooms of banks are overwhelmingly male across the world. In my own twenty-four years in financial services in India, I have come across just one woman trader. In the UK, women comprise a mere 13 per cent of bank traders.[1] Trading involves taking shorter-term risks repeatedly to make gains, with financial incentives heavily loaded in favour of those who deliver the big bucks, the winners.

The act of taking risks in the short term to achieve repeated gains has been widely studied by neuroscientists in several other domains—politics, sports, the military, and even animal behaviours relating to territorial gains. Aptly termed the 'winner effect', in the dealing rooms of banks it manifests when traders, initially successful in taking risks to achieve wins, are spurred to take increasingly larger risks for even bigger wins. The reverse holds true as well: losses often lead to risk aversion in all decisions. In these situations, carefully calibrated risk-taking gives way to emotional surges. Instances of 'rogue traders' causing financial institutions billions of dollars in losses make headlines with disturbing regularity.

The research on derivative traders was led by John Coates, who spent thirteen years on Wall Street trading desks at Deutsche Bank and Goldman Sachs.[2] Having both experienced and observed this effect on traders, he later turned to neuroscience and Cambridge to research the phenomenon. He found that women were largely immune to the effect, as were older men. Laboratory tests using saliva samples indicated a strong link to testosterone, a hormone found in larger concentrations in younger men.

Meanwhile, *Science Daily* published a report on a large-scale study led by neuroscientists at Rosalind Franklin University of Medicine and Science examining differences between men's and women's brains, including performance across a range of tasks.[3] Decades of research were coalesced into a single meta-synthesis, and the conclusion was: 'hardly at all'. Dr Lise Eliot, who led the study, states: '... this false impression that there is such a thing as a "male brain" and a "female brain" has had wide impacts on how we treat boys and girls, men and women'.[4] One such impact is the long-standing belief that girls have a biologically lower ability in mathematics.

Interestingly, research has also found a relationship between maths scores and gender equality in countries. The more gender-equal the country, the smaller the difference in scores. In Scandinavian countries, the gap is negligible; in Iceland—the most gender-equal country—girls outperform boys. It is noteworthy that for quite some time, testosterone was believed to play a role in mathematical thinking.

These two seemingly unrelated studies connect in interesting ways, and testosterone is not the only link. But let's start there. In popular discourse, testosterone is the much-maligned hormone associated with male aggression and overconfidence at one end, and with numerous supplements promising improved performance in sport and in the bedroom at the other. Less widely known, and contrary to popular perception, is scientific research showing that testosterone can encourage men to pursue with greater enthusiasm whatever brings them social kudos. As neurobiologist and primatologist Robert Sapolsky notes: '… boosting testosterone levels … can make people compete like crazy to do the most random acts of kindness' if social circumstances are engineered accordingly.[5]

This is one example of what scientists have long realized: the interplay between biology and environment is complex and nuanced, involving feedback loops that work both ways. In the case of derivatives traders in bank dealing rooms, apart from hormonal factors, the daily environment comprises risk management practices, financial incentives and predominantly men goading one another. One of John Coates's key policy prescriptions is to balance high-risk trading roles with more women and older men. Likewise, the study of girls' maths scores and gender equality underscores the importance of environment. In this instance, it is the larger cultural environment of a country that impacts girls' mathematical performance.

The immense popularity of the book *Men are from Mars, Women are from Venus* has made that phrase officially a meme and is '… an example of how incorrect and baseless ideas can displace good reasoned thinking based on research.'[6] Disproportionate media attention and countless seemingly innocuous jokes and memes help such false ideas take root in the popular imagination, with severely pernicious long-term effects.

Just as it has engendered the longstanding misconception that girls have biologically lower abilities in maths, it has also perpetuated the stereotype that women are not cut out for finance, implicitly influencing both men and women. In India, women constitute a mere 10 per cent of the workforce in microfinance—ironically, an industry where 98 per cent of its clientele are women.[7] And while research shows that women are both better investors for themselves and more effective investment managers, they account for an abysmal 11 per cent of those roles.[8]

Barring the stated 'no discrimination' policy in company manuals, there has been no real concerted action in terms of deliberate, affirmative steps to rectify this anomaly in organizations. Sadly, the science-based tools and techniques that have worked in certain contexts to correct such disparities are neither widely known nor widely practiced. Fragmented efforts—such as appointing a diversity champion or offering a dedicated women's training programme—may be better than doing nothing, but are unlikely to move the needle in any meaningful way. Sending a few people for short-term training programmes at Ivy League institutions is not of much use. It takes considerably longer to imbibe and assimilate a complex subject, and then a very different set of skills to share those learnings across an organization.

Good intent may lead organizations to hire consultants and pop psychologists with only superficial knowledge, resulting in a mishmash of initiatives—such as unconscious bias training or overtly women-centric policies—that empirical research shows are of little use and sometimes counterproductive. Unsurprisingly, in a speaker interview at the annual conference of the CFA Institute in 2018, Nobel laureate in Economics Daniel Kahneman when was asked for 'easy suggestions and advice' on applying behavioural insights for its 1,50,000-strong global membership of investment professionals, suggested simply reading a couple of books by his friend and fellow Nobel laureate Richard Thaler, highlighting that there are no 'easy solutions or advice'.

Clearly, there is a lack of effective mechanisms to transfer the wealth of evidence-based research to policymakers and business leaders. Meaningful options for organizations could be to draw on the expertise of the few behavioural science practitioners who have spent reasonable periods of time in both business and academia, or collaborations with academic institutions, that have a nuanced understanding of the subject and the ability to test it in specific organizational contexts.

21

The Power of Narrative

A Media Perspective

ANUPAMA MANDLOI

THE INDIAN OBSESSION WITH MOVIES rivals that of cricket and possibly even marriage. India produces more films than any other country, around 1900 films a year in approximately thirty-five different languages, attracting 157.4 million viewers and an annual business of $1.36 billion![1] Indian television, however, remains the dominant medium, reaching over 900 million households, particularly in tier 2 and tier 3 cities. In a country of 1.46 billion people, 48.42 per cent are female.[2] In this context, the role of media in shaping the representation of women on screen and their contribution to society cannot be ignored.

The dominant screen narrative has been the endorsement of patriarchy, objectification and the reinforcement of stereotypes: powerless female characters on the one hand and, on the other extreme, the goddess on a pedestal to be feared and revered. Traditional roles such as the virtuous wife, devoted mother and damsel in distress have been the hallmarks of female representation. Portrayals of women displaying independent thought and action or enjoying financial and sexual freedom have been far less common.

In the early days of the small screen, the national broadcaster Doordarshan did a lot to boost awareness about issues ranging from polio eradication and family planning, to the importance of educating girls and the value of agriculture. Eventually, in the 1990s, it was overtaken by the shiny, consumerist shows on satellite television.[3]

When Balaji shows, popularly known as K serials, ruled the roost, female protagonists held sway on television. The men were either obsessive stalkers demanding submission and obedience, or emotionally manipulated, spineless mama's boys. Playing one woman against the other was a consistent strategy used by men to control 'their' women. Meanwhile, women negotiated their interpersonal boundaries of power within the confines of their homes, were god-fearing and paid homage at the altar of martyrdom and sacrifice. If they ever lent a hand in business, it was superficial. They rarely crossed the line of modesty. If they did, they were cast as vamps. The separation between 'good' and 'bad' was clear and distinct.

The stories were voraciously consumed by homemakers who recognized themselves on screen and saw in the leading ladies a reflection of their own lives. They identified with the trials and tribulations, the domestic power negotiations, and the small victories. Their lives seemed more palatable when compared with what they saw on screen. Their lack of agency was mirrored in the plotlines, yet the over-the-top drama made their lives appear exciting and intriguing. The patriarchal legacy of rivalry and toxicity between women was played up. Realism was replaced by glamour. Female protagonists on television became trendsetters in fashion and were viewed as role models of ideal social behaviour. They were stars in their own right and had an enviable following. The influence of these shows was tremendous.

This was followed by a period of issue-based storytelling, in which men supported women in their education and professional goals. The horizons widened for women joining the police force, running a business or even aspiring to be sportspersons. It was an indulgent portrayal of women being 'allowed' to step outside the norm of convention. Issues such as child widowhood, corruption, bonded labour, dowry, the caste system and homosexuality were addressed within narrative stereotypes acceptable to the audience. These social issues were great marketing hooks, but rarely lasted in the storyline beyond the first few months. Having said that, it is important to recognize the extent and depth of effective, positive social messaging in shows like *Diya aur Baati Hum*, *Balika Vadhu,* and currently, *Anupamaa*, which have chosen to question the norm.

Then came aspirational India. Reality shows like *Kaun Banega Crorepati, Indian Idol, India's Got Talent* and *Dance India Dance*, among many others, mirrored vignettes from the interiors of India, showcasing aspirations, opportunities and local stories of grit and achievement. These shows opened a window to a changing India. A hallmark of these programmes was the youth who learnt and upskilled via YouTube, who were ambitious and desired the upwardly mobile lifestyle reflected in mainstream media. Television became a means of earning recognition, accessing celebrities, and attracting glamour and prosperity.

The trouble with all this is that mainstream media, by design, caters to the largest common denominator, resulting in homogenous content and the unfortunate exclusion of unique voices. The failure to encourage alternative narratives eventually produces a mediocre, unvarying viewpoint that never challenges the status quo. Over time, it erodes trust, transparency, and accountability. News channels and publications are no longer seen as reliable or accurate. Is this the result of the inherent belief of media executives who presume to know their audience, or does it stem from the viewers' own reluctance to engage with anything that doesn't conform to entertainment as they know it? This dilemma is real and far from simple.

Mass media is all about reach and profitability. It is a business, after all. While the business of entertainment is profitable, feeds frenzied consumers daily, and keeps the wheel of engagement, creation and monetization turning, it must also remain cognizant of its value creation in the social context. Star Plus, for example, introduced *Satyamev Jayate* and *TED Talks, India* into its programming mix. Shows otherwise deemed unprofitable because they were seen as too 'serious' needed the weight of Bollywood male superstars to ensure success. *Satyamev Jayate* provoked discussions on social issues like corruption, female foeticide, alcoholism, sexual abuse and discrimination. It inspired forums, donations and policy shifts, effectively creating impact through awareness building.

As screens shrank and consumers moved to their phones and hand-helds, OTT created a space for experimentation and alternative storytelling, although the focus on marketability, big stars and subscriptions still drives most programming decisions. Nevertheless, the opportunity to build differentiated content for varying verticals is being explored through new genres and narrative structures. Streamers have begun to play a fundamental role in reframing women-led narratives by giving female characters more multifaceted and complex roles, for example, *Panchayat, Kafas, Jubilee, Darlings, Kohhra, Gullak, Trial by Fire* and *Made in Heaven*.

A lot of this was already played out on the big screen. The previous decade brought a breath of fresh air to cinema. The introduction of strong, independent female characters broke the norm and challenged patriarchy, as seen in *Queen, Piku, Parched, Stree, Badhaai Ho, Laapata Ladies, Girls Will Be Girls, Humans in the Loop* and others. The possibility of women driving box office collections became a reality. The growth, however small, of women at the helm led to more nuanced and authentic portrayals of women on screen.

Independent films, documentaries and small-budget productions shed light on hidden issues, inequities and corruption, led by individualistic and experimental voices. These, however, tend to get sacrificed at the altar of business. Independent films are often unsupported by mainstream institutions because they are seen as unprofitable. Filmmakers must rely on film festivals, crowdfunding, government sanctions and grants to garner visibility.[4]

Along the way, much has altered. In India, the Films Division has ceased to be an independent entity. The central government's documentary and newsreel-making body, established in 1948, was merged with the National Film Development Corporation, closing an avenue that once allowed different voices to be heard.[5]

Independent production remains an untamed and provocative voice. It is the domain of innovation, disruption, and potent change. This vibrant alternative needs encouragement in a country where the jingoistic and the mainstream dominate. Some independent films are exceptionally well-made, with the power to shift awareness and even provoke policy change, but they lack distribution or marketing support. As a result, their exposure is limited, and their influence curtailed.

In a risk-averse, restrictive environment where producers are treated as work-for-hire, and intellectual property is controlled by the platforms and studios, where do women professionals feature? Approximately 15 per cent of women hold head-of-department positions across production design, direction, writing, editing and cinematography in the film industry. Similarly, only about 10 per cent of senior leadership roles in media corporations are held by women. Where does the fix lie?[6]

The Prevention of Sexual Harassment (POSH) at the Workplace Act was introduced in 2013, fortuitously before the MeToo movement in India in late 2018. The movement led to extreme discomfort and surprising reactions. Men scoffed at the movement while being overtly careful, exaggerating this caution around women in their interactions. Most women, especially those who spoke up, believe it achieved little. While Me Too did not yield tangible success and, in some cases, resulted in backlash, it shifted the conversation around sexual harassment and made it more vocal. Once the spotlight has revealed a problem, there is no going back. In this instance, the media served as both the spotlight and the muckraker.

Until the lens through which women are seen changes, their representation on screen and in the workplace will remain compromised.[7] Empowering their portrayal and rightful place in the economy lies in the hands of parents, the education system, the industry and the government. Women in positions of power owe it to the next generation to carry forward the legacy of the suffragettes, allowing young women to stand on their shoulders and reach for the stars. Waiting for men to sign off on women's empowerment is, in itself, an attestation of male power.

To this effect, there have been several worthwhile initiatives. Amazon Prime Video has introduced an inclusion policy playbook to ensure fair representation for women on and off the screen. The policies range from mandatory female representation in writers' rooms to evaluating every script on specific parameters, such as the Bechdel Test (is a simple measure of the representation of women in film based on three criteria. It must feature at least two women, the two women must speak with each other, and their conversation must be about something other than a man.) Another initiative is Maitri by Prime Video, where women at the helm convene to share challenges and consider new avenues to overcome them. Actor-producer Richa Chadha and Ali Fazal launched an incubation programme to train ten female gaffers (chief lighting technicians) to work in the Hindi film industry. Global streaming giant Netflix has been ranked a "PACESETTER" in gender equity for offering comprehensive healthcare benefits, generous parental leave, and initiatives like the Fund for Creative Equity that support and build female talent in the film industry.

As the number of women across the media industry grows, they pave the way for others. For generations, women have been encouraged to view one another as rivals. For centuries, they vied for the affection of men and struggled to survive the power dynamic in domestic spaces. It is this deep-seated conditioning that often manifests as a default mode of functioning at work. Yet, the power of sisterhood can shape an autonomous future.

Broadcasters, streamers and studios monopolize the media business. Film stars, social media influencers and television protagonists wield immense power. An important tier of power brokers and influencers is the executives within these companies, who are in a position to decide what shapes public thought. Some visionary leaders are beginning to allocate a small percentage of their programming budgets to create meaningful content. Decision-makers are realizing the need to reinvent their roles.

The business is in the midst of a transformation, driven by technology, content innovation and distribution. It can become a beacon of social change when it represents, employs, empowers and creates opportunities for women and minorities. This can be furthered through legislative changes, such as mandating women's representation on boards and ensuring salary transparency to achieve pay parity. Gender-sensitivity training to reveal unconscious bias and gender stereotypes can help create more respectful work environments. Recognizing the contributions and achievements of women through awards and accolades can inspire others, while regularly collecting and updating data on gender representation within the industry can highlight areas of progress.

The industry is run on the metrics of box office success, subscriptions, and ratings. A minority of organizations wield all the influence, creating an unhealthy power system that needs rebalancing. Unity and conviction between producers and creators is one way forward. A striking example is the fight for the rights of lyricists, singers and composers undertaken by Javed Akhtar at the cost of being isolated and banned by film producers and studios.[8] His efforts broke the unfair stranglehold of music companies and film producers. Today, creators enjoy 12.5 per cent of royalties earned outside of films. In 2018, as head of the Indian Performing Rights Society, Javed Akhtar distributed approximately Rs 13 crore among 2800 musicians from royalties generated through synchronization across ads, television and other media.[9]

We saw the impact of the Hollywood writers' strike, which began in May 2023. It brought the business to a grinding halt in the US. The fight was to establish guardrails against the use of artificial intelligence in contracts and to level the playing field for all participants in the business. The actors' union soon entered the fray. Collectively, the two unions were ready to ride out the storm.[10]

Producers have begun to negotiate stakes in intellectual property rights. They invest years in creative development, incubate writers and creative teams and incur significant costs, yet often end up as work-for-hire operators earning only a 10 per cent profit margin rather than being recognized as collaborators.

The media industry is facing a radical overhaul. India's OTT landscape is booming, with 547 million users, 60 per cent on mobile, with a projected growth to 634 million by 2029, reflecting highly fragmented yet expanding consumption. Cloud-based broadcasting and AI-driven recommendations are reshaping engagement through personalized, immersive content delivery. While urban regions drive adoption, rural markets present vast growth potential, fueled by affordable smartphones, cheap data and supportive government initiatives.

Radical solutions could lie in eliminating the need for upfront money in the creative process by focusing on the barter of services and skills, innovative profit-sharing models, time banking systems where credits earned can be exchanged for services from others, open-source projects, and reduced copyright restrictions.

Those who refuse to adapt may be doomed to failure. We are already seeing the signs. The film industry is undergoing change with its ridiculous fee structure, select and preferred inner circles and the resounding flops of many high-budget films in recent years. Smaller films with high concepts, real and relevant stories and innovative formats have been gaining traction.

As AI enters scriptwriting, editing and visual design, Indian media will need its own guardrails to protect creativity and IP, ensure fair contracts and train the workforce to adopt and adapt to the new wave of tech that is already reshaping the industry.

The parallel growth of independent cinema needs patrons. If administrative support has dried up, then businesses, HNIs (High Net Worth Individuals) and established media corporations must take the lead. Many organizations are in a position to introduce and implement fair contracts, train and empower employees, reward responsible and sustainable work ethics, and build a culture of responsibility and inclusivity. Such organizations will stand apart from the crowd and inevitably gain in both reputation and goodwill.

As for storytelling, those who respect its power and use it for the greater good will give this industry the same dignity that education and medicine inherently command.

22

The Changing Face of Brands and Communication

A Brand Perspective

KIRAN KHALAP

Discontinuity Exhibit A

I FIRST ENCOUNTERED THE CONCEPT of the noosphere in the famous book *The Phenomenon of Man* by the palaeontologist and priest Teilhard de Chardin.

I was captivated by the idea of a skin of consciousness enveloping the Earth, much as the atmosphere wraps it in a skin of air.

So captivated, in fact, that in December 2013 I wrote an opinion piece in *The Times of India* on how the internet would make the noosphere tangible.

It's 2025.

Elon Musk's Starlink satellites, currently providing the Internet to 100 countries plan to cover the entire Earth. It has deployed 7800 satellites (Starlink website, 2025), with a possible extension to 42,000.

The skin of consciousness and communication is now available in the middle of a desert, a forest, an ocean and tomorrow, on Planet Mars.

This is the first discontinuity in the history of the Earth that has created tectonic changes in the way business is conducted.

We will come back to its role in redefining business.

Discontinuity Exhibit B

Once upon a time, businesses owned tangible assets like factories and machinery. Reassuringly, they reflected on balance sheets

In the late eighties, firms started acknowledging a new asset class: intellectual property.

While we don't have similar data for India, here's a simple chart showing the subterranean shift in market value of businesses in the US. It's by Ocean Tomo, specialists in intellectual property since the 80s. Between 1975 and 2015, the value of intangible assets has reversed!

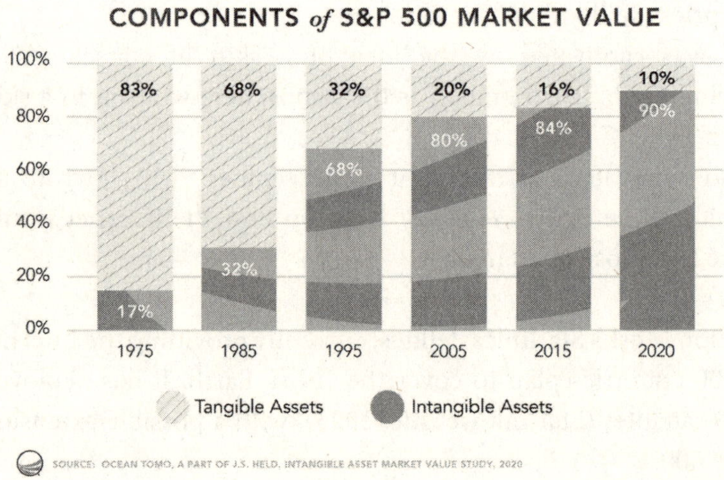

Unfortunately, not all intangible assets reflect on the balance sheet. Brands, for example. In 2025, Apple brand value was, depending on who was evaluating, between US $574 billion[1] and $ 1.3 trillion,[2] but this does not find place in the Apple Inc. balance sheet.

As things stand, a brand's value is realized when it is bought or sold. As of October 2025, the largest ever acquisition was the 1999 takeover of Mannesmann by Vodafone Airtouch plc at $183 billion ($297.7 billion adjusted for inflation).

Now let's stitch together the effects of the two discontinuities. The Internet did two things: opened up a totally new way of doing business: online. And it made the intangible assets called brands vulnerable to a new way of gaining or losing goodwill. And even if globalization stalled post-COVID,[3] e-globalization is an unstoppable force.

India's numbers in this arena are startling.

In 2023, over 1.2 billion Indians are accessing the Internet. By 2050, 1.6 billion Indians will be accessing it.[4]

India has the cheapest data rates and hence the highest consumption per month in the world.

This has opened a direct connect for businesses with their key stakeholders: they reach millions of employees, customers, investors, partners

Already, nearly 8 per cent of all retail sales in India is online commerce;[5] as of 2020, India accounted for the highest fintech adoption rate (87 per cent); 2.5 to 3.5 million Indians (individuals not business owners!) create content in India[6]: one of the easiest ways to make money online without any investment![7]

This is an explosive new way of doing business and reaching consumers with a range of products and services they had never experienced before.

And it is a new way for individuals to become business owners ... like the bloggers and the influencers!

But the Internet is not a one-way street.

The I in Internet represents three Is: interactive, international and instantaneous.

That's why, while businesses discovered a low-cost way of reaching customers, customers found a new way of exercising their choice of rights.

Before this network, businesses operated in their own cocoons, their borders impervious to stakeholder gaze.

You and I bought biscuits, insurance, bottled water or nappies without having any clue of where the factory was or the offices were and how the company was treating its workers.

Now consider this: in 2015 social activist jhatkaa.org roped in Indian rapper Sofia Ashraf to give voice to the victims of mercury poisoning in Kodaikanal, India. Hindustan Unilever was contaminating the environment by dumping tonnes of toxic waste: this was first detected in 2001. The rap song catapulted the issue to global social media platforms, including Hollywood stars.[8]

In 2016, Unilever granted compensation to 591 ex-employees, after a decade and a half of the event.

Or this: most prospective employees tend to check the scores of companies, executives and brands on sites like glassdoor.co.in. The reviews are by employees within the companies... and anything less than the average of 3.3 out of 5 will make the employer fairly unattractive.

Or this: As of 2025, TrustPilot.com has hosted 200 million reviews about more than 1.2 million brands since its birth in 2007.[9]

For the first time in the history of business, hiding is not possible.

Stakeholders have a role to play in how brands and businesses are run.

If brands represent enormous intangible value, and if stakeholders are directly able to affect that value, businesses need to rearrange their priorities to align with them and, moreover, prove that their priorities are aligned!

What should a business owner do? Lead societal change or follow it?

Let's look at the biggest challenge facing businesses today, whether in India or elsewhere.

Sustainability.

At least 60 per cent of consumers in India are willing to pay a premium for sustainability products, according to a Bain report in 2023.[10]

Simultaneously, in May 2021, SEBI made it mandatory for the top 1,000 listed companies to disclose non-financial information under SEBI's Business Responsibility and Sustainability Reporting (BRSR) norms.

Do brands get rewarded for leading by their conscience rather than following the regulation?

The Godrej Group has been at the forefront of sustainability, ahead of the regulatory threat, and you can see it getting rewarded on the same glassdoor.co.in with a score of 3.9.

Let's look at issues like diversity, inclusion, equality.

A Google Search ad about the reunion of Indian and Pakistani friends garnered 1.2 million views. HP's Diwali 2022 campaign, *#ThodisiJagahBanaLo*, celebrating artisans, reached 3.2 million views. Mia by Tanishq celebrates diversity in femininity and features Riza Reji, the first Indian with Down syndrome to appear in the 'Be Beautiful, Be Yourself' fashion show organized by the Global Down Syndrome Foundation in Colorado in November 2022.

These campaigns reflect the issues Millennials and Gen Z in India are grappling with, which is why brands that lead on these concerns are gaining distinctiveness on social media. One area that still requires far greater psychological investment is gender parity in advertising. While there have been notable exceptions, women continue to be portrayed primarily as caregivers, while men are cast as breadwinners.

A laudable, very consistent and long-term investment made by Campaign magazine is the curation by Dr A.L. Sharada of Population First. She has been doing a creative critique of ads from the gender lens for decades now.[11]

The next set of nudges are coming from technology!

Apps like Good on You, Think Dirty, Shop Ethical rate all the brands by the most sustainable-worthy levels—labour conditions, environmental policies, and usage of animal products in manufacturing. Choosing these apps means choosing conscious retailers making an effort to reduce their carbon footprint.

On the other hand, Rent the Runway, allows you to rent clothing to avoid buying items that you'll only wear once.

And yet.

Managing businesses online in India is a funambulist's job, a tight ropewalk.

India as a society and as a market has three peculiarities.

1. Pseudo-maturity©

A pseudomature© market or society is one where all levels of evolution co-exist.

358 billionaires worth $1.67 trillion (Hurun Rich List, 2025) co-exist with a large number of people below poverty line.[12]

India is the largest two-wheeler and three-wheeler market globally—this number co-exists with the poor who travel on foot.

The same pseudo-maturity© exists in attitudes towards the big themes of sustainability, diversity, inclusivity, equality.

The WEIRD (Western, Educated, Industrialized, Rich, Democratic) culture co-exists with the non-WEIRD culture: interestingly they co-exist in metros and villages both.

The Gen Z are busy defining 'self against vertical conformity and horizontal homogeneity' while Gen X are busy adapting received norms to new realities of technology.

When businesses attempt to live up to the aspirations of one group, they alienate the other.

The FEM Dabur ad in 2021 showed Karva Chauth celebrations in a same sex marriage. For one end of the market, it was pushing the envelope for equality; for another, it was sacrilege.

The Tanishq ad for interfaith marriage in 2021 had to be pulled down finally because of the severe backlash from segments of society.

What should businesses do, lead or follow?

2. The echo chamber of English

The language of business in India is English, but the language of the consumer is not English.

Less than 0.05 per cent Indians use English as their first language.[13]

Businesses have translated their web sites into Mandarin and Spanish for their international clients, but they will need to translate them into Indian languages for their prospective Indian employees.

Around 98 per cent of current Indian internet users accessed it through Indic languages over English.[14]

Facilitators like Google Research have set an ambitious goal of building a single, unified model that will be capable of handling over 100 Indian languages across both speech and text.

This is the next level of inclusion for Indian businesses: including the 99.05 per cent of non-English users in their offerings.

In Spotify's first year in India, 70 per cent of the music consumed on the platform was international; in 2023, 70 per cent was from India. Astonishingly, Spotify's Weekly Top Songs list for India for the week of 7 March 2024 shows all of the top ten spots held by Indian artists![15]

RummyCircle, the largest online rummy game site with 50 million users, rode to the top by offering the game in regional languages.

One of the best sources of connect for businesses in regional languages are regional influencers. Regional influencers help anchor the brand in local culture and realities.

The Tamil VillageCooking Channel (VCC) on YouTube has over 28 million subscribers (May 2025).

Five brothers and their grandfather cook traditional food outdoors and the audience is never sated!

STAGE, 'The Netflix of Bharat', now has more than 20 million users and 4.4 million paid subscribers, achieved since 2019 by offering content in hyper-local languages like Haryanvi and Rajasthani for non-metro audiences![16]

Businesses and brands need to pivot quickly to embrace languages and with them, local cultures, for faster business conversion.

3. The oral culture

For thousands of years, Indian music, sciences and philosophical texts have been transmitted orally.

We trust our ears more than we trust our eyes.

And don't even for a moment believe that this is a tradition that's no longer relevant. Because it is not to do with illiteracy; it is to do with a deep civilizational rhythm.

Even today, all communication in Indian languages is rhymed: because rhyming enhances memorability in an oral culture.

The English-speaking passenger types the destination address on Google Maps, the Ola driver talks to Google Maps on his phone.

This is one continuity that Indian businesses have leveraged well over the years.

The feature film industry knows that songs (an average of five today; in 1932, *Indrasabha* had 72)! are the key to success.

There is a restaurant in Candolim, Goa, that plays jingles of Indian advertising films, making all the patrons participate wholeheartedly at the top of their voices!

And T-Series, the Indian record label/film production company, is the owner of the second-most subscribed YouTube channel on Earth … at 303 million (September 2025)![17]

All because of their unparalleled collection of songs!

While these peculiarities present new challenges to business and brand owners, across the world, as the boundaries between businesses and their stakeholders crumble, the one virtue that wins over all others is authenticity. However, enticing your stand on issues like sustainability, purpose, diversity, equality and inclusiveness, the online universe is quick to punish the gap between claim and action.

The most famous brand living up to its claim is Patagonia. The owner Yvon Chouinard and his family transferred their ownership of Patagonia, valued at about $3 billion, to a specially designed trust and a nonprofit organization. For forty-nine years he has been espousing that the most important stakeholder is the earth, and all businesses must finally contribute to its health. And now he has proven his commitment in a manner unheard of in the world of business.

In India, the most inspiring businesses are those that display real time metrics. The Parle Agro web site says, 'All PET bottles produced by us including our paper-based packaging material are 100 per cent recyclable.' The Marico web site has numbers that measure water consumption, green manufacturing, social impact. Ditto with ITC, pioneer of the Triple Bottomline reporting in India since 2004.

On the other hand, the commonest form of gap between claim and performance is in digital advertising. ASCI (Advertising Standards Council of India) says that 94 per cent of all misleading ads that they receive complaints about are now digital ads.[18]

The term 'radical transparency' (invented by Ray Dalio of Bridgewater) was embraced by the brand Everlane in 2010.

Its website revealed its pricing markups, its clothing suppliers, its ecological footprint.

It became the darling of Hollywood stars and investors among San Francisco's liberal elite—until July 2020, when *The New York Times* broke the story of employees complaining about anti-Black behaviour, union busting and, most damning of all, fake transparency.[19]

As Luke Smitham, a sustainability expert at Kumi Consulting in London, said, 'They do some good work, but I wouldn't describe it as radical. The most radical thing about Everlane is the marketing.'[20]

In the short term, when the audiences are not aware of the gaps, the businesses thrive. Over time, the misleading brands die.

The dominant nudge in India for diversity and inclusion, beyond technology, beyond laws, beyond regulatory bodies, is likely to be the 'unheard voices' of the non-English speaking consumers.

As one of the greatest physicists, Freeman Dyson said, 'In the last five hundred years, we have had six major concept driven scientific revolutions ... and there have been about twenty tool-driven revolutions.'

That tool in India is the adoption of Indian languages by the Internet: it is the new freedom since 1947.

Every voice can now be heard. Consumers have become influencers bigger than film stars and politicians and sport heroes. They will force businesses to decrease the gap between promise and delivery, between exclusion and inclusion, between diversity and monoculturalism.

Which in the end brings us to the biggest discontinuity not just businesses but we all experienced: the COVID-19 pandemic.

Suddenly, the interconnectedness of all of us on Earth is no longer a concept, it is an experienced reality. What happens in a small market in Wuhan, China, affects all but four nations out of the 193, as recognized by the UN.

The 'noosphere' now is proven physically and both business owners and individuals have to make the right decisions together towards that one great stakeholder: our planet.

There really is no choice.

It's co-existence or no existence.

PS: The greatest discontinuity is around the corner: Artificial intelligence. Its implications are so wide-ranging and transformative that the subject will need a much longer discourse, but here is a glimpse!

Ray Kurzweil, the scientist seer, predicted PCs that would fit into pockets by 2009 (iPhone in 2007); he predicted the cloud; Siri, drones, streaming movies ... His prediction for 2029, just four years hence, is this: '2029 is the consistent date I have predicted for when an AI will pass a valid Turing test and therefore achieve human levels of intelligence.'

So imagine this in 2029.

Your health adviser asks you to wear an AI-powered ('Think Humane' AI pin) sensor under your skin to keep track of all your health markers.

The sensor communicates with your fridge, your phone and your AC (think Google Nest) through the Internet of Things (IoT).

Your fridge has run out of the apple-cranberry-ginger juice deemed vital to your health by your AI adviser.

You have fed strict carbon-footprint guidelines into the dashboard of your smart sensor. Your phone has access to the 'field-to-glass' production journeys of various brands of apple-cranberry-ginger juice.

Your phone scans products across brands online, pulling information commonly found on the back of the pack.

Together, these intelligent machines analyse calories, carbon footprint, fibre content, purity and provenance—and place the order for you

Yes, the AI-driven discontinuity for brands and businesses will be real and all-encompassing. It will overshadow everything else. It will be the best of times; it will be the worst of times.

23

Behavioural Tools to Reshape Social and Market Norms

SUTAPA BANERJEE

THE FACT THAT TECHNOLOGIES LIKE AI and social media are double-edged swords, meaning they hold immense potential for both good and harm, is no surprise. But the examples in this section of how it plays out contextually in India are telling.

AI: The good and the bad

The Good

Some key takeaways from the very insightful first chapter in this section include the value of AI in diagnostic accuracy in healthcare in remote areas, in catering to the needs of the disabled, in efficient access to e-government services and more. The future potential of these and many more such initiatives could be mind-boggling. AI, with its ability to cater to the linguistic diversity of India, may well be one of the biggest tools of inclusion by democratizing the digital landscape.

The Bad

On the other hand, legal suits and huge penalties imposed on some of the largest entities in this area bear evidence of the disproportionately large impact errors and biases from AI and machines have, making the case for checks and balances both critical and urgent. Safeguards are not only necessary but need to be embedded early in the development of AI. The European Union's AI Act in this respect is significant. But regulations in a large heterogenous country like India, where the potential for both use and abuse is enormous, will need to tread the fine line of preventing harm without throttling innovation. What may help is a collaborative committee coming together to oversee the approach comprising as the first chapter aptly puts it, 'ethicists, sociologists, technologists and users' and, if I may add, behavioural science practitioners.

Diversity

My essay 'Bringing Threads Together Using Evidence-Based Tools' highlights the role of the board chair in creating cohesion while ensuring diversity of views, including the gender diversity mandated by the EU's Women on Boards legislation. I will delve here into other aspects of diversity that the corporate sector should put to use.

Hidden 'bonus': Cognitive diversity

The literature on diversity is replete with research on the correlation of cognitive diversity with innovative thinking and robust decision making. The different mental models, frameworks, assumptions and problem-solving abilities that a set of cognitively diverse people collectively bring to the table help create the diversity 'bonus' as it were. Yet banks tend to appoint retired senior bankers as directors and FMCG company boards look for directors with consumer marketing experience. Age diversity too is shunned due to misplaced notions of 'fit' and the tendency to equate experience with skills.

Fostering cognitive diversity

It's worth noting that simply bringing on board cognitively diverse people does not suffice. 'Conformity bias' is deeply wired in our brains as part of the evolutionary design. The use of evidence-based tools and techniques that allow different ways of thinking to be expressed need to be practiced. 'Premortem', thinking the opposite' and 'perspective taking' are only some among the many design interventions that may help legitimize expression of dissent much-needed to make the decision process robust at board and senior leadership levels. This whole area of behavioural insights-led thinking and interventions has started to become mainstream in the West but is barely known in corporate India.

Lack of risk-taking

As pointed out in one of the essays, television and commercial cinema in India, barring a few exceptions, largely continue with hackneyed formulaic plots perpetuating the existing stereotypes. Recent initiatives like the 'inclusion policy playbook' of Amazon Prime and Netflix, with 49 per cent women employees, partnering with the UN for equality are among the handful of companies trying to spearhead change. OTT platforms provide edgier content, and 'Independent cinema' needs to be supported for its role in injecting new thinking, creativity and challenging norms, but the fact remains that both cater to an infinitesimally small segment of the population.

Role of mainstream cinema, television and celebrities

To make a dent in existing norms and stereotypes, it is mainstream cinema and television watched by millions that need to play the central role. Celebrities from the world of entertainment and sports sometimes wield disproportionate power when it comes to influencing masses. It is heartening to see it being used to create a perceptual shift regarding for instance, menstruation. Board committees discussing CSR initiatives about providing sanitary napkins to girls in villages is progress considering just a few years ago, in one of the most reputed co-ed schools in Mumbai catering to the upper middle class, girls were actually taught how to carefully conceal sanitary napkins they took to the washroom so the boys wouldn't see! Celebrities and mainstream media can play a crucial role in reshaping many such norms.

Stereotypes and memes: Perpetuation of biases

As I highlight in my essay, research in neuroscience has shown that risk-taking jobs, like the derivative desks in banks, need to hire more women, as their presence improves the quality of risk taking. Sadly, it is precisely in these areas that the number of women, even in the Western countries, is abysmal due to the deeply entrenched inaccurate stereotype of men being decisive risk-takers. Breaking stereotypes and celebrating it across media is key to countering the pernicious effects that memes like 'Men are from Mars and Women from Venus' have helped reinforce and perpetuate over the years.

In this regard it is interesting to note that when women in the armed forces offered themselves for the 'command' and 'combat' forces, it took the Supreme Court's intervention to overrule the objections raised by the government and chief of army. They felt that soldiers from traditional households may be unwilling to accept female officers in command. Precisely the reason for the government and chief of army to have extended full support as it was the perfect opportunity to reshape a deep-set social norm.[1]

Here's what may help. 'Women taking on symbolically powerful roles—army, police, fighter pilots, CEOs and men taking on jobs as nurses, airline stewards, primary school teachers and the sharing of domestic responsibilities and childcare both need to be highlighted in media. The numbers in both categories are low not due to natural i.e., biological reasons as mistakenly assumed by many but as a fall-out of the definitions masculine and feminine that have got deeply rooted in culture over the years'.[2]

The green shoots of hope

Women excelling in sports supported and sponsored by businesses—especially those traditionally associated with men, such as wrestling, boxing and weightlifting—have far-reaching multiplier benefits. The very successful launch of the Women's Premier League in a country where cricket tops the popularity roster like no other has had a similar impact, not dissimilar to the evidence found in villages in West Bengal in the early 1990s on introduction of the reservation for women in Panchayati Raj amendments.[3]

Here too the economic rewards may induce similar behaviour change in parents and the community. In addition, their success in winning the country laurels and medals in prestigious international events and popularity as cricket stars amplified by mass and social media can help shift perception and stereotypes like no other. It can help break the stranglehold of objectifying women as scantily clad sexualized cheerleaders or the demure self-sacrificing wife and mother stereotype. If more and more businesses lured by television viewership ratings and the growing popularity of sportswomen stepped in to nurture and support female sporting talent images of strong, fit, powerful women may take root in popular imagination replacing existing stereotypes.

PART V
The Outcome

24

Towards a New Playbook

SUTAPA BANERJEE

THIS BOOK BEGAN FOR ME as an interesting experiment with three expected outcomes.

First: an interesting collection of chapters

A set of perspectives on three complex problems, shared by practitioners and domain experts, makes for interesting reading, both as standalone pieces and as a set of diverse views on a subject. The chosen areas are complex, significantly impacted (both positively and negatively) by businesses, and ones where I also have a perspective.

Second: insights from diverse perspectives on a complex problem

Do any new insights emerge from bringing together these varied perspectives on a theme? My essays at the end of sections 2, 3 and 4 encapsulate these findings.

Third: cross-domain applications

Does anything surface, something that may not be self-evident or known widely, when all three subjects are brought together under the umbrella of one book? Are there connections, insights or successes in a particular domain that can be applied to another?

This chapter addresses the third outcome. And indeed a number of key insights worthy of discussion and consideration emerge.

1. Make it central to business strategy

Be it sustainability or inclusion, success lies in making it central to strategy and including it in the key performance indicators (KPIs) of the top team rather than treating it as a peripheral side agenda. A striking example from one chapter describes an investor who tied the bonus payment of an investee company's CEO to hiring female loan officers in the Middle East, where the talent availability was low. This drove the adoption of a successful, out-of-the-box approach.

Another case involved a global BPO company that saw clear business benefits in hiring people with disabilities, stemming from the belief that those who have had to solve problems all their lives would bring the same problem-solving mindset and resourcefulness to the workplace. The company made this a key part of its strategic agenda, setting measurable goals that met with great success.

Similarly, an Internet food marketplace innovated by turning wheelchairs into 'road-worthy electric vehicles', enabling wheelchair users to become delivery partners, demonstrating once again the power of making inclusion part of the strategic agenda.

2. Reshaping norms and breaking stereotypes using evidence-based research

The pernicious effects of social norms and stereotypes were highlighted in my own chapter in Section 4 and in my essays at the end of both Sections 2 and 3. While the far-reaching benefits of changing social norms and stereotypes may be appreciated by some, what is barely known, let alone used, is the evidence-based research showing that behavioural insights, when used judiciously with legislation and/or incentives, can be a potent tool to hasten change in cultural norms.

In my *Economic Times* article,[1] I referenced empirical studies conducted in India:

1. In villages where, over three years, recruitment services for BPOs were provided by women, not only did female employment increase, but girls in those villages saw greater improvements in health and were more likely to be in school.
2. In West Bengal, villagers who initially opposed voting for women when quotas were introduced (as part of the Panchayati Raj amendments in the early 1990s) overcame their long-standing bias after being exposed to two female chiefs. They subsequently rated men and women leaders equally. The simple insight here is that just seeing women in power 'normalized' it, reshaping a social norm one would have expected to take decades to change.

In the same article[2] (also discussed in my 'Behavioural Tools to Reshape Social and Market Norms' section in Chapter 23), I expressed disappointment that when women offered themselves for command and combat positions, it took the Supreme Court's intervention to make it a reality, when the army should have supported it for the very reasons it opposed it.

As I write today, however, I'm encouraged by a news report on rural women being trained to be become 'drone didis'—a pioneering initiative of IFFCO backed by the government.[3]

This programme trains women to remotely operate heavy-duty fertilizer-spraying drones for farmland cultivation. The benefits go well beyond economic gains for rural women. As IFFCO's marketing director aptly put it, it's about 'not just employment but empowerment' for women who, due to 'deep-rooted patriarchal attitudes', have been homebound. Many more such initiatives are needed to put women in the driver's seat (literally!) rather than leaving them as passive beneficiaries—and businesses need to step in to initiate and support them.

The WPL, now in its second year as I write this, has benefits that extend well beyond sports and monetary gains. As I mentioned in the 'Bringing Threads Together Using Evidence-based Tools' chapter in Section 3, apart from cricket being the crowd-puller that it is in India, substantial television viewership makes it a viable business opportunity, attracting significant advertising spend. In line with the WPL, advertising content must evolve in its portrayal of women. Not only is the apparel industry now focusing on strong, fit women in sporting attire, but other businesses are also cashing in on this lucrative opportunity and are likely to portray women in ways that could go a long way in changing existing stereotypes.

Other simple ways for businesses to break stereotypes and reshape social norms worth considering include:

1. Orienting corporate social responsibility (CSR) initiatives towards the upliftment of girls and women in ways that break stereotypes and reshape social norms. For example, in skilling programmes, the focus for women—especially younger women—could be on non-traditional jobs such as carpentry, electrical work, plumbing, healthcare roles, farming, driving tractors, three-wheelers and taxis.

Likewise, encouraging counter-stereotypical roles for men, such as pickle-making or stitching uniforms, can help remove deep-rooted notions of what constitutes 'men's work' and 'women's work'.

2. When it comes to hiring women, organizations need to intentionally focus on P&L roles—business heads, sales and roles in risk—to reduce the stark 'occupational bias' evident in corporate workspaces across sectors. These are 'hard', decisive roles historically dominated by men due to implicit biases, even when empirical evidence shows women to be equally proficient, or better (see my article 'Men and Money' in Section 4).
3. Prestigious corporate awards such as 'Best CEO of the Year', 'Best Company of the Year', and other categories given annually with much fanfare by media houses generate phenomenal visibility and publicity, with leading industrialists, CEOs, key ministers and policymakers in attendance. Just as sustainability and inclusion must be made part of a company's strategic agenda to succeed, they should also be integral to the selection criteria for these awards—particularly the most coveted categories. If net sales, net profit, ROE and market capitalization are the current benchmarks for selecting 'Best Company of the Year', then sustainability and diversity must feature as equally important criteria. Incorporating these into award frameworks, and stating it upfront, can powerfully 'nudge' businesses in the right direction. It is an opportunity missed when environmental, social and governance (ESG) remains a stand-alone category, relegated to the periphery as it is today.

3. Multi-stakeholder collaboration and getting the stakeholders right

That multi-stakeholder collaboration is necessary to find solutions for complex problems is widely known. What may not be is the kind of expertise required. For pioneering initiatives or innovative projects, it is imperative to deploy the available evidence-based research, contextualize it through pilots that gather data at every stage and then replicate and scale carefully, using both the learnings and research data. Partnering with reputed research institutions is key to the success of such collaborations.

The striking example in the 'What Works, What Doesn't' chapter of Section 2 highlights the pioneering Emissions Trading Scheme (ETS), cited internationally as an excellent example of evidence-based policymaking. Piloted in Surat in 2019, it is the world's first pollution market for particulate matter, creating a win-win by reducing costs for industries while also cutting pollution emissions. Using the learnings from the Surat pilot, the scheme was launched in Ahmedabad in 2023. While every stakeholder—including the regulator, the Gujarat government and private industries—deserves kudos for coming together, the success of this pioneering initiative also underscores the importance of quality research partners, in this case Energy Policy Institute at the University of Chicago (EPIC) and J-PAL South Asia.

In sectors where the pace of change is rapid having an outsize impact both immediate and longer term on society, as in high-tech spaces like AI, the committee should comprise not just policymakers, tech businesses and industry bodies, but also, as the chapter on AI biases in Section 4 suggests, 'ethicists, sociologists, technologists and end-users' and (as I would add) behavioural sciences practitioners. The wisdom lies in the sheer breadth of diversity and interdisciplinarity suggested, and in recognizing why it is critical.

Also featured in one of the chapters in Section 2, and reiterated in my essay for the same section, is the high-tech domain of space data analytics. Here, the author notes a 'crying need for policymakers, climate scientists, remote sensing analysts, data scientists and software engineers' and (as I would add) end-users, including potential business users, to come together to create a conducive ecosystem of policies, incentives and interdisciplinary learning formats and curriculum design. This is essential to action high-impact societal use cases such as adaptation to climate change and conservation of biodiversity.

4. Observe, test, pilot, measure, learn and use the learnings

It is intriguing to note, including in this book, that several highly successful businesses began with founders simply observing the behaviour of people around them. Behavioural sciences and behavioural economics similarly emerged from systematic observation of human behaviour in varied contexts. While the practical applications of these disciplines have become mainstream internationally—through behavioural insights units informing public policy in many countries—in India they remain largely unfamiliar within business and policymaking circles.

Since social science research is not an exact science like the physical sciences, and context plays a key role, it is imperative to rely on empirical evidence to run pilots, gather data at all stages and apply the learnings to scale and replicate within organizations. Policies and codes of conduct alone are rarely sufficient to change behaviour in organizations or society. As mentioned in my essay at the end of Section 3, drawing on my article published in *The Economic Times*, examples such as paternity leave and the role of 'norm entrepreneurs' show how norms can shift.

Other measures suggested in the book and encapsulated in my chapters for each section may also help spark thinking in this regard. Since both empirical evidence and its optimal application in specific contexts have remained largely within the silo of academia, it may make sense to use behavioural science practitioners (not pop psychologists) to delve deeper into it. As I have cited repeatedly, the use of behavioural insights and interventions—sometimes alone, sometimes in conjunction with legislation and incentives—can hasten change in norms and expectations. While by no means a silver bullet, its role has been deliberately reiterated, as it has been used far too rarely in India.

5. The longer-term view and how to make it happen

As is apparent, the book suggests approaches that may entail businesses taking a longer-term view, something that may run counter to the quarter-on-quarter results pressure from shareholders with shorter-term interests. Apart from enlightened self-interest (unlikely to be universal), the measures already in place and those suggested in this book, one possible way to bridge this gap could be to link voting rights not only to the volume of shares held but also to the duration of the investment. While this idea raises several issues worth debating, it merits further exploration. It was, in fact, elaborated in a *Harvard Business Review* article as far back as 2011.[4]

Finally, it would have been foolhardy to be prescriptive in a book dealing with such complex problems. Instead, the aim has been to offer examples, best practices and a diverse set of perspectives to suggest ways of thinking and approaches that may have a higher likelihood of success in both understanding and finding paths to resolve complex societal problems and to 'nudge' businesses in that direction.

Notes

The Experiment

1. Nudges constitute one amongst several practical tools that behavioural insights provide. It gained popularity with Richard Thaler (winner of the Nobel Prize in Economics in 2017) and Cass Sunstein's book titled *Nudge*, first published in 2008.

2. Sustainability and Inclusion: An Economist's View

1. Sustainability and Inclusion: An Economist's Perspective
2. *Composite Water Management Index*, Niti Aayog, June 2018, p. 27, https://www.niti.gov.in/sites/default/files/2023-03/CompositeWaterManagementIndex-CWMI.pdf, accessed 5 October 2025.
3. *Global Gender Gap Report 2025*, *World Economic Forum*, June 2025, p. 33, https://reports.weforum.org/docs/WEF_GGGR _2025.pdf, accessed 5 October 2025.
4. Ibid.
5. 'Analysis: Which countries are historically responsible for climate change?', Carbon Brief, 5 October 2021, https://www.carbonbrief.org/analysis-which-countries-are-historically-responsible-for-climate-change/, accessed 1 November 2025.

6. Ibid.
7. Priyadarshi R. Shukla et al, ed., *Climate Change 2022: Mitigation of Climate Change (Working Group III Contribution to the Sixth Assessment Report)*, Intergovernmental Panel on Climate Change (IPCC), April 2023, https://www.ipcc.ch/report/ar6/wg3/downloads/report/IPCC_AR6_WGIII_FullReport.pdf, accessed 28 October 2025.
8. Tensie Whelan, Ulrich Atz and Casey Clark, CFA, 'ESG and Financial Performance: Uncovering the Relationship by Aggregating Evidence from 1,000 Plus Studies Published between 2015–2020', NYU Stern: Centre for Sustainable Business, 2021. https://www.stern.nyu.edu/sites/default/files/assets/documents/NYU-RAM_ESG-Paper_2021.pdf, accessed 5 September 2025.
9. 'Profits with Purpose: How Organizing for Sustainability can Benefit the Bottom Line', McKinsey Sustainability, 1 July 2014, https://www.mckinsey.com/capabilities/sustainability/our-insights/profits-with-purpose-how-organizing-for-sustainability-can-benefit-the-bottom-line#/, accessed 12 March 2024.

3. From Compliance to Leadership: A Climate Educator's View

1. Simran Arora, '7 decades of wellness: How life expectancy increased in India the last 75 years', *Times Now*,11 August 2022, https://www.timesnownews.com/health/7-decades-of-wellness-how-life-expectancy-increased-in-india-the-last-75-years-article-93489497, accessed 18 September 2023.
2. Health Data overview for Republic of India, *World Health Organisation*, https://data.who.int/countries/356, accessed 18 September 2023.
3. 'One of The Youngest Populations in the World – India's Most Valuable Asset', *Economic Diplomacy Division*, 13 June 2021, https://indbiz.gov.in/one-of-the-youngest-populations-in-the-world-indias-most-valuable-asset/, accessed 18 September 2023.
4. Manoj Kumar, 'One-tenth of India's population escaped poverty in 5 years - government report', *Reuters*, 17 July 2023, https://www.reuters.com/world/india/one-tenth-indias-population-escaped-

poverty-5-years-government-report-2023-07-17/, accessed 18 September 2023.

5. Ministry of Jal Shakti, '1st All India Annual State Ministers Conference On Water To Deliberate Water Vision@2047', *Press Information Bureau,* Press Release ID: 1888514, 4 January 2023, https://pib.gov.in/PressReleseDetail.aspx?PRID=1888514, accessed 18 September 2023.
6. E. Somanathan, 'The Environment and Climate Change' in Abhijit Banerjee et al., *What the Economy Needs Now*, Juggernaut Books, New Delhi, 2019, p. 211.
7. Michael Braungart and William McDonough, *Cradle to Cradle: Remaking the Way We Make Things,* North Point Press, New York, 2002.
8. There is no concept of waste in nature, everything gets recycled, this concept is referred to as circularity. Circular economy refers to a system that reuses byproducts and materials in the production processes rather than discarding them as waste.
9. Speeches and statements, Ministry of External Affairs, Government of India, https://www.mea.gov.in/Speeches-Statements.htm?50/Speeches__amp;_Statements, accessed 18 September 2023.
10. Rupali Handa, 'What India's net-zero announcement means for businesses', *India Matters,* Observer Research Foundation, 8 March 2021,https://www.orfonline.org/expert-speak/what-indias-net-zero-announcement-means-for-businesses/#:~:text=Net%2Dzero%20targets%20must%20be,support%20for%20SME%20partners%20and, accessed 18 September 2023.
11. Indira Gandhi's Speech at the Stockholm Conference in 1972, *Plenary Session of United Nations Conference on Human Environment*, Stockholm, 14 June 1972, http://lasulawsenvironmental.blogspot.com/2012/07/indira-gandhis-speech-at-stockholm.html, accessed 18 September 2023.
12. Principle 16 of the Rio Declaration on Environment and Development states that 'National authorities should endeavour to promote the internalization of environmental costs and the use of economic instruments, taking into account the approach that the polluter should, in principle, bear the cost of pollution, with due regard to the public interest and without distorting international trade and investment.'

United Nations. (1992). *Report of the United Nations Conference on Environment and Development*. In A/CONF.151/26 (Vol. I).

13. Principle 7 of the Rio Declaration on Environment and Development states that 'States shall cooperate in a spirit of global partnership to conserve, protect and restore the health and integrity of the Earth's ecosystem. In view of the different contributions to global environmental degradation, States have common but differentiated responsibilities. The developed countries acknowledge the responsibility that they bear in the international pursuit of sustainable development in view of the pressures their societies place on the global environment and of the technologies and financial resources they command.'
United Nations. (1992). Ibid.
14. About Major Groups and other stakeholders: Sustainable Development Knowledge Platform. (n.d.). https://sustainabledevelopment.un.org/aboutmajorgroups.html
15. United Nations, *The Future We Want: Outcome Document of the* Rio+20 United Nations Conference on Sustainable Development, Rio de Janeiro, Brazil, 20-22 June 2012, https://sustainabledevelopment.un.org/content/documents/733FutureWeWant.pdf, accessed 18 September 2023.
16. Ibid.
17. *Pravinbhai Jashbhai Patel vs State of Gujarat*, August 1995, https://indiankanoon.org/doc/783573/, accessed 18 September 2023.
18. 'Sustainability Targets Of Arvind – A Talk With Abhishek Bansal', *Denim and Jeans,* 31 January 2019, https://www.denimsandjeans.com/environment/sustainability-targets-of-arvind-a-talk-with-abhishek-bansal/, accessed 18 September 2023.
19. 'We Help Businesses Weave Environment Sustainability Into Business Profitability', *Envisol,* https://www.arvindenvisol.com, accessed 18 September 2023.
20. JSW Times of India & Centre for Environment Education. (2016). *Earth Care Awards 2016: Awards for Excellence in Climate Change Mitigation and Adaptation, 7th Edition*. Centre for Environment Education.
21. Reghu Balakrishnan, 'Mahindra's renewables biz set to launch Rs 3,500-crore InvIT', *Economic Times,* 16 March 2023,

https://economictimes.indiatimes.com/industry/renewables/mahindras-renewables-biz-set-to-launch-rs-3500-crore-invit/articleshow/98674721.cms, accessed 20 September 2023.

22. 'Green Supply Chain', Godrej, https://www.godrejcp.com/sustainability/green-supply-chain, accessed 20 September 2023.
23. Rakteem Katakey, 'ONGC Gets Credits for Mumbai High Waste Heat Project', *Bloomberg,* 5 April 2010, https://www.bloomberg.com/news/articles/2010-04-05/ongc-gets-emission-credits-for-waste-heat-recovery-project-at-mumbai-high#xj4y7vzkg, accessed 20 September 2023.
24. ICRA, *Report on TATA Sponge Iron Limited*, ICRA, 5 January 2018, https://www.icra.in/Rationale/ShowRationaleReport?Id=66245#:~:text=The%20company%20has%20two%20power%20plants%20based%20on,ensure%20availability%20of%20power%20at%20a%20low%20cost, accessed 20 September 2023.
25. ITC, 'Reimagining Future Towards the NEXT Horizon', *Sustainability and Integrated Report 2022*, https://www.itcportal.com/sustainability/sustainability-integrated-report-2022/ITC-Sustainability-Integrated-Report-2022.pdf, accessed 20 September 2023.
26. 'Mother Dairy Reaffirms Its Commitment Towards Environment Safety', Mother Dairy, https://www.motherdairy.com/pdf/PR/2021/2021-06-04.pdf, accessed 20 September 2023.
27. Hindustan Unilever Limited, *Our commitment to a waste-free future,* https://www.hul.co.in/planet-and-society/waste-free-world, accessed 20 September 2023.
28. 'Environment and Climate', Proctor & Gamble, https://www.pginvestor.com/esg/environmental/climate/default.aspx, accessed 20 September 2023.
29. 'Reliance planted mangroves on 875 acres in FY 2020-21, Read in depth story', *IndiaCSR,* 25 July 2021, https://indiacsr.in/reliance-planted-mangroves-on-875-acres-in-fy-2020-21-read-in-depth-story/, accessed 20 September 2023.
30. 'RIL to develop mangrove forest at Marine National Park', *The Times of India,* 7 July 2023, https://timesofindia.indiatimes.com/city/ahmedabad/ril-to-develop-mangrove-forest-at-marine-national-park/articleshow/101558852.cms, accessed 20 September 2023.

31. 'Godrej & Boyce announces "The India Mangroves Coalition" with CII and WWF India on International Day for the Conservation of the Mangrove Ecosystem', Godrej, https://www.godrejenterprises.com/newsroom/press-releases/press-release-the-indian-mangroves-coalition, accessed 20 September 2023.
32. Mangrove Coalition launched to strengthen India's coastal cities from. (n.d.). https://www.wwfindia.org/?27802/Mangrove-Coalition-launched-to-strengthen-Indias-coastal-cities-from-climate-risks, accessed 3 December 2025.
33. HCL Foundation, https://www.hclfoundation.org/hcl-harit, accessed 20 September 2023.
34. 'Introducing Wipro Impact, our sustainability services portfolio to help clients measure, reduce and create value', *Wipro,* https://www.wipro.com/sustainability/#:~:text=New%20York%2C%20USA%20and%20Bangalore,line%20with%20the%20objective%20of, accessed 20 September 2023.
35. 'Net zero by 2050', Birla Carbon, https://www.birlacarbon.com/net-zero-by-2050/, accessed 20 September 2023.
36. 'Climate Change', JSW, https://www.jsw.in/groups/sustainability-framework-measuring-success-climate-change#:~:text=As%20India's%20leading%20steel%20producer,tCO2%2Ftcs%20by%202030, accessed 20 September 2023.
37. 'UltraTech commits to Net Zero Concrete Roadmap announced by GCCA', UltraTech Cement, https://www.ultratechcement.com/corporate/media/press-releases/ultratech-commits-to-net-zero-concrete-roadmap-announced-by-gcca, accessed 20 September 2023.
38. 'Adani Transmission To Become Net Zero By 2050', Adani Energy Solutions, https://www.adanitransmission.com/newsroom/media-releases/adani-transmission-to-become-net-zero-by-2050, accessed 20 September 2023.
39. 'Bridging Sustainability and Growth', Reliance India Limited, https://www.ril.com/ar2020-21/natural-capital.html, accessed 20 September 2023.
40. 'Environmentally Friendly And Sustainable', Dalmia Cement, https://www.dalmiacement.com/esg/environment, accessed 20 September 2023.

41. 'Environment and Climate', P&G, https://www.pginvestor.com/esg/environmental/climate/default.aspx, accessed 20 September 2023.
42. 'Mahindra Lifespaces launches India's first net zero energy homes in Bengaluru', Mahindra, Press Release, 4 December 2022, https://www.mahindra.com/news-room/press-release/en/mahindra-lifespaces-launches-indias-first-net-zero-energy-homes-in-bengaluru, accessed 20 September 2023.
43. 'Dabur Digital Annual Report – 2021-22', Dabur, https://www.dabur.com/digital-annual-report-2021-22/natural-capital.html,accessed 20 September 2023.
44. 'Tata Steel Joins UN initiative "LeadIT" to Drive Net-Zero Emissions in Heavy Industry', Tata Steel, Press Release, 12 July 2023, https://www.tatasteel.com/media/newsroom/press-releases/india/2023/tata-steel-joins-un-initiative-leadit-to-drive-net-zero-emissions-in-heavy-industry/#:~:text=Tata%20Steel%20has%20set%20a,enhancing%20its%20own%20climate%20initiatives, accessed 20 September 2023.
45. 'IndianOil to go Net Zero by 2046', Indian Oil, https://iocl.com/pages/NetZeroone, accessed 20 September 2023.
46. '*ESG is an opportunity: ESG Report 2022-23*', https://www.infosys.com/sustainability/documents/infosys-esg-report-2022-23.pdf, accessed 20 September 2023.
47. CDP, https://www.cdp.net/en/, accessed 20 September 2023.
48. GRI, 2022.
49. Nidhi Singal, 'India Inc.'s Big Bet on Net Zero', *Business Today,* 10 July 2022, https://www.businesstoday.in/magazine/corporate/story/india-incs-big-bet-on-net-zero-340471-2022-07-06, accessed 20 September 2023.
50. Neha Chaliwala, 'Many India Inc majors may be Net-Zero by 2050', *The Economic Times,* 17 October 2022, https://economictimes.indiatimes.com/industry/renewables/many-india-inc-majors-may-be-net-zero-by-2050/articleshow/94902337.cms, accessed 20 September 2023.
51. 'India Will Require Investments worth over USD 10 Trillion to Achieve Net-Zero by 2070: CEEW-CEF', *CEEW,* Press Release, https://www.ceew.in/sites/default/files/CEEW-CEF-Press-Release-Investment-Sizing-Indias-2070-Net-Zero-Target.pdf, accessed 20 September 2023.

52. 'A Report of the High-Level Policy Commission on Getting Asia to Net Zero, Asia Society Policy Institute, https://asiasociety.org/sites/default/files/2022-09/ASPI_Getting%20India%20to%20Net%20Zero_Report.pdf, accessed 20 September 2023.
53. Piyush Shukla, 'Achieving 2070 Net-Zero Target Could Boost India's GDP', *Current Affairs Adda 247,* 27 August 2022, https://currentaffairs.adda247.com/achieving-2070-net-zero-target-could-boost-indias-growth/, accessed 20 September 2023.
54. 'A Report of the High-Level Policy Commission on Getting Asia to Net Zero, Asia Society Policy Institute, https://asiasociety.org/sites/default/files/2022-09/ASPI_Getting%20India%20to%20Net%20Zero_Report.pdf, accessed 20 September 2023.
55. India Infoline News Service, 2022
56. Bhawna Ahuja, Ananya Chakraborty, Vivek Venkataraman, 'Greening of MSMEs key in India's journey towards climate-resilience' *Down to Earth,* 22 March 2023, https://www.downtoearth.org.in/blog/climate-change/greening-of-msmes-key-in-india-s-journey-towards-climate-resilience-88404, accessed 20 September 2023.
57. CII, *Toolkit for MSMEs Nature-based Solutions and Controlling Air Pollution*, 2022, https://sustainabledevelopment.in/wp-content/uploads/2022/06/Toolkit-for-MSMEs-24-March-2022-1.pdf, accessed 20 September 2023.
58. Amar Munnolimath, Camilla Shearman, Dr Shilpi Kapur Bakshi, Mehar Kaur, Shweta Gautam, 'Fostering the Circular Economy: Role of MSMEs | Policy Landscape Paper India', *Policy Landscape Paper, SEED,* 1 September 2021, https://seed.uno/articles/reports/fostering-the-circular-economy-role-of-msmes-policy-landscape-paper-india, accessed 20 September 2023.
59. Matt McGrath and Mark Poynting, 'Climate change: July set to be world's warmest month on record', *BBC,* 27 July 2023, https://www.bbc.com/news/science-environment-66322608, accessed 20 September 2023.

4. The Chemicals Industry: A Business View

1. Ministry of Environment, Forest and Climate Change, Government of India, *India's Long-Term Low-Carbon Development Strategy*

2022, https://moef. gov. in/wp-content/uploads/2022/11/Indias-LT-LEDS-2. pdf

2. International Council of Chemical Association, *ICCA Responsible Care® Leadership Group (RCLG) Status Report 2021,* https://icca-chem. org/wp-content/uploads/2021/12/RCLG-2021-Status-Report-FINAL. pdf
3. Consultivo, *Trustea Impact Report August 2020,* https://trustea. org/uploads/publication/16714396741. pdf
4. John W. Phair, 'Green chemistry for sustainable cement production and use', *Green Chemistry,* Vol. 8, 2006, pp. 763-780, https://doi. org/10. 1039/B603997A
5. Albert Lin, 'Fixing Net Zero Leakage', *Wake Forest Law Review,* 20 September 2022, http://dx. doi. org/10. 2139/ssrn. 4225087
6. 'Global climate action from cities, regions and businesses: Impact of individual actors and cooperative initiatives on global and national emissions', NewClimate Institute, Data-Driven Lab, PBL, Deutsches Institut für Entwicklungspolitik (DIE), Blavatnik School of Government, University of Oxford, 2019, https://newclimate. org/sites/default/files/2021/06/NewClimate_GCC_June21_2. pdf
7. 'Outcomes of the United Nations Climate Action Summit (Summary Analysis)', Institute European Environmental Policy, 2019, https://www.un.org/en/climatechange/2019-climate-action-summit
8. Angel Hsu, Niklas Höhne, Takeshi Kuramochi, Virginia Vilariño and Benjamin K. Sovacoo, 'Beyond states: Harnessing sub-national actors for the deep decarbonisation of cities, regions, and businesses', Energy Research & Social Science, Vol. 70, 2020, https://doi. org/10.1016/j.erss.2020.101738
9. Haley Wiebel, Kevin Moss and Emily Neagle, 'From Pledges to Action: What's Next for COP26 Corporate Commitments', World Resources Institute, 22 November 2021, https://www. wri.org/insights/pledges-action-whats-next-cop26-corporate-commitments
10. Maha Faisal Alsayegh, Rashidah Abdul Rahman and Saeid Homayoun, 'Corporate Economic, Environmental, and Social Sustainability Performance Transformation through ESG Disclosure', *Sustainability,* Vol. 12, 2020, https://doi.org/10.3390/su12093910
11. Ellen Pei-yi Yu, Christine Qian Guo and Bac Van Luu, 'Environmental, social and governance transparency and firm value', *Business Strategy*

and the Environment, Vol. 27 (7), 2018, pp. 987-1004, https://doi.org/10.1002/bse.2047

12. D.V. Verneul, 'Candid climate efforts or empty promises? Analyzing NSA's voluntary commitments and efforts', unpublished MSc Thesis, Delft University of Technology, 2021, https://repository.tudelft.nl/record/uuid:12a972fc-5358-4c7e-a477-1bf3fb3a5da0
13. Venkata Mrudula Bhimavarapu, Shailesh Rastogi, Rajani Gupte, Geetanjali Pinto and Sudam Shingade, 'Does the Impact of Transparency and Disclosure on the Firm's Valuation Depend on the ESG?' *Journal of Risk and Financial Management*, Vol. 15 (9), 2022, https://doi.org/10.3390/jrfm15090410
14. Jason Potts, 'Sustainability in the Coffee Sector: Exploring Opportunities for International Cooperation—Assessment and Implementation', International Institute for Sustainable Development, 2003.
15. Steven Bernstein, Benjamin Cashore, 'Can non-state global governance be legitimate? An analytical framework', *Regulation & Governance*, Vol. 1 (4), 2007, pp. 347–71, https://doi.org/10.1111/j.1748-5991.2007.00021.x
16. Natalie J. Langford, 'The governance of social standards in emerging markets: an exploration of actors and interests shaping Trustea as a Southern multi-stakeholder initiative', *Geoforum*, Vol. 104, 2019, pp. 81-91, https://doi.org/10.1016/j.geoforum.2019.06.009
17. Pytsje Bakker, 'Do Smallholders Benefit from Group Certification? A Case Study on the Social and Economic Effects of Rainforest Alliance Group Certification on Small-Scale Tea Farmers in Misiones, Argentina', Unpublished MSc Thesis, Submitted to Wageningen University, 2014, https://edepot.wur.nl/308496
18. Joke Aerts, Divya Mudappa and T.R. Shankar Raman, 'Coffee, Conservation, and Rainforest Alliance Certification: Opportunities for Indian coffee', *Planters Chronicle*, Vol. 106 (12), 2010, pp. 15–26, https://www.ncf-india.org/education-and-public-engagement/306
19. Domenico Dentonia and H. Christopher Peterson, 'Multi-Stakeholder Sustainability Alliances in Agri-Food Chains: A Framework for Multi-Disciplinary Research', *International Food and Agribusiness Management Review*, Vol. 14 (5), 2011, pp. 83–108, https://www.ifama.org/resources/Documents/v14i5/Dentoni-Peterson.pdf

20. Commonland and United Nations Development Programme et al, '1000 landscapes for 1 billion people: Strategy for scaling sustainable landscape solutions for people and planet', March 2021, https://landscapes.global/wp-content/uploads/2021/04/1000L-strategy-for-scaling-sustainable-landscape-solutions-for-people-and-planet.pdf
21. Martina Vidovic, Neha Khanna and Michael Delgado, 'Third Party Certification and the Effectiveness of Voluntary Pollution Abatement Programs: Evidence from Responsible Care', Agricultural and Applied Economics Association, Annual Meeting, 2013, https://ideas.repec.org/p/ags/aaea13/150706.html
22. Peter Topalovic, 'The Challenges in Implementing Responsible Care', MSc Thesis, Submitted to McMaster University, 2007, https://www.eng.mcmaster.ca/sites/default/files/uploads/responsible_care.pdf
23. John Moffet, François Bregha and Mary Jane Middelkoop, *Responsible Care: A Case Study of a Voluntary Environmental Initiative*, 2015.
24. Terry F. Yosie, 'Responsible Care at 15 Years,' *Environmental Science and Technology*, Vol. 37 (21), 2003, https://doi.org/10.1021/es032631+
25. Lindsey A. Greene, 'Responsible Care Goes Online', *Environmental Health Perspectives*, Vol. 108, 2000, https://doi.org/10.1289/ehp.108-a448a

Endnotes

1. SAICM is a policy framework adopted in 2006 to promote the sound management of chemicals globally. Its goal is to minimize adverse impacts on human health and the environment by ensuring that chemicals are produced and used in ways that significantly reduce harm. The SAICM secretariat is hosted by the United Nations Environment Programme (UNEP).

5. Building Sustainably: A Cement Industry Perspective

1. IBEF, *Indian Cement Industry Analysis*, https://www.ibef.org/industry/cement-presentation
2. Global Cement and Concrete Association India, *Blended Cement-Green, Durable & Sustainable, 2022*, 13 April 2022, https://

gccassociation.org/wp-content/uploads/2022/04/Report_Blended-Cement-Green-Duratable-Sustainable_13Apr2022. pdf

3. International Energy Agency & World Business Council for Sustainable Development-Cement Sustainability Initiative, *Technology Roadmap: Low Carbon Transition in the Cement Industry*, https://www.wbcsd.org/contentwbc/download/4586/61682/1
4. World Business Council for Sustainable Development, *Low Carbon Technology Roadmap for the Indian Cement Sector: Status Review 2018*, https://docs.wbcsd.org/2018/11/WBCSD_CSI_India_Review.pdf
5. Christian Hoffmann, Michel Van Hoey and Benedikt Zeumer, 'Decarbonization challenge for steel', McKinsey & Company, 3 June 2020, https://www.mckinsey.com/industries/metals-and-mining/our-insights/decarbonization-challenge-for-steel
6. JSW Cement, *Environmental Product Declaration (EPD) of Average PSC of JSW Cement*, 2019, https://api. environdec. com/api/v1/EPDLibrary/Files/d20934da-2b0c-40e3-b029-4da5f1ad4d6e/Data
7. JSW Cement, *Environmental Product Declaration (EPD) of GGBS of JSW Cement*, 2019, https://api.environdec.com/api/v1/EPDLibrary/Files/eeed72e7-274a-47dd-8918-79a67427064a/Data
8. Department of Science and Technology, Government of India, *Carbon Capture, Utilisation and Storage (CCUS)*, https://dst.gov. in/carbon-capture-utilisation-and-storage-ccus
9. Yash Kashyap, 'Analysis: Costs and Impacts of Low-Carbon Technologies for Steel and Cement Sectors in India', *Climate Policy Initiative*, 5 December 2022, https://www. climatepolicyinitiative. org/report-summary-costs-and-impacts-of-low-carbon-technologies-for-steel-and-cement-sectors-in-india/
10. Cement Capacity: 554 MT (FY22), 'India Cement', Citigroup Global Markets India Equity Research Desk, 22 July 2022.
11. Cement Demand: 365 MT (FY22), 438 MT (FY25), 'Sector Update – Cement', Research Report by IDBI Capital Markets & Securities Equity Research Desk, 29 August 2022
12. '80 MT cement capacity addition in next 3 years, a ten year high', *CRISIL Ratings*, 28 July 2021, https://www.crisil.com/en/home/newsroom/press-releases/2021/07/80-mt-cement-capacity-addition-in-next-3-years-a-ten-year-high.html

13. Annual Report 21–22 of the Department for Promotion of Industry and Internal Trade, Ministry of Commerce and Industry, Government of India, https://commerce.gov.in/wp-content/uploads/2022/02/English-Annual-Report-2021-22-Department-of-Commerce.pdf
14. 'Experiences with alternative fuels', *Cemnet,* 12 June 2020, https://www.cemnet.com/News/story/169021/experiences-with-alternative-fuels. html

Endnotes

1. Leadership in Energy and Environmental Design by the US Green Building Council
2. Green Rating Integrated Habitat Assessment
3. Indian Green Building Council

7. Fuelling the Future: A Policy Perspective on Biofuel

1. 'How India could rise to the world's second biggest economy', *Goldman Sachs*, 6 July 2023, https://www.goldmansachs.com/intelligence/pages/how-india-could-rise-to-the-worlds-second-biggest-economy.html, accessed 22 September 2023.
2. 'Electricity Sector: Vital Stats', PRS Legislations, https://prsindia.org/policy/vital-stats/electricity-sector, accessed 22 September 2023.
3. *India Energy Outlook 2021*, Flagship Report, International Energy Agency, February 2021, https://www.iea.org/reports/india-energy-outlook-2021, accessed 22 September 2023.
4. Ibid.
5. 'Report of the Sub-Committee for the Assessment of Financial Requirements for Implementing India's Nationally Determined Contribution (NDC)', Department of Economic Affairs, Ministry of Finance, Government of India, New Delhi, June 2020, https://dea.gov.in/sites/default/files/Sub%20Committee%20Report%20Final.pdf, accessed 22 September 2023.
6. 'National Policy on Biofuels', Ministry of Petroleum and Natural Gas 2018, *The Gazette of India*, New Delhi, 2018, https://mopng.gov.in/files/uploads/NATIONAL_POLICY_ON_BIOFUELS-2018.pdf, accessed 22 September 2023.

7. Ibid.
8. Ibid.
9. First generation (1-G) biofuels are produced by traditional technologies using food sources as raw materials, including sugarcane, vegetable oils and animal fats. Second generation (2-G) biofuels are produced through biochemical reactions and use non-food crops or waste as raw materials. Third generation (3-G) biofuels use micro-organisms such as algae. Fourth generation (4-G) biofuels use genetically modified crops having larger biomass.
10. 'National Policy on Biofuels', *The Gazette of India*.
11. Sukalp Sharma, 'India's reliance on imported crude oil at record high of 87.3% in FY23', *Indian Express,* 25 April 2023, https://indianexpress.com/article/business/commodities/india-reliance-on-imported-crude-oil-at-record-high-of-87-3-in-fy23-8573996/, accessed 22 September 2023.
12. *India Energy Outlook 2021*.
13. 'Annual Report 2020-2021', Department of Agriculture, Cooperation & Farmer's Welfare, Ministry of Agriculture & Farmer's Welfare, Government of India, https://agricoop.gov.in/Documents/annual-report-2020-21.pdf, accessed 22 September 2023.
14. Young Ju Lee et al, 'Water-food-energy challenges in India: political economy of the sugar industry', *Environmental Research Letters,* IOP Publishing, 24 July 2020, https://iopscience.iop.org/article/10.1088/1748-9326/ab9925, accessed 22 September 2023.
15. P. Mookherjee, 'The Implications of India's Revised Roadmap for Biofuels: A Lifecycle Perspective', Observer Research Foundation, No. 526, 8 March 2022, https://policycommons.net/artifacts/2273619/the-implications-of-indias-revised-roadmap-for-biofuels/3033480/, accessed 22 September 2023.
16. Ibid.
17. 'Roadmap for Ethanol Blending in India 2020-25', Report of the Expert Committee, NITI Ayog; Ministry of Petroleum and Natural Gas, Government of India, New Delhi, 2021, https://mopng.gov.in/files/uploads/Ethanol_blending_in_India_(7).pdf), accessed 22 September 2023.
18. Ibid.
19. Ibid.

20. Mookherjee, 'The Implications of India's Revised Roadmap for Biofuels'.
21. 'Review of Progress in Production of Non-Conventional Fuels with specific reference to Bio-Fuels', Standing Committee Report Summary, PRS Legislative Research, 2021, https://prsindia.org/policy/report-summaries/review-of-progress-in-production-of-non-conventional-fuels-with-specific-reference-to-bio-fuels#:~:text=It%20noted%20that%20the%20target,litre%20-from%20grain%2Dbased%20distilleries, accessed 22 September 2023.
22. Mookherjee, 'The Implications of India's Revised Roadmap for Biofuels'.
23. 'Pradhan Mantri JI-VAN Yojana', Ministry of Petroleum and Natural Gas, Government of India, Press Information Bureau, 2022, https://pib.gov.in/PressReleasePage.aspx?PRID=1843441, accessed 22 September 2023.
24. 'National Policy on Biofuels', *The Gazette of India*.
25. 'Government amends export policy for biofuels', *The Economic Times*, 22 March 2023, https://economictimes.indiatimes.com/news/economy/foreign-trade/government-amends-export-policy-for-biofuels/articleshow/98921190.cms, accessed 26 September 2023.

8. Emerging Business Models for Environmental Change: The Catalysts

1. Ministry of Power, Government of India, 'Revised Policy for Biomass Utilisation for Power Generation through Co-firing of biomass in Coal based Power plants', No. 11/86/2017-Th. II, 8 October 2021, https://powermin.gov.in/sites/default/files/Revised_Biomass_Policy_dtd_08102021.pdf, accessed 11 September 2023.
2. Ministry of Petroleum and Natural Gas, Government of India, 'India's National Biofuels Policy 2018', *The Gazette of India*, 4 June 2018, https://mopng.gov.in/files/uploads/NATIONAL_POLICY_ON_BIOFUELS-2018.pdf, accessed 11 September 2023.
3. 'SATAT' scheme on Compressed Bio Gas (CBG) encourages entrepreneurs to set up CBG plants, produce & supply CBG to Oil Marketing Companies (OMCs) for sale as automotive & industrial fuels, https://satat.co.in/satat/#/.

4. Ministry of New and Renewable Energy, Government of India, 'Renewable Energy Policy for bioenergy Supply Chain', *Bio-Energy Schemes*, https://mnre. gov. in/bio-energy/schemes, accessed 11 September 2023.
5. Ministry of Environment, Forest and Climate Change, Government of India, 'Voluntary Green Credits Mechanism', https://moef.gov.in/wp-content/uploads/2023/06/Draft-GCP-Notification-Inviting-Comments-27062023.pdf, accessed 11 September 2023.
6. International Energy Agency, 'New report on biofuel policy in Brazil, India and the US presented to ministers from around the world as governments seek to step up co-operation', https://www.iea.org/news/iea-shares-recommendations-for-the-global-biofuel-alliance-at-g20-energy-transitions-ministerial-meeting, accessed 11 September 2023.

Endnotes

1. 'Global Space Budget – A Country level Analysis', *Space in Africa*, 10 March 2021, https://africanews.space/global-space-budgets-a-country-level-analysis/, accessed 18 September 2023.

9. What Works, What Doesn't

1. Ministry of Corporate Affairs, Government of India, *National Guidelines on Responsible Business Conduct*, https://www.mca.gov.in/Ministry/pdf/NationalGuildeline_15032019.pdf, accessed 24 January 2024.
2. Ministry of Corporate Affairs, Government of India, *Report of the Committee on Business Responsibility Reporting*, https://www.mca.gov.in/Ministry/pdf/BRR_11082020.pdf, accessed 24 January 2024.
3. *BRSR Core: New guidelines around assurance*, Deloitte, November 2023, https://www2.deloitte.com/content/dam/Deloitte/in/Documents/audit/in-audit-Business-Responsibility-and-Sustainability-Report-Core_10-11-2023.pdf, accessed 24 January 2024.
4. 'Major construction and cement players join forces with Xynteo to accelerate India's decarbonization efforts', *PR Newswire*, 23 August 2022, https://www.prnewswire.com/in/news-releases/

major-construction-and-cement-players-join-forces-with-xynteo-to-accelerate-india-s-decarbonization-efforts-807269299.html, accessed 24 January 2024.

5. Michael Greenstone quoted in 'World's First Particulate Pollution Market Reduced Pollution and Increased Industry Profits', University of Chicago, 15 April 2025, https://climate.uchicago.edu/news/worlds-first-particulate-pollution-market-reduced-pollution-and-increased-industry-profits/, accessed 20 June 2025.
6. 'Gujarat opens emissions market in Ahmedabad, building on collaboration with EGC', *Yale Economic Growth Center,* 5 September 2023, https://egc.yale.edu/news/emissions-trading-ahmedabad-india, accessed 24 January 2024.

10. Being a Good Ancestor

1. Jonas Salk, inventor of the polio vaccine, reflected on the moral responsibility of present generations to future ones, stating that our most significant duty is to be 'good ancestors'.
2. United Nations Population Fund (UNFPA), *World Population Dashboard* (2024), accessed November 3, 2025, https://www.unfpa.org/data/world-population-dashboard.
3. Sofia Bapna and Russell J. Funk, '*The Unintended Consequences of Maternity Leave Policy: Evidence from India's 2017 Maternity Benefit (Amendment) Act*," University of Minnesota, 2024, SSRN, https://papers.ssrn.com/sol3/papers.cfm?abstract_id=4973853

12.Show Me the Money: Corporate Motivation

1. The Equality pillar is about ensuring that women have the same opportunities as men to be hired, to be recognized and to advance. The Inclusion pillar focuses on creating an environment in which women are heard and valued, and the realities of their lives are considered and respected. The Representation pillar relates to achieving a 50/50 gender split in leadership, and across all functional areas and at all levels or job bands.
2. U.S. Department of Justice, *Investigation of the City of Minneapolis and the Minneapolis Police Department* (Washington, DC: Civil

Rights Division, June 2023), https://www.justice.gov/d9/2023-06/minneapolis_findings_report.pdf

'The Murder of George Floyd: A Case Study Examining How the Criminal Justice System Responds to Police Violence', *Digital Commons @ Concordia University, St. Paul*, https://digitalcommons.csp.edu/cgi/viewcontent.cgi?article=1037&context=edd.

US Congress, House of Representatives, *George Floyd Justice in Policing Act of 2020*, House Report 116–434 (Washington, DC: U.S. Government Publishing Office, 2020), https://www.congress.gov/116/crpt/hrpt434/CRPT-116hrpt434.pdf.

3. Megan Armstrong, Eathyn Edwards and Duwain Pinder, 'Corporate commitments to racial justice: An update', McKinsey Institute for Economic Mobility, 21 February 2023, https://www.mckinsey.com/institute-for-economic-mobility/our-insights/corporate-commitments-to-racial-justice-an-update
4. Lily Zheng, 'The Failure of the DEI-Industrial Complex', Harvard Business Review, 1 December 2022, https://hbr.org/2022/12/the-failure-of-the-dei-industrial-complex
5. Alexis Krivkovich, Drew Goldstein and Megan McConnell, *Women in the Workplace Report 2025*, McKinsey & Company, 9 December 2025, https://www.mckinsey.com/capabilities/people-and-organizational-performance/our-insights/women-in-the-workplace
6. 'Women in the boardroom: A Global Perspective', Deloitte Global Boardroom Program, Eighth edition, 2024, https://boardreadywomen.com/wp-content/uploads/2024/05/ca-women-in-the-boardroom-8th-edition-2024-en-aoda.pdf?utm
7. Ibid.
8. World Economic Forum, *Global Gender Gap Report 2020*, https://www3.weforum.org/docs/WEF_GGGR_2020.pdf, accessed 20 September 2023.
9. Umma Kannan, 'Women hold only 76 of 1,314 board seats across 116 unicorns', 8 March 2025, https://www.newindianexpress.com/business/2025/Mar/07/women-hold-only-76-of-1314-board-seats-across-116-unicorns

   Swagat Dash, 'When Women Join the Boardroom, But Don't Get a Seat at the Table', Impact and Research Institute, 27 July 2025, https://www.impriindia.com/insights/when-women-boardroom-seat-table/

10. 'Are you ready for change? Gender equality attitudes study 2019', United Nations Entity for Gender Equality and the Empowerment of Women (UN Women), 2020, https://www.unwomen.org/sites/default/files/Headquarters/Attachments/Sections/Library/Publications/2020/Research-paper-Are-you-ready-for-change-Gender-equality-attitudes-study-2019-en.pdf, accessed 20 September 2023.
11. 'Nasdaq Board Diversity Disclosure Rules No Longer in Effect After Overturning by Court', White & Case, 13 December 2024, https://www.whitecase.com/insight-alert/nasdaq-board-diversity-disclosure-rules-no-longer-effect-after-overturning-court?utm
12. *2024 Sustainability Report and TCFD Report*, NASDAQ, https://www.nasdaq.com/nasdaq-2024-sustainability-report
13. Kantar's Gender Equality Attitudes Study 2021
14. Facts and figures: Women's leadership and political participation', UN Women, 15 September 2025, https://www.unwomen.org/en/articles/facts-and-figures/facts-and-figures-womens-leadership-and-political-participation?utm
15. Fareeha Iftikhar, 'Number of women MPs elected to the Lok Sabha drops', *Hindustan Times*, 6 June 2024, https://www.hindustantimes.com/india-news/number-of-women-mps-elected-to-the-lok-sabha-drops-101717616188425.html
16. PTI, '74 Women Won Lok Sabha Polls This Time, Slight Dip From 78 Elected In 2019', NDTV, 5 June 2024, https://www.ndtv.com/india-news/lok-sabha-election-results-2024-74-women-won-lok-sabha-polls-this-time-slight-dip-from-78-elected-in-2019-5826172?utm
17. Nitheesh Kumaar MV, 'Women in Parliament', Vikaspedia, 6 June 2024, https://socialwelfare.vikaspedia.in/viewcontent/social-welfare/women-and-child-development/women-development-1/women-in-parliament?lgn=en&utm
18. 'Government is promoting greater participation of women in local governance and political leadership roles', Ministry of Women and Child Development, https://www.pib.gov.in/PressReleasePage.aspx?PRID=2150216&utm
19. *Women in the Boardroom: A Global Perspective.*

15. Hiring People with Disabilities: A Global Call Centre View

1. Robert D. Austin and Gary P. Pisano, 'Neurodiversity as a Competitive Advantage Why you should embrace it in your workforce', *Harvard Business Review,* March-June 2017, https://hbr.org/2017/05/neurodiversity-as-a-competitive-advantage, accessed 13 March 2024.
2. Thomas Aichner, 'The economic argument for hiring people with disabilities', *Humanities and Social Sciences Communication*, vol. 8 (22) , 2021, https://doi.org/10.1057/s41599-021-00707-y, accessed 29 September.
3. *Getting to Equal: The Disability Inclusion Advantage*, Accenture Report, 2018, https://www.accenture.com/content/dam/accenture/final/a-com-migration/pdf/pdf-89/accenture-disability-inclusion-research-report.pdf

16. Women as Economic Actors and Decision-Makers: An Investor Perspective

1. Anu Madgavkar et al, 'Covid-19 and Gender Equality: Countering the Regressive Effects', McKinsey & Company, https://www.mckinsey.com/featured-insights/future-of-work/covid-19-and-gender-equality-countering-the-regressive-effects, accessed 20 September 2023.
2. 'Women in Financial Services', Oliver Wynman, 2020, https://www.oliverwyman.com/our-expertise/hubs/gender-diversity-in-financial-services.html, accessed 20 September 2023.
3. Emily Thomas, 'Why Gender Lens Investing May Lead to Better Returns', Morgan Stanley, 21 February 2023, https://www.morganstanley.com/articles/gender-diversity, accessed 20 September 2023.
4. Ewens Michael, Richard Townsend, 'Are Early Stage Investors Biased Against Women?', Harvard Law School Forum on Corporate Governance, 20 September 2019, https://corpgov.law.harvard.edu/2019/09/20/are-early-stage-investors-biased-against-women/, accessed 20 September 2022.

5. Oliver Wyman, Rock Creek, and International Finance Corporation, 'Moving toward gander balance in private equity and venture capital', 2019, pp. 27 (https://www.oliverwyman.com/content/dam/oliver-wyman/v2/publications/2019/mar/Moving-toward-gender-balance-3_21.pdf#page=27, accessed 20 September 2023.
6. Lawrence, Stephen, *Diversity Matters: The Role of Gender Diversity on US Active Equity Fund Performance*, 23 March 2022, http://dx.doi.org/10.2139/ssrn.4081494, accessed 20 September 2023.
7. Chaturvedi, Seema, 'Why we need more women investing in women', *Forbes*, 9 March 2021, (https://www.forbes.com/sites/forbesfinancecouncil/2021/03/09/why-we-need-more-women-investing-in-women/?sh=141f4a255775, accessed 20 September 2023.
8. Ewens Michael, Richard Townsend, 'Are Early Stage Investors Biased Against Women?', Harvard Law School Forum on Corporate Governance, 20 September 2019, https://corpgov.law.harvard.edu/2019/09/20/are-early-stage-investors-biased-against-women/, accessed 20 September 2023.
9. Women's World Banking, *Women's World Banking Annual Report*, 28 July 2022, https://www.womensworldbanking.org/tag/annual-report/, accessed 20 September 2023.
10. Women's World Banking Capital Partners, LP. *Annual Financial & Social Performance Report, 2021*, Women World Banking Asset Management, https://womensworldbanking.box.com/s/ixny4k4bihc37x0jpy7q9q75dfaym58f, accessed 20 September 2023.
11. Abouzahr, Katie, Frances Brooks Taplett, Matt Krentz and John Harthorne, ' Why Women-Owned Start-ups are a Better Bet,' The Boston Consulting Group, Inc. 2018.
12. World Bank Group, Unlocking the Potential of Women Entrepreneurs: Mainstreaming Gender in Private Sector Development, Gender Thematic Policy Note (Washington, DC: World Bank, 2023),
13. Ibid.
14. Hunt, Vivian, Dennis Kayton, Sara Prince, 'Diversity Matters', McKinsey & Company, 2 February 2015, https://www.mckinsey.com/~/media/mckinsey/business%20functions/people%20and%20organizational%20performance/our%20insights/why%20

diversity%20matters/diversity%20matters.pdf, accessed 20 September 2023.

15. Women's World Banking, *Women's World Banking Impact Report 2021*, https://www.womensworldbanking.org/wp-content/uploads/2022/07/Impact-Report_WWB_2021.pdf, accessed 20 September 2023.

17. Bringing Threads Together Using Evidence-Based Tools

1. 'Global Gender Gap Report 2025', World Economic Forum, 11 June 2025, https://www.weforum.org/publications/global-gender-gap-report-2025/in-full/benchmarking-gender-gaps-2025/, accessed January 2026.
2. Luis A. Andres, Basab Dasgupta, George Joseph, Vinoj Abraham and Maria Correia, 'Precarious Drop Reassessing Patterns of Female Labor Force Participation in India', Policy Research Working Paper 8024, April 2017, https://documents1.worldbank.org/curated/en/559511491319990632/pdf/WPS8024.pdf, accessed 2 February 2024.
3. Bansari Kamdar, 'India's Women Bear the Burden of Unpaid Work – With Costs to Themselves and the Economy', *The Diplomat*, 2 November 2020, https://thediplomat.com/2020/11/indias-women-bear-the-burden-of-unpaid-work-with-costs-to-themselves-and-the-economy/#:~:text=While%20Indian%20men%20spend%2080,working%20hours%20on%20unpaid%20labor.&text=One%20of%20the%20repercussions%20of,of%20participation%20in%20paid%20work, accessed 2 February 2024.
4. Robert Jensen, 'Do Labor Market Opportunities Affect Young Women's Work and Family Decisions? Experimental Evidence from India.' *The Quarterly Journal of Economics* 127, no. 2 (2012): 753–92, http://www.jstor.org/stable/23251997, accessed 2 February 2024.
5. Indian Women Network, *Women Matter*, Volume 3, 2018, https://indianwomennetwork.in/wp-content/uploads/2018/12/IWN-E-Newsletter.pdf, accessed 2 February 2024.
6. Purna Banerjee, Shreya Biswas, and Debojyoti Mazumder, '*Maternity Leave and Labour Market Outcomes*', SSRN, 23 July 2022, https://ssrn.com/abstract=4159552

7. Iris Bohnet, What Works: Gender Equality by Design (Cambridge, MA: Belknap Press of Harvard University Press, 2016), 51–54.

18.Artificial Intelligence: A Perspective on Bias and Inclusion

1. Jeffrey Dastin, 'Insight - Amazon scraps secret AI recruiting tool that showed bias against women', *Reuters,* 11 October 2018, https://www.reuters.com/article/us-amazon-com-jobs-automation-insight/amazon-scraps-secret-ai-recruiting-tool-that-showed-bias-against-women-idUSKCN1MK08G/, accessed 18 January 2024.
2. Jillian D'Onfro, 'Google CEO: We're headed towards an "AI first" world', *Business Insider,* 22 April 2016, https://www.businessinsider.in/google-ceo-were-headed-towards-an-ai-first-world/articleshow/51935048.cms, accessed 18 January 2024.
3. 'World-class AI for Education', Khan Labs, https://www.khanacademy.org/khan-labs, accessed 18 January 2024.
4. 'AI powered diagnostic systems show promise in predicting the clinical status of patients with COVID-19-induced pneumonia', *Qure.ai*, 18 September 2023, https://www.qure.ai/news_press_coverages/AI-powered-diagnostic-systems-show-promise-in-detecting-covid19-pneumonia, accessed 18 January 2024.
5. 'Seeing AI: An app for visually impaired people that narrates the world around you', Microsoft, https://www.microsoft.com/en-us/garage/wall-of-fame/seeing-ai/#:~:text=With%20this%20intelligent%20camera%20app,along%20with%20its%20original%20formatting, accessed 18 January 2024.
6. Ibid.
7. Jordan Ellenberg, *Read How Not to Be Wrong: the Power of Mathematical Thinking,* Penguin, 2014.
8. Oliver Balch, 'BrandWatch: Companies "woefully behind" in grappling with ethics risks of AI', *Reuters,* 13 June 2023, https://www.reuters.com/sustainability/boards-policy-regulation/brandwatch-companies-woefully-behind-grappling-with-ethics-risks-ai-2023-06-13/, accessed 18 January 2024.
9. To delve deeper into the concepts and practices of Responsible AI, further insights can be found in Ashna Taneja and Sray Agarwal,

'Embracing Responsible AI: Building trust, ethical use, and fairness in a dynamic business landscape', Whitepaper, Fractal Analytics, 2023, https://fractal.ai/embracing-responsible-ai/, accessed 18 January 2024.

10. 'EU AI Act: First Regulation on Artificial Intelligence', European Parliament, 19 December 2023, https://www.europarl.europa.eu/news/en/headlines/society/20230601STO93804/eu-ai-act-first-regulation-on-artificial-intelligence, accessed 18 January 2024.
11. Joyce Hakmeh, 'Balancing China's role in the UK's AI agenda', Chatham House, 30 October 2023, https://www.chathamhouse.org/2023/10/balancing-chinas-role-uks-ai-agenda, accessed 18 January 2023.
12. 'NASSCOM Responsible AI Resource Kit', *Indiaai,* https://indiaai.gov.in/responsible-ai/homepage, accessed 18 January 2024.

19. Diversity in Boardroom Decision-Making

1. *Women in Business 2024: Pathways to Parity,* Grant Thornton, 2024, https://www.grantthornton.in/insights/women-in-business-2024/

20. Men and Money: Behavioural Insights on Mitigating Gender Stereotypes

1. Eva Szalay, 'Trading floor culture remains a barrier for senior female staff', *Financial Times,* 10 August 2019, https://www.ft.com/content/16cbf8da-b9d7-11e9-96bd-8e884d3ea203, accessed 5 January 2024.
2. 'Better Trading Through Science', *Bloomberg,* https://www.bloomberg.com/news/articles/2011-08-31/better-trading-through-science, accessed 21 December 2023.
3. The Rosalind Franklin University of Medicine and Science, 'Massive study reveals few differences between men's and women's brains,' *Science Daily,* www.sciencedaily.com/releases/2021/03/210325115316.htm, accessed 21 December 2023.
4. Ibid.

5. Robert Sapolsky, *Behave: The Biology of Humans at our Best and Worst*, Penguin Random House, 2017.
6. Jo Howarth Noonan, 'Men are from Mars, Women are from Venus: An Analysis of a Potential Meme', *Scholar Works@ Georgia State University*, unpublished Master's Thesis, 2007, https://scholarworks.gsu.edu/cgi/viewcontent.cgi?article=1024&context=communication_theses, accessed 5 January 2024.
7. Sa-Dhan: the Association of Community Development Finance Institutions, The Bharat Microfinance Report 2021, https://www.sa-dhan.net/wp-content/uploads/2022/11/BMR-2021.pdf, accessed 21 December 2023.
8. Tim Maurer, 'Why Women are Better (Investors) than Men', *Forbes*, 30 April 2023, https://www.forbes.com/sites/timmaurer/2023/04/30/why-women-are-better-investors-than-men/?sh=4b22e7dd799d, accessed 21 December 2023.

21.The Power of Narrative: A Media Perspective

1. Carol, 'Bollywood Music and Movies', *Asia Highlights*, 11 September 2023, https://www.asiahighlights.com/india/bollywood#:~:text=With%20almost%202%2C000%20movies%20a,and%20characterized%20by%20musical%20numbers%20..., accessed 21 September 2023.
2. 'India-Population, Female (% of total)', Trading Economies, https://tradingeconomics.com/india/population-female-percent-of-total-wb-data.html#:~:text=Population%2C%20female%20(%25%20of%20total%20population)%20in%20India%20was%20reported,compiled%20from%20officially%20recognized%20s-ources, accessed 21 September 2023.
3. '13 million households, constituting 5% of projected TV universe, to be cord-cutters by 2026 in India: KPMG', Best Media Info, Delhi, 17 November 2022, https://bestmediainfo.com/2022/11/13-million-households-constituting-5-of-projected-tv-universe-to-be-cordcutters-by-2026-in-india-kpmg, accessed 21 September 2023.
4. 'How does Europe boost its independent film production', European Audiovisual Observatory, 2019 Press Release, Strasbourg, France, 18 July 2019, https://www.obs.coe.int/en/web/observatoire/press-

releases-2019/-/asset_publisher/BJtZb1m5z7vu/content/how-does-europe-boost-its-independent-film-production-sector-, accessed 21 September 2023.

5. Mohamed, Khalid, 'Unease at Film Division after merger with NFDC', *Hindustan Times*, 31 December 2022, https://www.hindustantimes.com/cities/mumbai-news/unease-at-films-division-after-merger-with-nfdc-101672510654215.html, accessed 21 September 2023.
6. Ramchandran, Naman, 'Female Representation Report is a "Wake-Up Call" for Indian Film and TV sector', *Variety*, 4 August 2022, https://variety.com/2022/film/news/female-representation-report-india-film-tv-streaming-1235333155/, accessed 21 September 2023.
7. 'As India's population soars, number of women in workforce shrinks', *Al Jazeera*, 10 April 2023, https://www.aljazeera.com/gallery/2023/4/10/as-indias-population-soars-number-of-women-in-workforce-shrinks, accessed 21 September 2023.
8. 'Javed Akhtar's speech in Rajya Sabha on Copyright Amendment Bill 2010', *Lyrics Mint*, https://lyricsmint.com/articles/javed-akhtars-speech-in-rajyasabha-on, accessed 21 September 2023.
9. Sharma, Priyanka, 'Javed Akhtar distributes Rs 13 crore worth TV synchronisation royalty to musicians,' *Indian Express*, 23 April 2018, https://indianexpress.com/article/entertainment/bollywood/javed-akhtar-indian-performing-rights-society-iprs-5148564/, accessed 21 September 2023.
10. Nolan, Hamilton, 'The Hollywood strike can and must win- for all of us, not just writers and actors', *The Guardian*, 19 July 2023, https://www.theguardian.com/commentisfree/2023/jul/19/the-hollywood-strike-can-and-must-win-for-all-of-us-not-just-writers-and-actors, accessed 21 September 2023.

22.The Changing Face of Brands and Communication: A Brand Perspective

1. 'Apple Is the 2025 Most Valuable Brand in the World; NVIDIA Breaks into the Top Ten', Brand Finance press release, 21 January 2025, https://brandfinance.com/press-releases/apple-is-the-2025-most-valuable-brand-in-the-world-nvidia-breaks-into-top-ten

2. Chris Morris, 'Apple Is the World's Most Valuable Brand for the Fourth Year in a Row', *Fortune*, 16 May 2025, https://fortune.com/2025/05/16/apple-worlds-most-valuable-brand-2025/
3. 'Coronavirus: Impact on the Global Economy', Statista, 2023, https://www.statista.com/topics/6139/covid-19-impact-on-the-global-economy/#topicOverview
4. 'Number of Internet Users in India', Statista, 2025, https://www.statista.com/statistics/255146/number-of-internet-users-in-india/
5. 'India's E-Commerce Market Growth: Trends & Key Data 2024–2025', PaymentsCMI, https://paymentscmi.com/insights/india-ecommerce-market-growth-trends/
6. 'Rise of Social Media Influencers in India: Who's Leading in 2024', Kofluence, 12 June 2024, https://www.kofluence.com/rise-of-social-media-influencers-in-india/
7. 'Market News and Insights', JM Financial Services, https://www.jmfinancialservices.in/market-news-and-insights/1612672
8. 'Victory – Hindustan Unilever Settles with 591 Kodaikanal Workers', IPEN, 9 March 2016, https://ipen.org/news/victory- per centE2 per cent80 per cent93-hindustan-unilever-settles-591-kodaikanal-workers/
9. 'Trustpilot Trust Report 2025', Trustpilot, 29 May 2025, https://corporate.trustpilot.com/trust/trust-report-2025/
10. 'Consumers Say Their Environmental Concerns Are Increasing Due to Extreme Weather; Study Shows They're Willing to Change Behaviour, Pay 12 per cent More for Sustainable Products', Bain & Company press release, 4 October 2023, https://www.bain.com/about/media-center/press-releases/2023/consumers-say-their-environmental-concerns-are-increasing-due-to-extreme-weather-study-shows-theyre-willing-to-change-behavior-pay-12-more-for-sustainable-products/
11. 'Creative Critique from a Gender Lens: 6–10 February', *Campaign India*, 10 February 2025, https://www.campaignindia.in/article/creative-critique-from-a-gender-lens-6-10-february/482320
12. Jocelyn Fernandes, 'Hurun India Rich List 2025: Not Dubai or New York. The richest non-resident Indians live in these cities', Livemint, 7 October 2025, https://www.livemint.com/companies/people/hurun-india-rich-list-2025-non-resident-indian-nris-

live-in-this-city-london-gopichand-hinduja-ln-mittal-anil-agarwal-11759825587198.html

13. 'How Many People in India Speak English', *The History of English*, 20 March 2025, https://www.thehistoryofenglish.com/how-many-people-in-india-speak-english/
14. 'Internet in India Report 2024', Internet and Mobile Association of India (IAMAI) and Kantar, 2024, https://www.iamai.in/sites/default/files/research/Kantar_ per cent20IAMAI per cent20report_2024_.pdf
15. Daniel Tencer, 'Global consumption of music from India soared 2,000 per cent in 5 years on Spotify', *Music Business Worldwide*, 12 March 2024, https://www.musicbusinessworldwide.com/global-consumption-of-indian-music-soared-2000-in-5-years-on-spotify12/
16. Debarghya Sil, 'How STAGE Is Shaking Up Netflix & Amazon with Its Regional Originals,' *Inc42*, 24 March 2025, https://inc42.com/startups/how-stage-is-shaking-up-netflix-amazon-with-its-regional-originals/
17. Alec Chillingworth, 'The most-subscribed and most-viewed YouTube channels in 2026', Epidemic Sound, 2 January 2026, https://www.epidemicsound.com/blog/most-subscribed-and-viewed-youtube-channels/
18. *Annual Complaints Report 2024–25*, The Advertising Standards Council of India, https://www.ascionline.in/wp-content/uploads/2025/05/Digital-ASCI-Annual-Complaints-Report-2024-2025.pdf
19. Jessica TestaVanessa Friedman and Elizabeth Paton, 'Everlane's Promise of "Radical Transparency" Unravels', *New York Times*, 26 July 2020, https://www.nytimes.com/2020/07/26/fashion/everlane-employees-ethical-clothing.html
20. 'Vol 12: Work Culture, Everlane, and Sustainability', Sustainability & Fashion, 4 August 2020, https://embrace.substack.com/p/vol-12-work-culture-everlane-and

23. Behavioural Tools to Reshape Social and Market Norms

1. Sutapa Banerjee, 'To reverse women leaving the workforce, policies must change behaviour before they change beliefs', *Economics Times*, 13 October 2017, https://economictimes.indiatimes.com/blogs/et-commentary/to-reverse-women-leaving-the-workforce-policies-must-change-behaviour-before-they-change-beliefs/?frmapp=yes Sutapa Banerjee, 'Why women are invisible in the workplace', *Medium,* 13 October 2017, (https://medium.com/@sutapaban65/why-women-are-invisible-in-the-workplace-b4a5c91a29ea
2. Ibid.
3. Ibid.

24. Towards a New Playbook

1. Sutapa Banerjee, 'To reverse women leaving the workforce, policies must change behaviour before they change beliefs', *The Economics Times*, 13 October 2017, https://economictimes.indiatimes.com/blogs/et-commentary/to-reverse-women-leaving-the-workforce-policies-must-change-behaviour-before-they-change-beliefs/?frmapp=yes, accessed 12 March 2024; Sutapa Banerjee, 'Why women are invisible in the workplace', *Medium,* 13 October 2017, https://medium.com/@sutapaban65/why-women-are-invisible-in-the-workplace-b4a5c91a29ea, accessed 12 March 2024.
2. Ibid.
3. AFP, 'How "drone didis" are piloting farming and social change in India', *The Times of India*, 7 March 2024. https://timesofindia.indiatimes.com/india/how-drone-didis-are-piloting-farming-social-change-in-rural-india/articleshow/108279528.cms, accessed 7 March 2024.
4. Roger L. Martin, 'How to Make Companies Think Long-Term', *Harvard Business Review*, 3 October 2021, https://hbr.org/2011/10/fixing-corporate-short-termism, accessed 11 March 2024.

Notes on the Contributors

Abheek Barua is a visiting professor of economics at Ashoka University, Sonepat. He was previously the chief economist and senior executive vice-president at HDFC Bank, with thirty-two years of experience in the financial sector. His career includes senior roles at CRISIL (Standard & Poor's India), Merrill Lynch Asia and ABN AMRO Bank, where he served as the chief economist. Barua has been a member of consultative committees of the Planning Commission, NITI Aayog and the Reserve Bank of India, and served on HDFC Bank's apex Asset–Liability Committee. A regular television commentator, Barua writes for *The Economic Times* and has been voted among Asia's top currency forecasters and bond analysts by Bloomberg, Reuters and *Asset* magazine.

Samir Kumar Barua is a former professor and director of the Indian Institute of Management, Ahmedabad (IIMA).

Prateep Basu is the founder and CEO of SatSure, a Bengaluru-based spacetech and AI startup founded in 2017. He has over thirteen years of experience in the space industry, spanning both business and technology. An aerospace engineer from the Indian Institute of Space Science and Technology, Thiruvananthapuram, he began his career as a propulsion systems engineer at ISRO's Satish Dhawan Space Centre and later worked as an Earth observation consultant before founding SatSure. Under his leadership, the company has grown to 200 employees across India, the US and the UK, serving enterprise clients in twelve countries and raising $20 million in equity capital.

Suhas Baxi is co-founder and CEO of BiofuelCircle, a digital platform building reliable supply chains for bioenergy. With over thirty-five years of experience, including two decades in CEO roles, he has worked across the energy, manufacturing, and software technology sectors. A mechanical engineer from VNIT Nagpur, he has also undergone management training at IIM Ahmedabad and Harvard Business School. His venture promotes farmer participation and digitally empowers rural enterprises to create an agri-waste-based circular economy.

Sanjeev Bikhchandani is the founder of Info Edge, one of India's pioneering internet companies, and the creator of Naukri.com, the country's first job portal. He studied economics at St Stephen's College and earned his MBA from IIM Ahmedabad before leaving a corporate career to start Naukri in 1997. Under his leadership, Info Edge launched 99acres, Jeevansathi and Shiksha, and invested early in unicorns such as Zomato and PolicyBazaar.com. He is also co-founder of Ashoka University. Bikhchandani received the Padma Shri in 2020 and the Ernst & Young Entrepreneur of the Year award in 2008.

Praveen Garg served in the Indian Administrative Service for over three decades. He held key positions in the Government of India and the Government of Madhya Pradesh, including in the Ministries of Law and Justice, Finance, and Environment, Forest and Climate Change. As district magistrate and later as secretary (finance), managing director of the Madhya Pradesh State Industrial Development Corporation and revenue commissioner, he introduced major administrative reforms. He has served on the boards of Air India; the Solar Energy Corporation of India; the Indian Renewable Energy Development Agency and the Industrial Development Bank of India; and, as chairman and managing director of the Security Printing and Minting Corporation of India, led the remonetization effort. He has also served on the governing bodies of the Indian Council of Forestry Research and Education, the Wildlife Institute of India and the National Tiger Conservation Authority, among others.

Currently, he is the president of the Mobius Foundation. He serves as an independent director on the boards of LIC Mutual Fund Asset Management Company, Lemon Tree Hotels, Asset Care & Reconstruction Enterprise and Ambuja Cements. He is also a member of the Investor Education and

Protection Fund Authority and an honorary senior adviser (finance and resource mobilization) to the International Big Cat Alliance.

Nadir Godrej is Chairman and Managing Director of Godrej Industries and Godrej Agrovet, and a key leader of the Godrej Group. A chemical engineer from MIT with a master's from Stanford and an MBA from Harvard Business School, he has led the group's expansion across chemicals, agriculture and consumer goods. Deeply committed to sustainability and innovation, he champions environmental responsibility and inclusive growth in Indian industry. He serves on several corporate and academic boards and was honoured with the *Chevalier de la Légion d'Honneur* by the Government of France.

Pirojsha Godrej is Executive Chairperson of Godrej Properties, Godrej Capital and Godrej Fund Management. A graduate of the Wharton School, he holds a Master's in International Affairs and an MBA from Columbia University. Godrej Properties, under his leadership, has undergone a period of rapid expansion, becoming India's largest real estate developer by sales in FY21. From 2020 to 2022, the Global Real Estate Sustainability Benchmark ranked the company first globally among listed residential developers for its sustainability and governance practices.

Deepinder Goyal is the founder and CEO of Zomato, one of India's largest startups and a global leader in the food-tech industry. Founded in 2008, Zomato has become a defining name in India's startup ecosystem. Before starting Zomato, Deepinder worked as a management consultant at Bain & Company. He holds an integrated master's in mathematics and computing from the Indian Institute of Technology, Delhi.

Mary Ellen Iskenderian is president and CEO of Women's World Banking, a global nonprofit expanding financial access for low-income women. Since 2006, she has led the organization's global strategy and investment initiatives. Featured in *Forbes* magazine's '50 Over 50: Investment' list, she is also the author of *There's Nothing Micro About a Billion Women*, which highlights the transformative power of women's financial inclusion.

Parth Jindal is managing director of JSW Cement and JSW Paints, and Director at JSW Energy, JSW Ventures and JSW USA. He holds a BA in Economics and Political Science from Brown University and an MBA from Harvard Business School. He founded JSW Sports, which owns Bengaluru FC, Haryana Steelers and co-owns Delhi Capitals, and established the Inspire Institute of Sport to nurture India's Olympic talent. He has been recognized among *Economic Times*'s '40 Under Forty,' *GQ*'s '50 Most Influential Young Indians' and *Forbes*' 'Next-Gen Entrepreneurs.'

Christina (CJ) Juhasz is managing partner and chief investment officer of WWB Asset Management (WAM), overseeing $150 million in gender-lens equity investments. Before co-founding WAM, she held senior roles at Deutsche Bank and Merrill Lynch. A graduate of the US Military Academy at West Point, she completed her MBA from Stanford Graduate School of Business and was named an Eisenhower Fellow in 2013.

Kiran Khalap is co-founder and managing director of chlorophyll, a brand consultancy that has shaped over 400 brands since 1999. His novels, *Halfway Up the Mountain*, *Two Pronouns and a Verb* and *Black River Run*, explore the theme of unification. He practices yoga and Vipassana, guided by Pierre Teilhard de Chardin's philosophy of conscious evolution.

Anupama Mandloi is an impact producer and a leading advocate for sustainability in the film and television industry. Through initiatives such as India GreenSet and the India Sustainable Entertainment Alliance, she promotes sustainable production practices and the use of storytelling as a catalyst for social and environmental change. She currently serves as Regional Ambassador for the Global Impact Producers Alliance (GIPA). Her producing debut was the award-winning documentary *Aunty Sudha Aunty Radha* (2019). She has held senior leadership roles at Sony, SAB and STAR, was Managing Director of Fremantle India and later worked as an independent content consultant with clients, including Zee5.

M.D. Ramesh has over thirty years of financial and operational experience in the agriculture and food sectors, with a deep specialization in Africa. Currently based in Rwanda as CEO of Africa Improved Foods BV, he previously served as President at Olam International for 28 years, managing businesses across Africa, India, and Europe. A regular speaker at global forums and guest faculty at Harvard Business School and the University of Cape Town, he is the author of *Amazing Africa: A Corporate Journey*, chronicling his experiences of building agri-businesses across the continent.

R. Mukundan is the managing director and CEO of Tata Chemicals Limited. A Fellow of the Indian Chemical Society, he joined the Tata Administrative Service in 1990 after earning his MBA from FMS, Delhi University and BTech from IIT Roorkee. An alumnus of Harvard Business School, he has served across the chemical, automotive, and hospitality sectors during his 33-year Tata career and contributes actively to several industry and impact forums.

Preeti Reddy was CEO and chairwoman, South Asia, at Kantar, one of the company's 'Big Six' global markets. A member of Kantar's global leadership team, she drove business growth and led diversity and inclusion initiatives in South Asia. Recognized five times among *Impact*'s '50 Most Influential Women in Indian Media, Marketing and Advertising,' she holds a BA (Hons) in Economics from Lady Shri Ram College, Delhi University, and an MBA from XLRI Jamshedpur.

Manish Sabharwal is a non-executive, non-independent director of TeamLease Services, India's largest staffing and human capital firm. He has served as an Independent Director on the Reserve Bank of India's Board, a Member of the Advisory Board to the Comptroller and Auditor General, and a Governing Board member of NCAER. Managing Trustee of the New India Foundation, he also writes a regular column for *The Indian Express*. An alumnus of SRCC, Delhi, and Mayo College, Ajmer, he holds an MBA from The Wharton School.

Kartikeya V. Sarabhai is founder-director of the Centre for Environment Education (CEE) and Chairman of Ambalal Sarabhai Enterprises. He was part of India's delegation to the 1992 Earth Summit at Rio and has contributed to multiple UN and COP dialogues. Co-author of the UNESCO report on Climate Change Education in India, he also chairs the group designing environmental content for India's new school textbooks under

NEP 2020. Educated at Cambridge University and MIT, he received the Padma Shri in 2012.

Sandip Sen is managing director of Litmus World, a leading SaaS platform for customer experience. A pioneer of India's outsourcing industry, he founded Customer First Services in 2001, which was later acquired by Aegis, where he served as Global CEO. He helped scale Aegis into a $700 million enterprise with 60,000 employees in multiple countries and later played a key role in its $1 billion sale. He now advises global private equity firms and high-growth companies in the BPM sector, and is a frequent speaker and writer.

Dilip Soman is Canada Research Chair in Behavioural Science and Economics at the Rotman School of Management, University of Toronto. He founded Behavioural Economics in Action at Rotman (BEAR) and the India Innovation Institute. Author and editor of several books and research papers, he previously taught at the University of Colorado and the Hong Kong University of Science and Technology. Educated at IIT Bombay, IIM Ahmedabad and the University of Chicago, his interests include music, theatre, cricket and old Hindi cinema.

Srikanth Velamakanni is co-founder and executive vice-chairman of Fractal, a global AI firm helping enterprises make better decisions. An alumnus of IIT Delhi and IIM Ahmedabad, he is passionate about client-centric innovation and long-term thinking in business. He is a founder-trustee at Plaksha University, Punjab; and serves as the vice chairperson of Nasscom, a non-governmental trade association, and an independent director on several boards. An avid reader, he finishes over 100 books a year.

About the Editor

Sutapa Banerjee is a business leader with over three decades of experience spanning financial services, corporate governance and behavioural science. She began her leadership career at multinational banks and was recognized among the Top 20 Global Rising Stars of Wealth Management by the Institutional Investor Group in 2007 and shortlisted for *Fortune India's* 50 Most Powerful Women in 2012. She serves on the boards of several leading companies. An Advanced Leadership Fellow at Harvard University, Banerjee has taught postgraduate students at IIM Ahmedabad as a visiting professor, applying behavioural insights to questions of gender and economic participation. She is also an adjunct faculty member in corporate governance at the Indian Institute of Corporate Affairs, an autonomous think tank under the Ministry of Corporate Affairs.

HarperCollins *Publishers* India

At HarperCollins India, we believe in telling the best stories and finding the widest readership for our books in every format possible. We started publishing in 1992; a great deal has changed since then, but what has remained constant is the passion with which our authors write their books, the love with which readers receive them, and the sheer joy and excitement that we as publishers feel in being a part of the publishing process.

Over the years, we've had the pleasure of publishing some of the finest writing from the subcontinent and around the world, including several award-winning titles and some of the biggest bestsellers in India's publishing history. But nothing has meant more to us than the fact that millions of people have read the books we published, and that somewhere, a book of ours might have made a difference.

As we look to the future, we go back to that one word—a word which has been a driving force for us all these years.

Read.